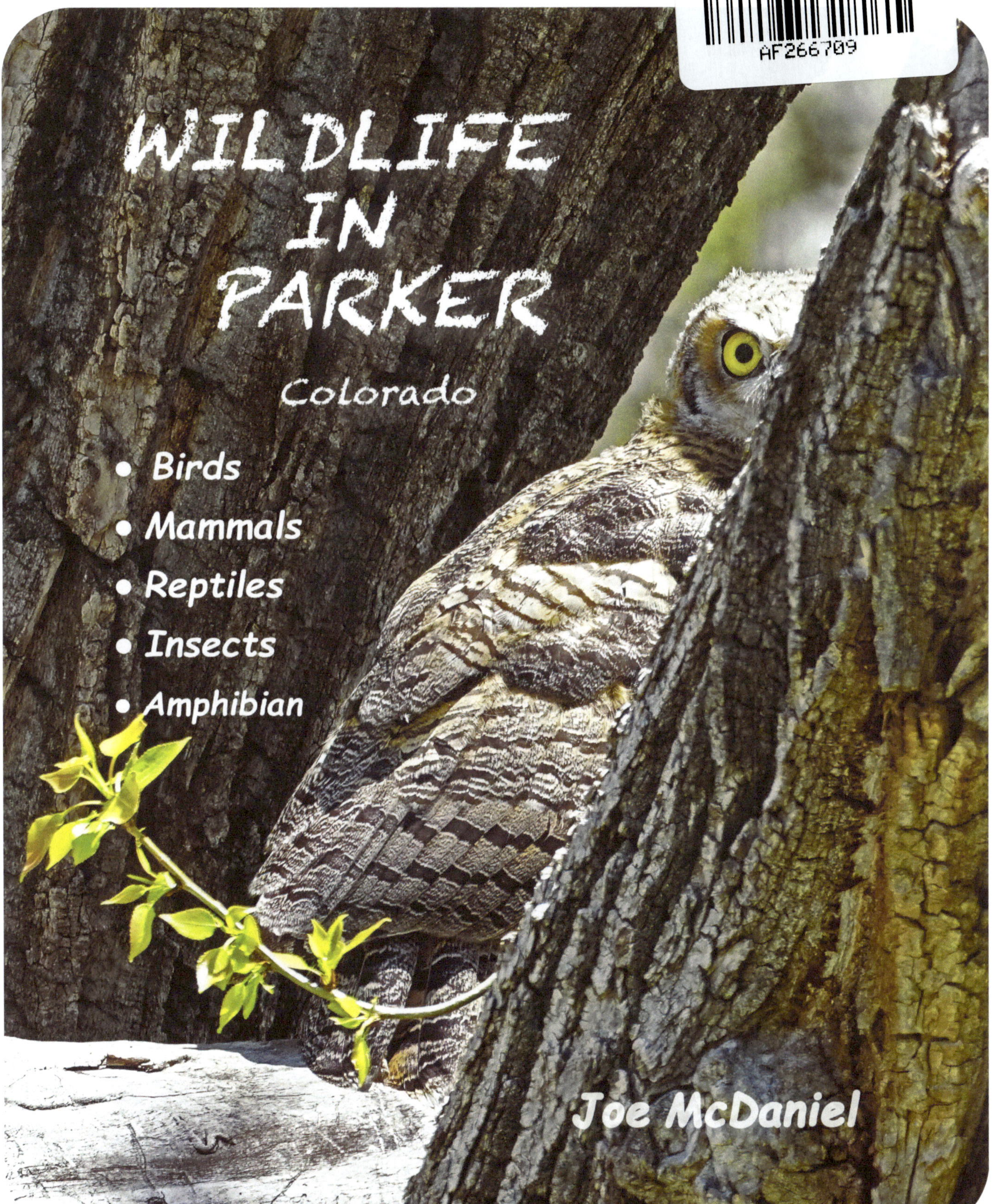

WILDLIFE
IN
PARKER
Colorado
• Birds
• Mammals
• Reptiles
• Insects
• Amphibian
Joe McDaniel

Publisher's Cataloging-in-Publication Data

Names: McDaniel, Joe G., author.
Title: Wildlife in Parker : Colorado / Joe McDaniel.
Description: Includes bibliographical references. | Parker, CO: BookCrafters, 2024.
Identifiers: ISBN: 978-1-957077-93-2 hardcover
                       978-1-957077-96-3 softcover
Subjects: LCSH Colorado--Parker--Wildlife. | Wildlife watching--Colorado. |
Animals--Colorado. | BISAC NATURE / Animals / Wildlife
Classification: LCC QL165 .M33 2024 | DDC 599/.09788--dc23

Front cover - Juvenile Great Horned Owl
Back cover - Three month old Mule Deer fawns
meet a Desert Cottontail on the street

Published by BookCrafters, Parker, Colorado.
www.bookcrafters.net

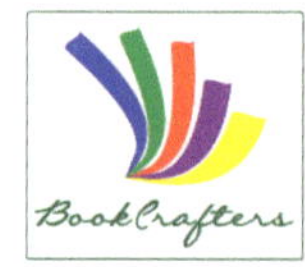

bookcrafterscolorado@gmail.com

Table of Contents

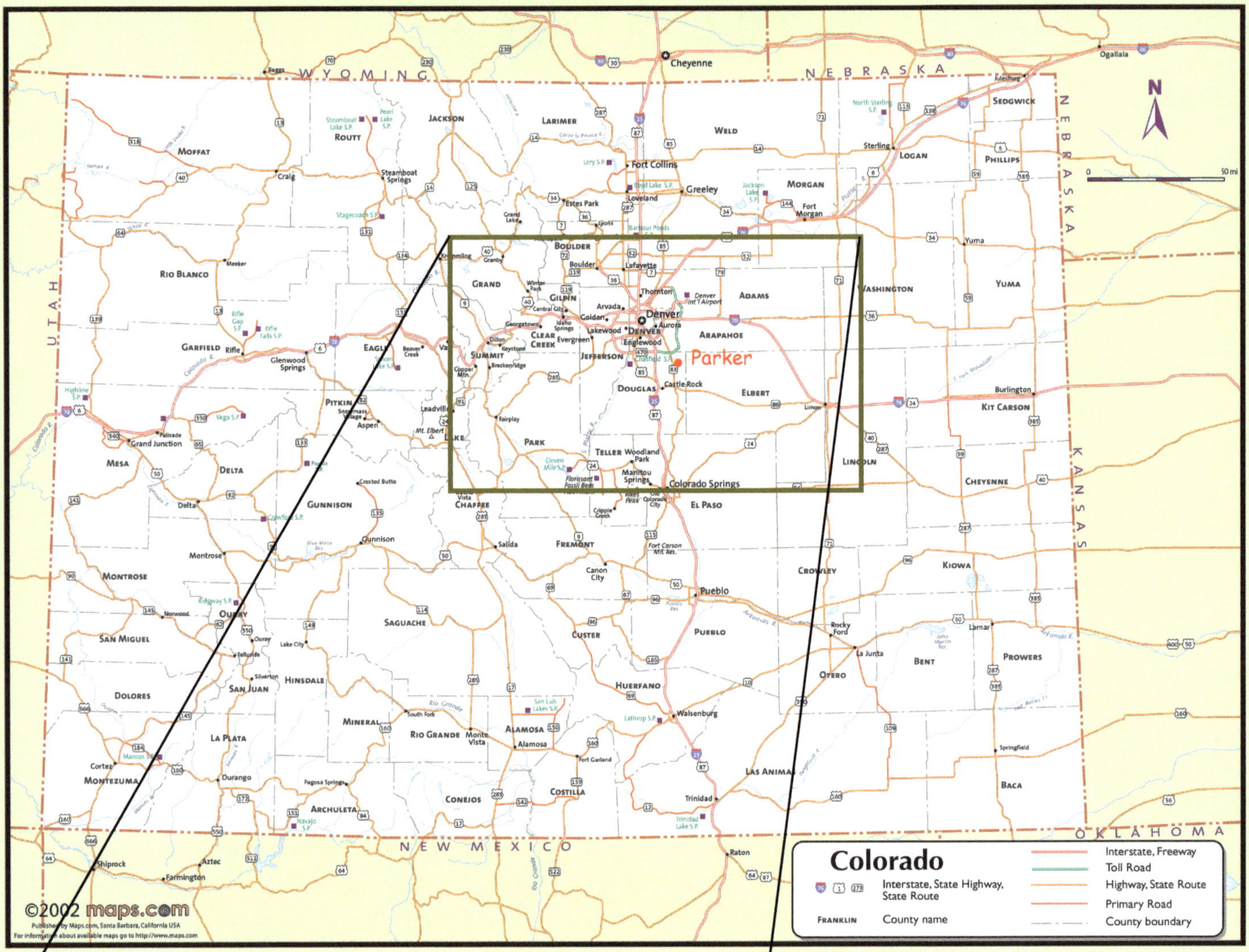

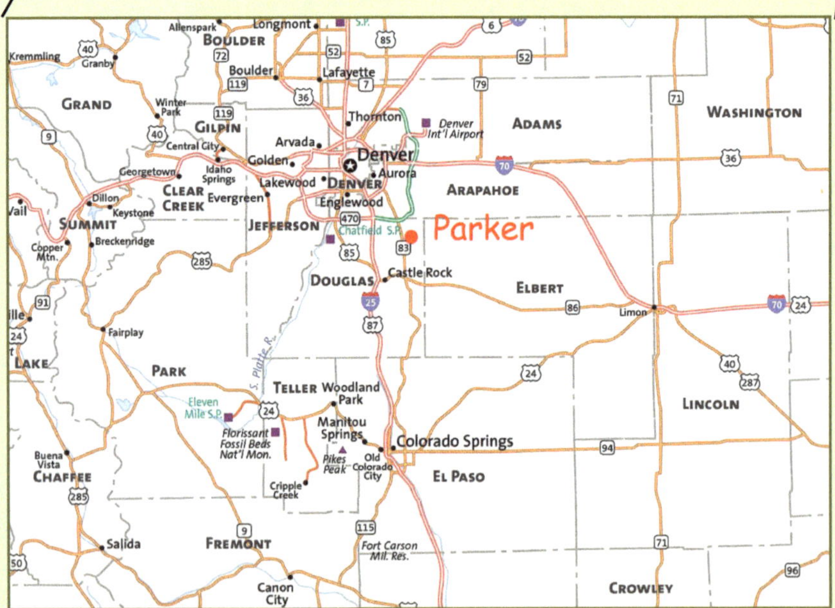

Parker is a home rule municipality in Douglas County, Colorado, United States, with a population of approx. 60,000. It is located approximately 22 miles (35km) southeast of downtown Denver.

Altitude is 1789M (5,815 ft).

The Town of Parker maintains more than 398 acres of Town-owned and proposed parkland, 41 miles of concrete and soft surface trails, 14 parks and 1,144 acres of open space.

(ii)

Introduction

Wildlife is plentiful in many Denver, Colorado suburbs such as The Town of Parker. (See The Parker Town Location Map on the opposite page.) At times our encounters can be brief and unexpected.

Wildlife shown in this book was photographed over several years • in our neighborhood, • in our back yard, • out of our office window, • in the nearby Public Open Spaces • and on the trails where we walk regularly.

In the Table of Contents I have listed each species alphabetically using the common name for each. For example, the **Black-capped Chickadee** is listed as **Chickadee, Black-capped**. The scientific name (genus and species) is indicated on the main photograph of each.

I have added a few notes on many photos and hope these will be of some interest and helpful to readers.

As a photographer I have learned the value of making adjustments to my camera *ahead of time* so that it is ready to use at a moment's notice. So, if it is dark, I adjust the ISO to allow for that quick shot that inevitably presents itself. As light conditions change, I re-adjust the camera from time to time. Many of my best captures were made with just one or two quick shots when a subject unexpectedly appeared. If I had not had the camera close at hand, and already set correctly, I would have missed those opportunities.

Photographer's Rules:

#1: Never go anywhere without your camera!

#2: Share your images.

There are almost certainly wildlife enthusiasts and/or photographers in your neighborhood who want to learn about local wildlife. Facebook, Nextdoor, etc. are good social media sites to share and exchange notes with neighbors.

This is a collection of personal memories and experiences. It is most certainly not intended to be a book of outstanding wildlife photographs. My hope is that you can gain a little knowledge and enjoy nature more.

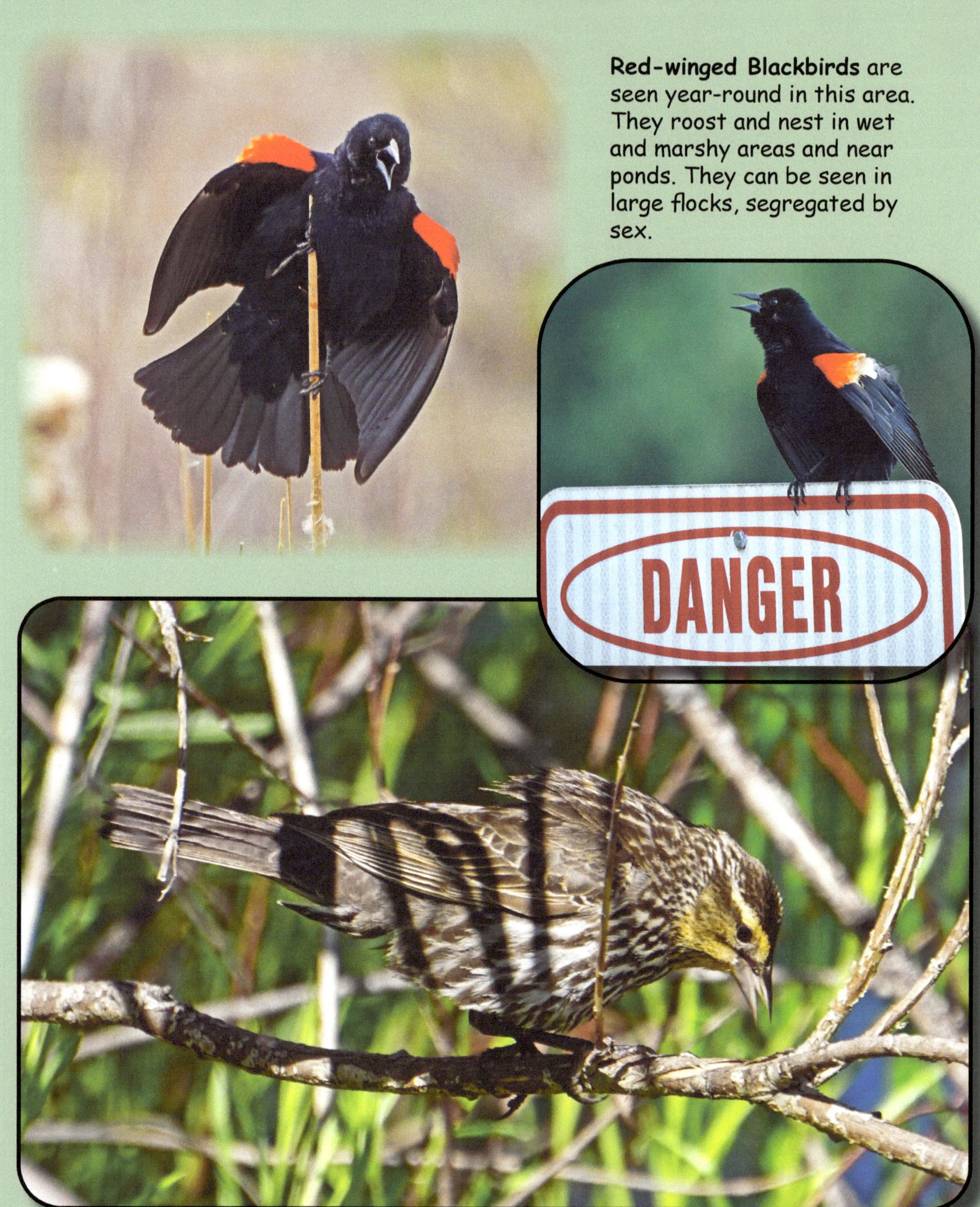

Red-winged Blackbird, female

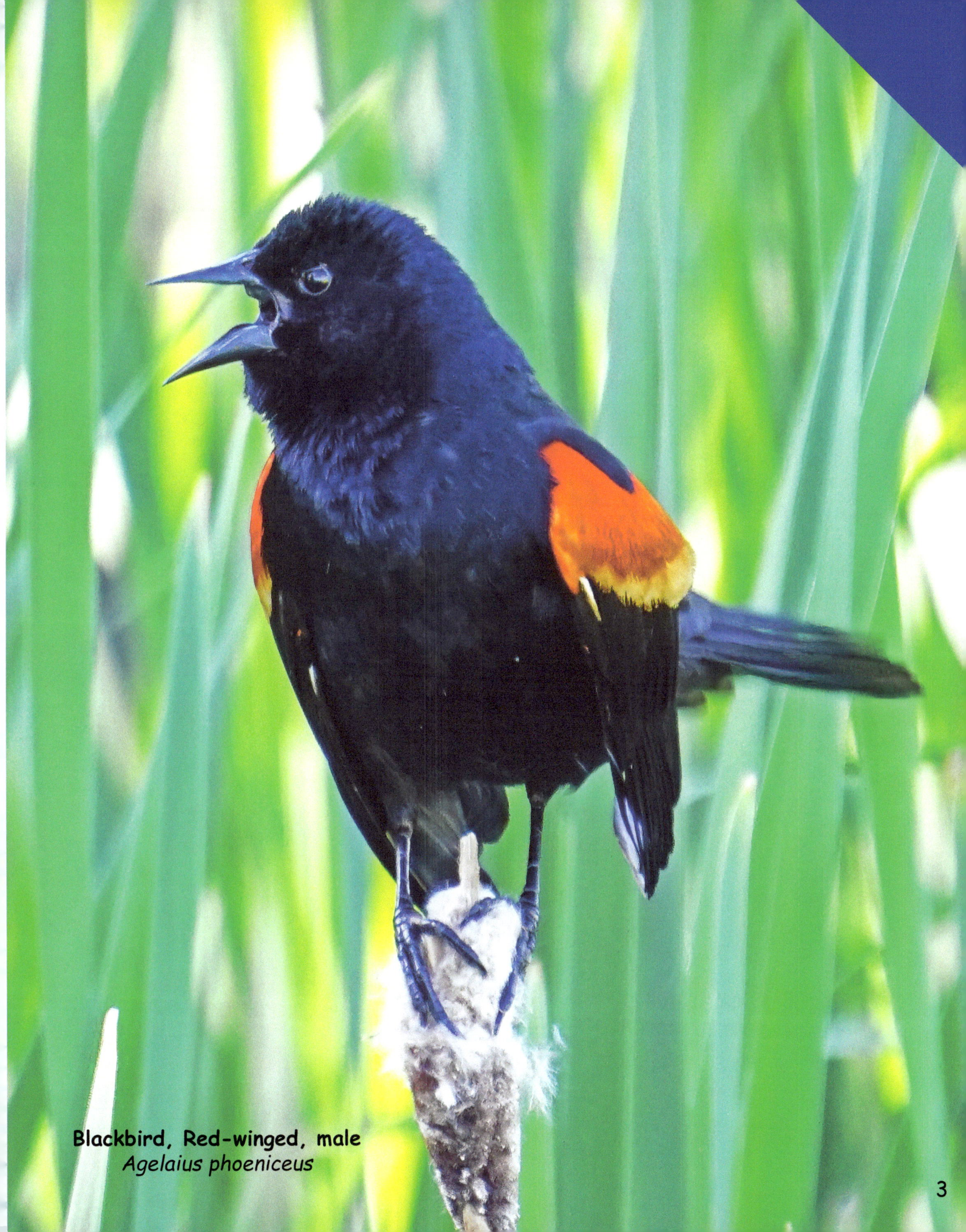

Blackbird, Red-winged, male
Agelaius phoeniceus

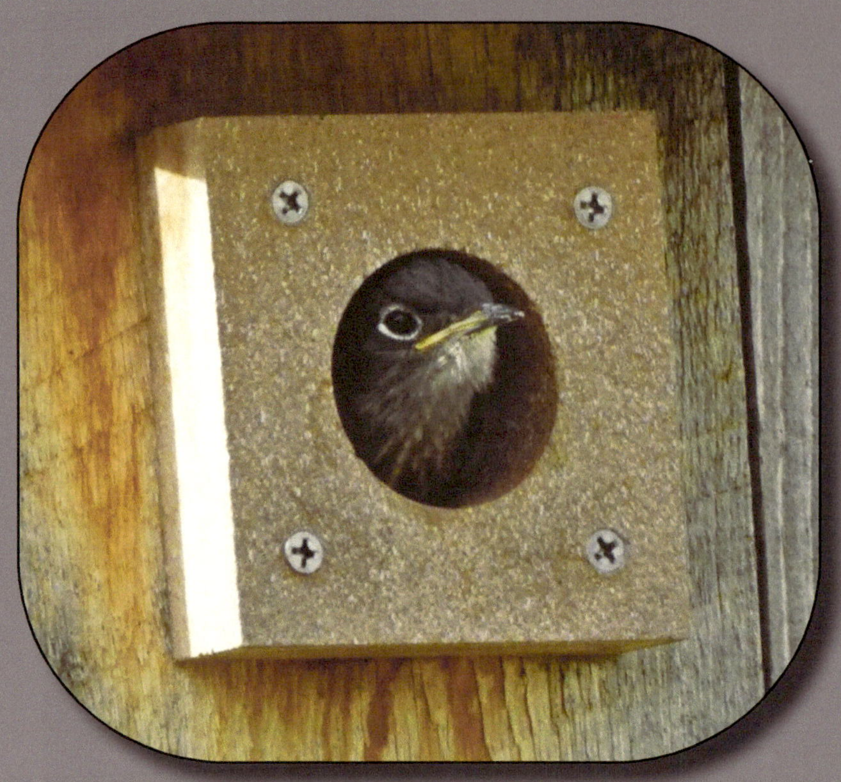

Western Bluebird chick

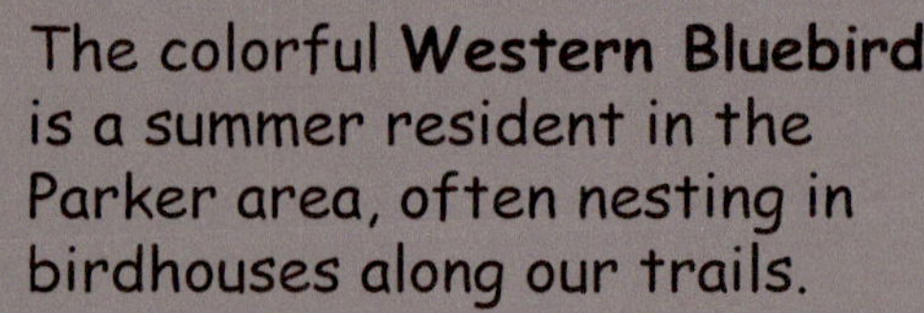

The colorful **Western Bluebird** is a summer resident in the Parker area, often nesting in birdhouses along our trails.

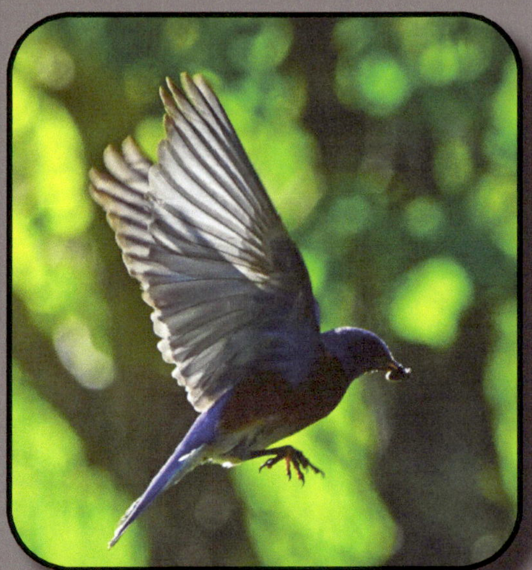

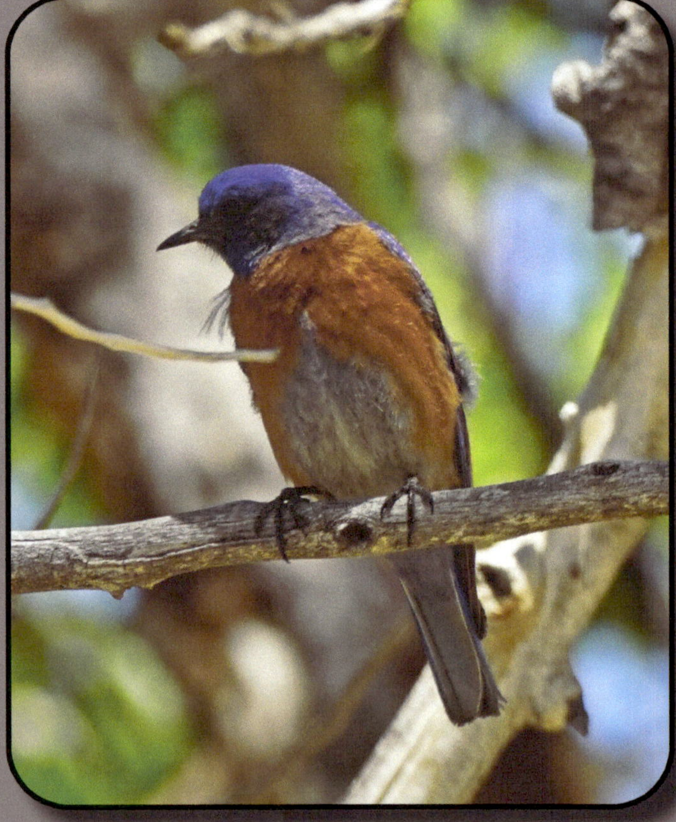

Western Bluebirds, male (left) female (right)

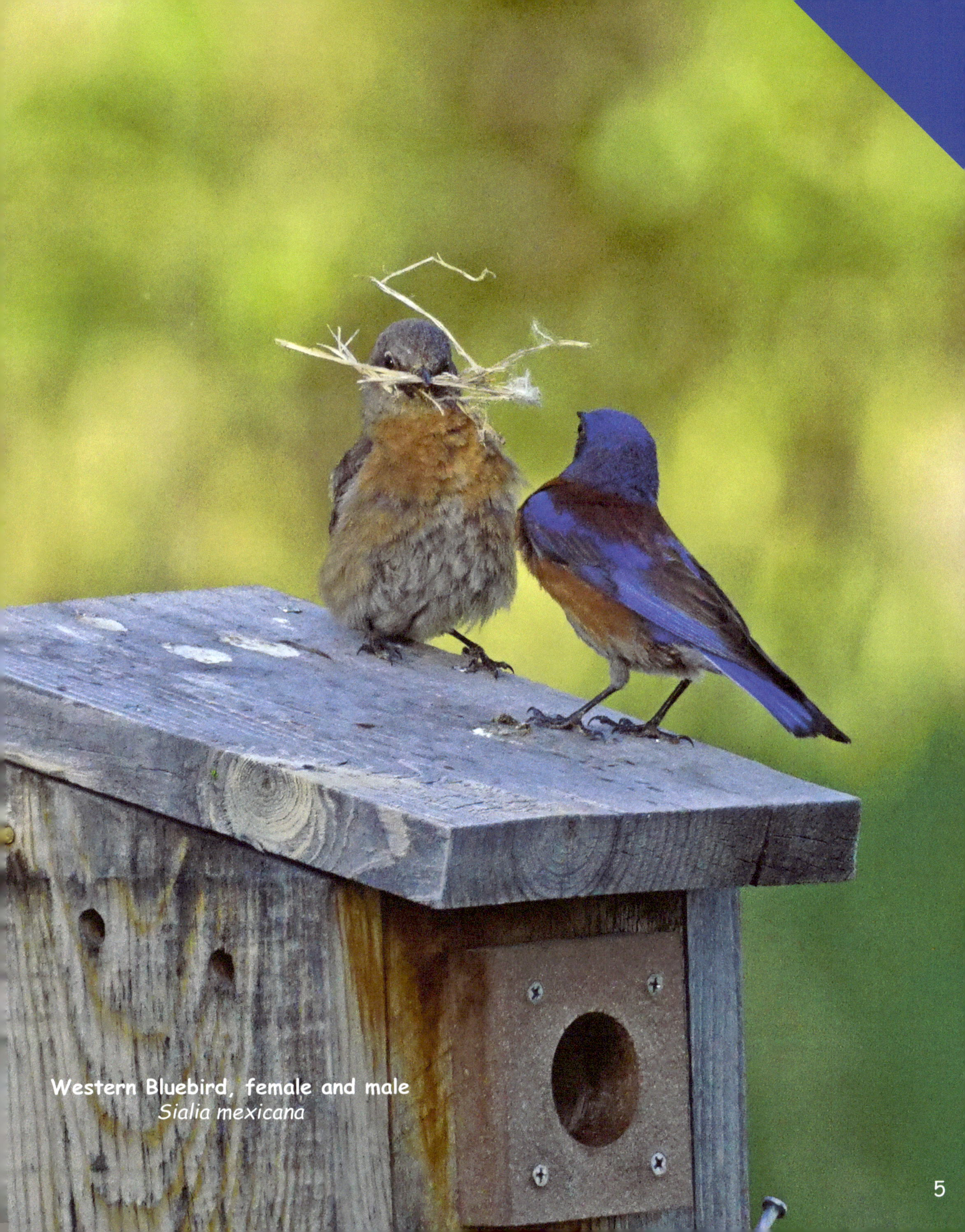

Western Bluebird, female and male
Sialia mexicana

The **Lazuli Bunting** is usually solitary and can be seen in the summer months (Apr-Jul) in Parker. Rarely, as seen here, we may be lucky enough to see one on our bird feeders.

Male coloration is distinctive. As in many bird species, the female is less colorful.

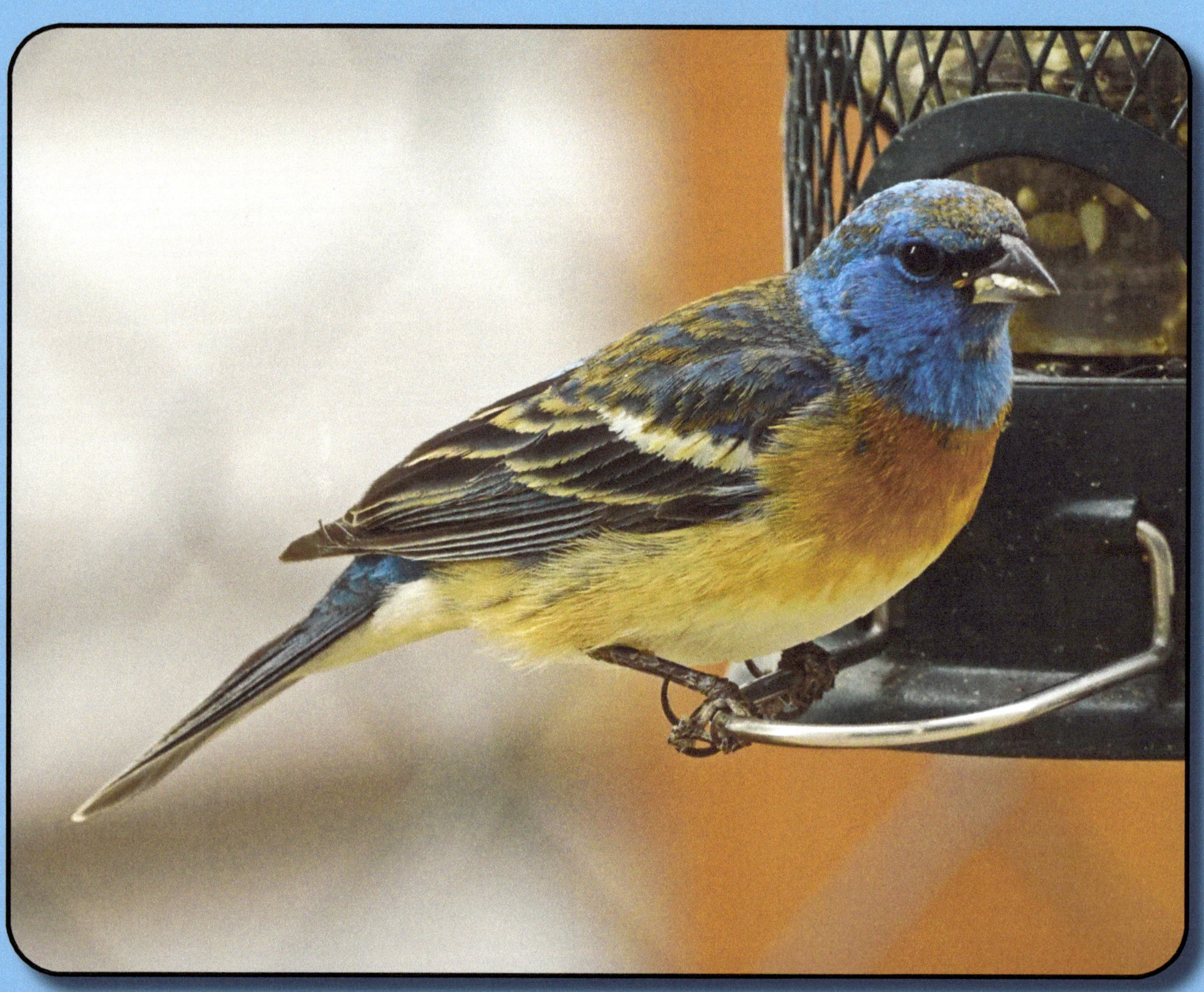

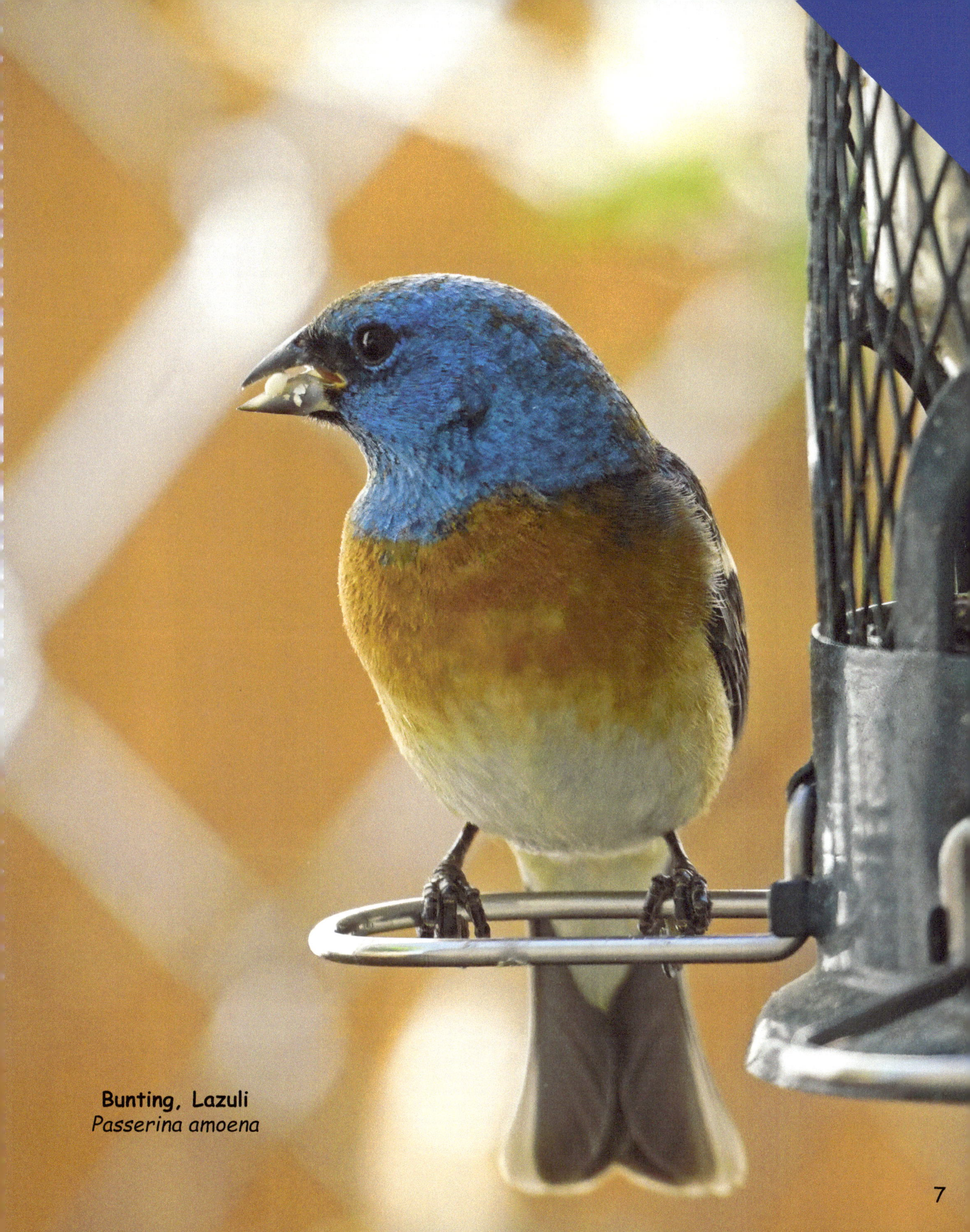

Bunting, Lazuli
Passerina amoena

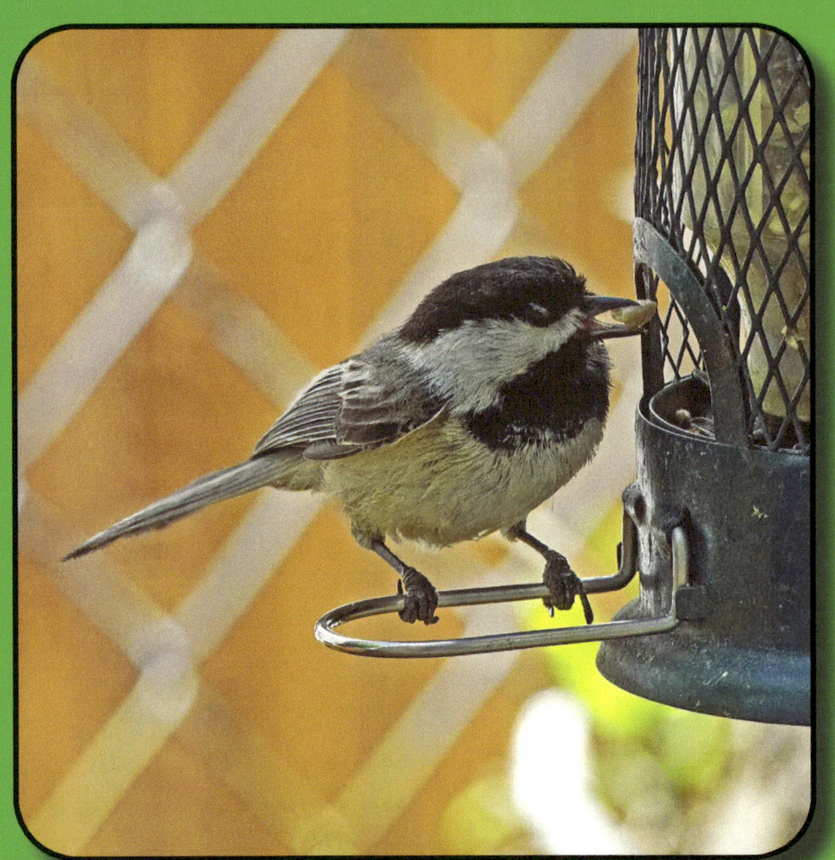

Black-capped Chickadees are year-round residents in this area and often visit bird feeders. Males and females are similar in color,

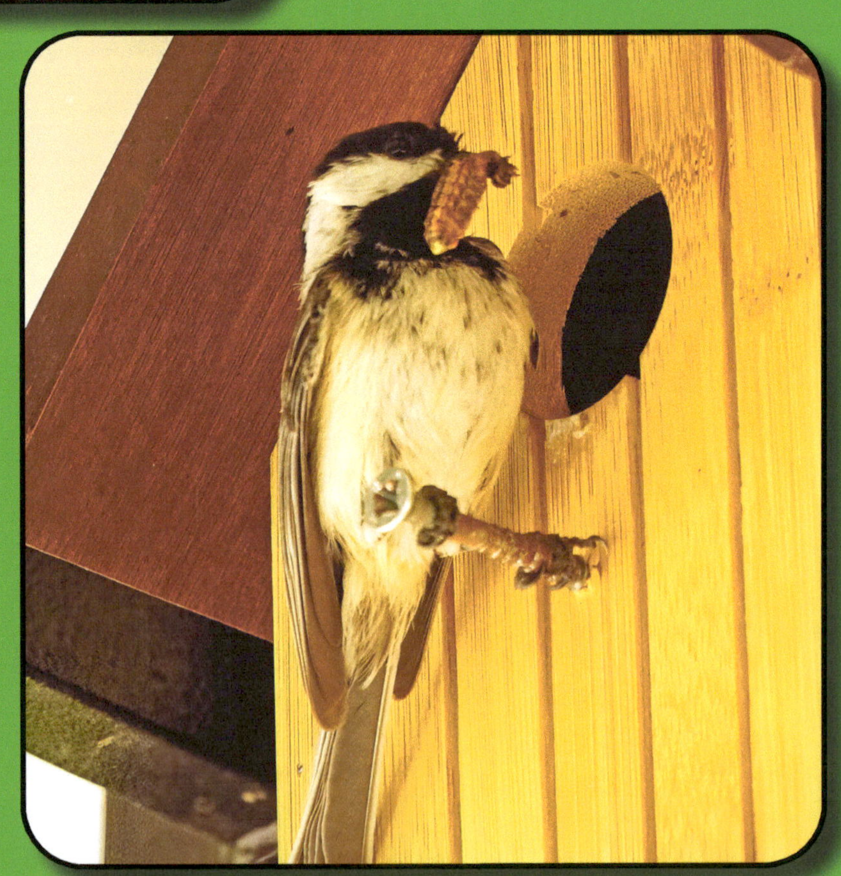

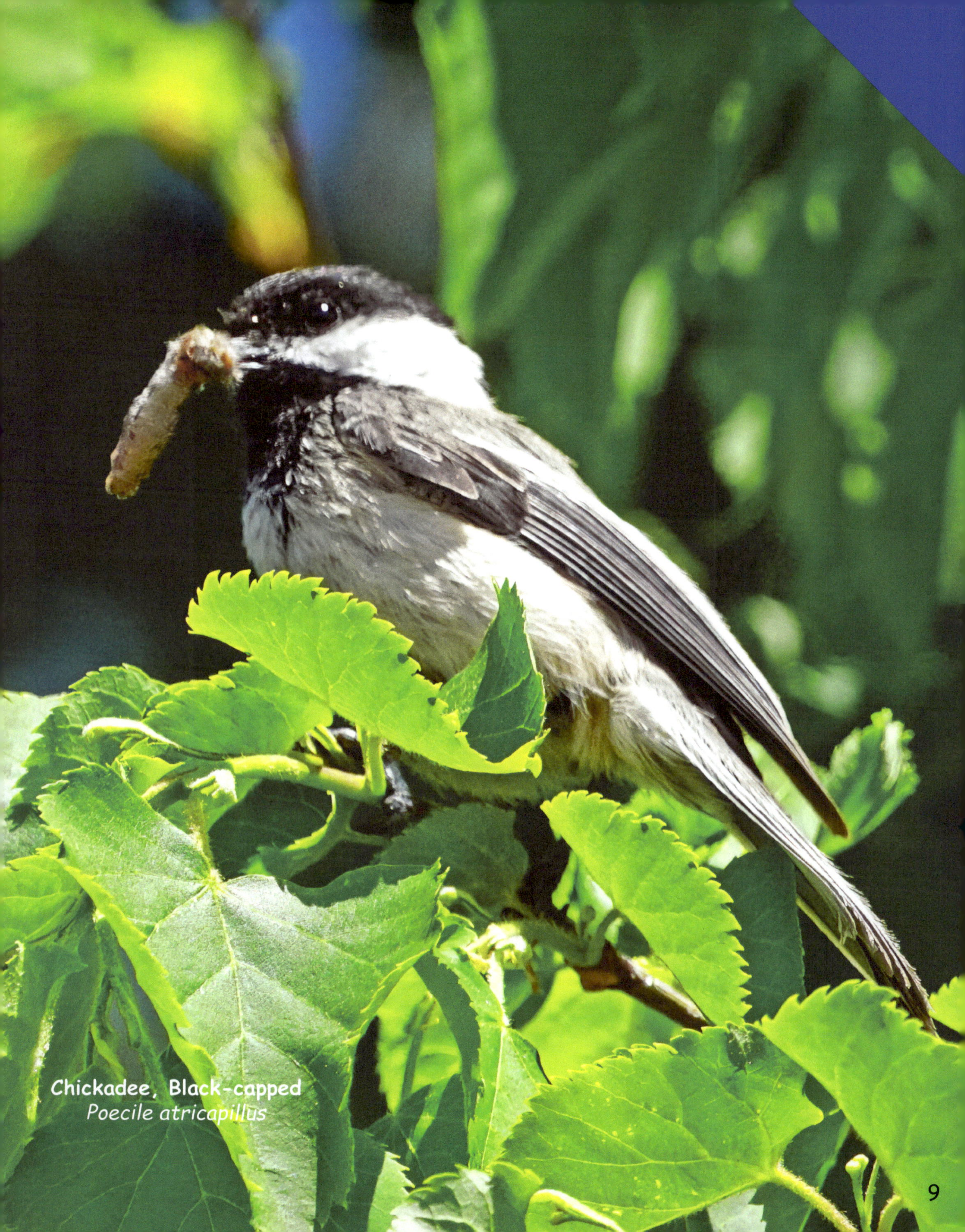

Chickadee, Black-capped
Poecile atricapillus

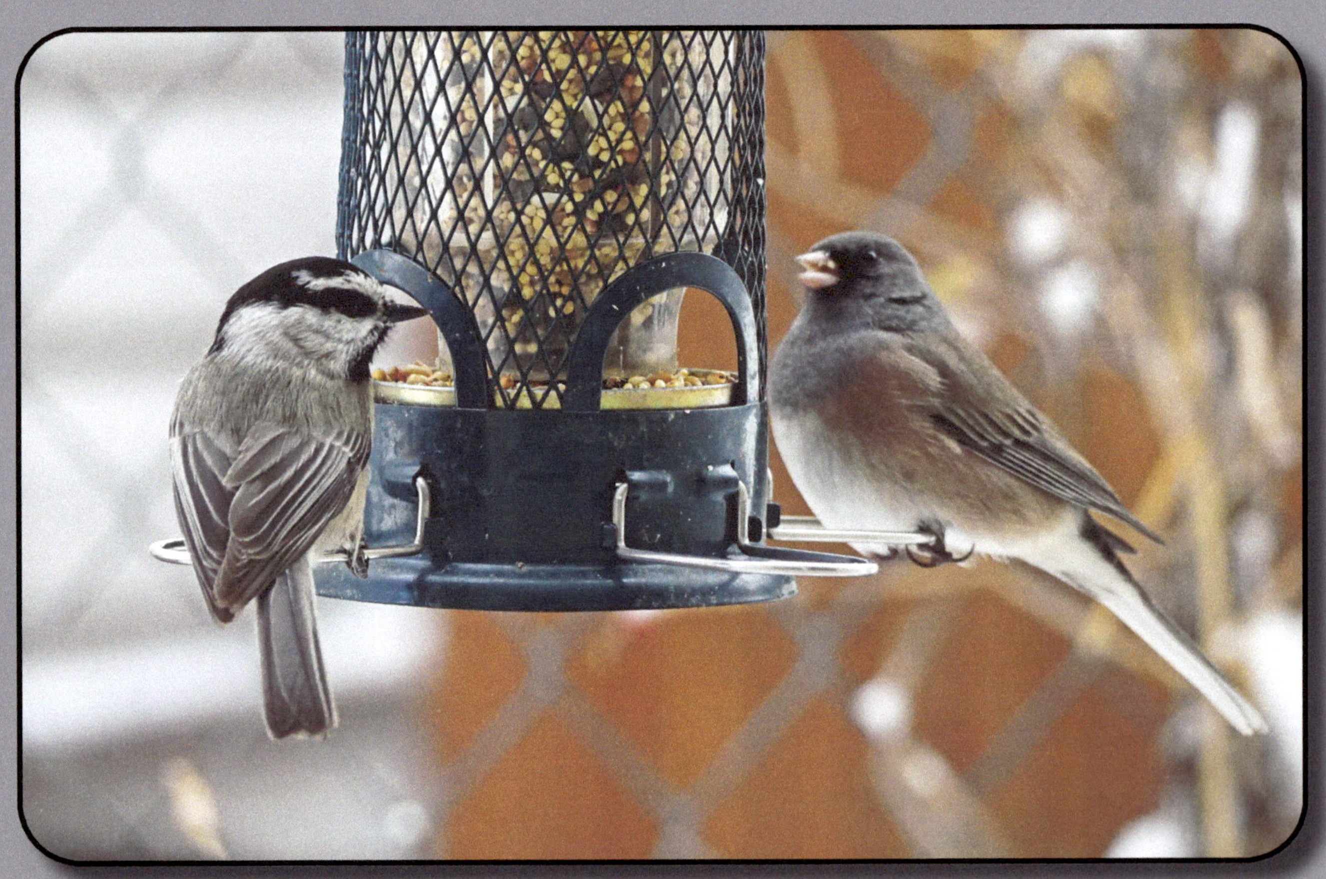

A Mountain Chickadee and a **Dark-eyed Junco** share the bird feeder

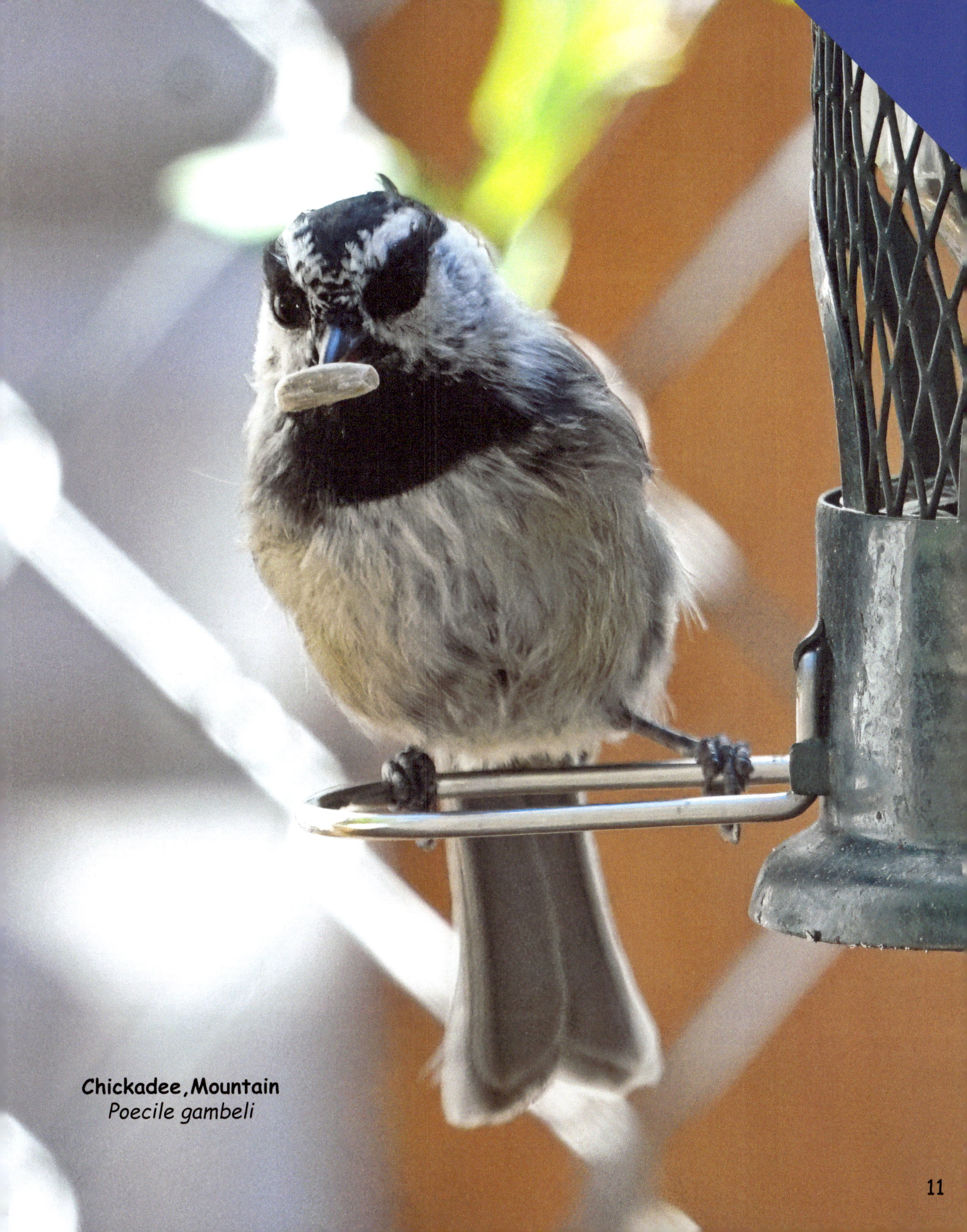

Chickadee,Mountain
Poecile gambeli

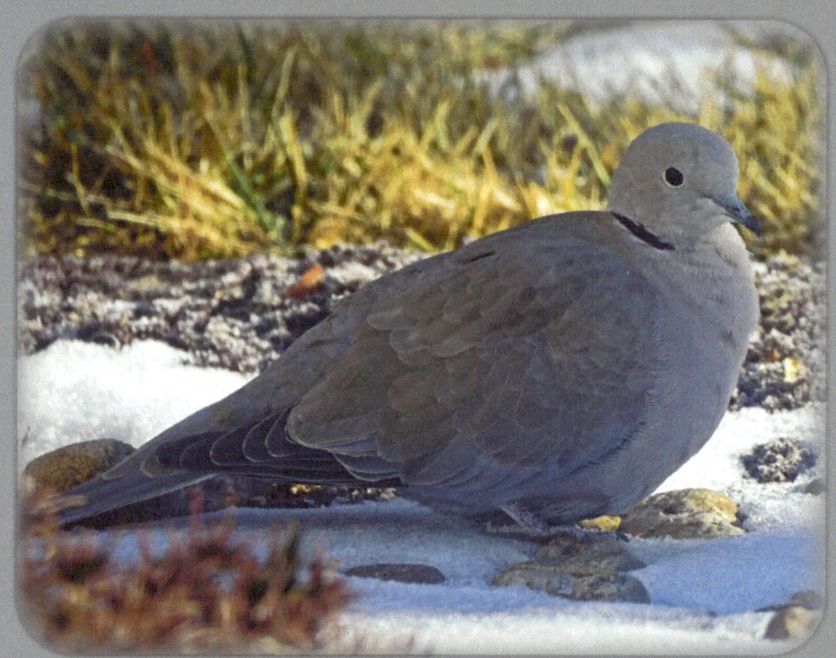

Eurasian Collared-Doves were introduced from Europe and are found across most of the country year-round. They are often seen on roof tops and in gardens in Parker suburbs.

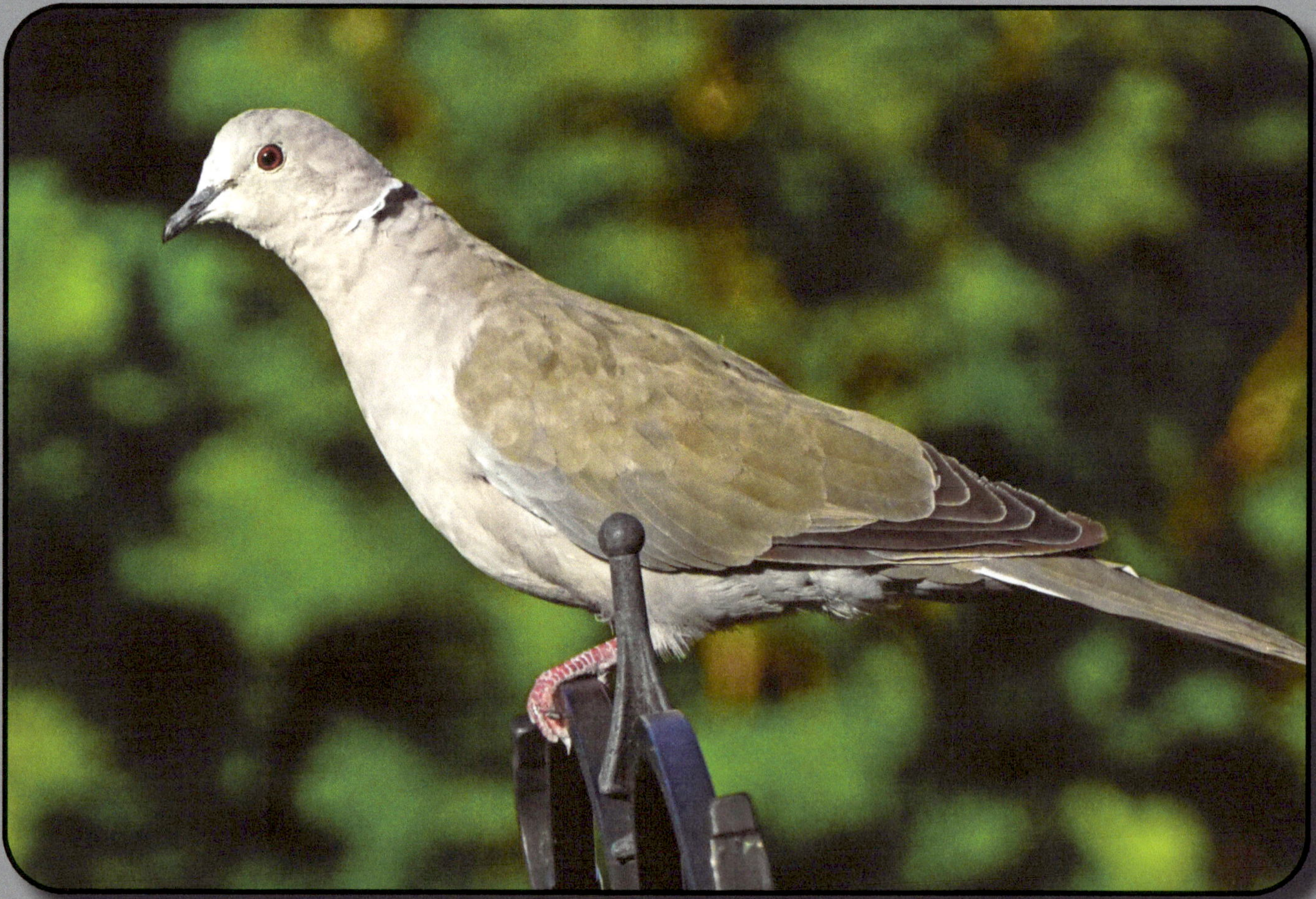

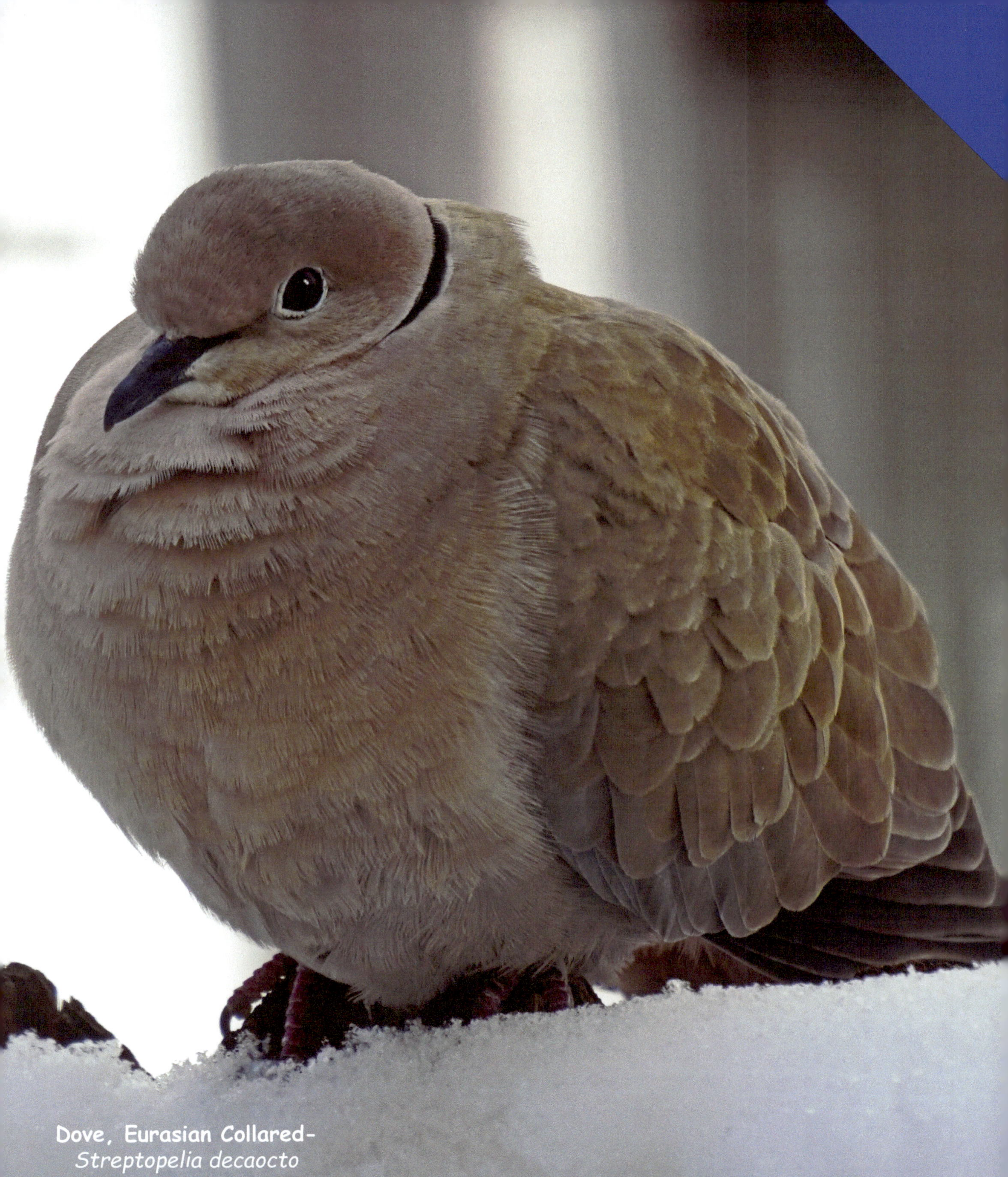

Dove, Eurasian Collared-
Streptopelia decaocto

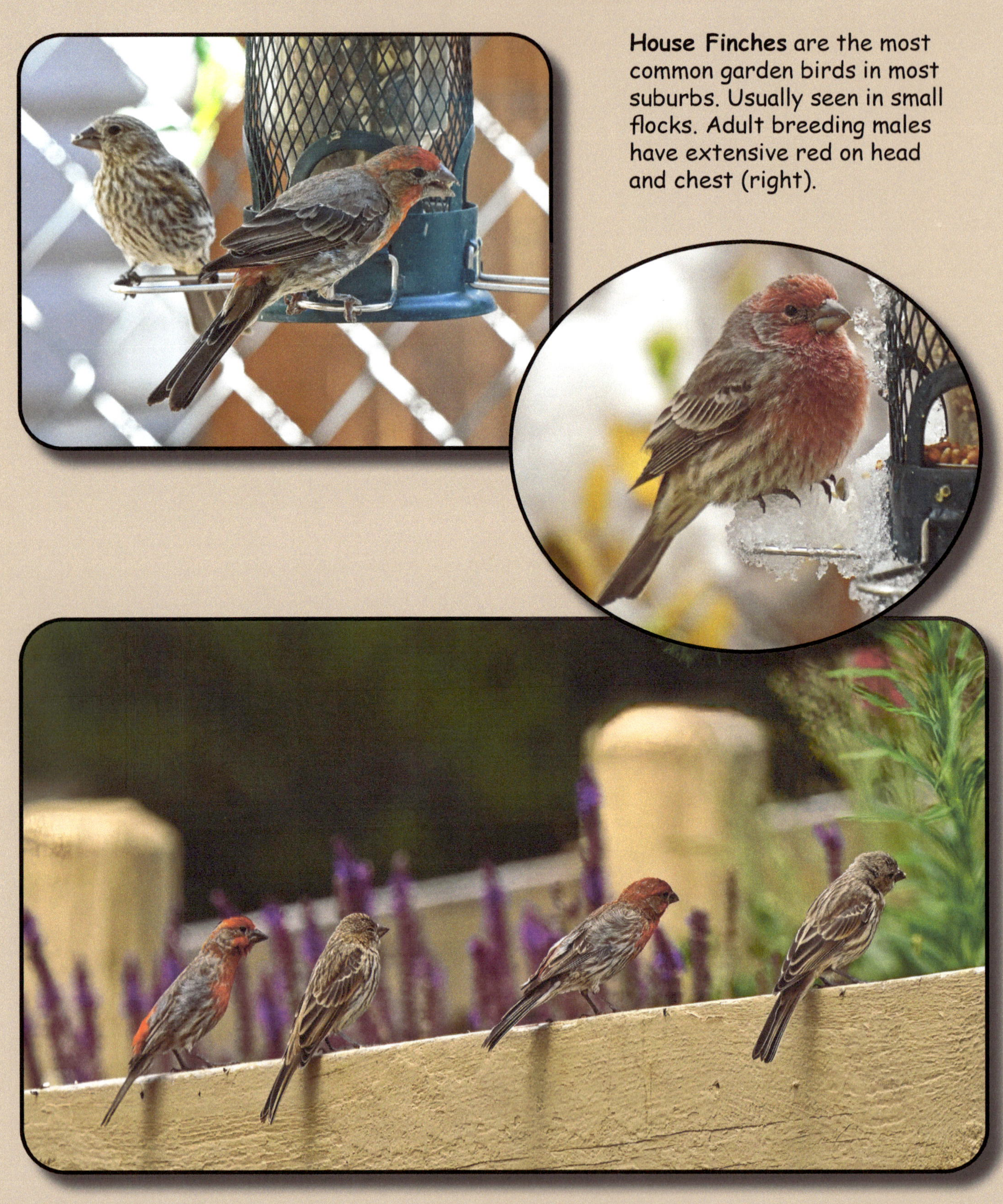

House Finches are the most common garden birds in most suburbs. Usually seen in small flocks. Adult breeding males have extensive red on head and chest (right).

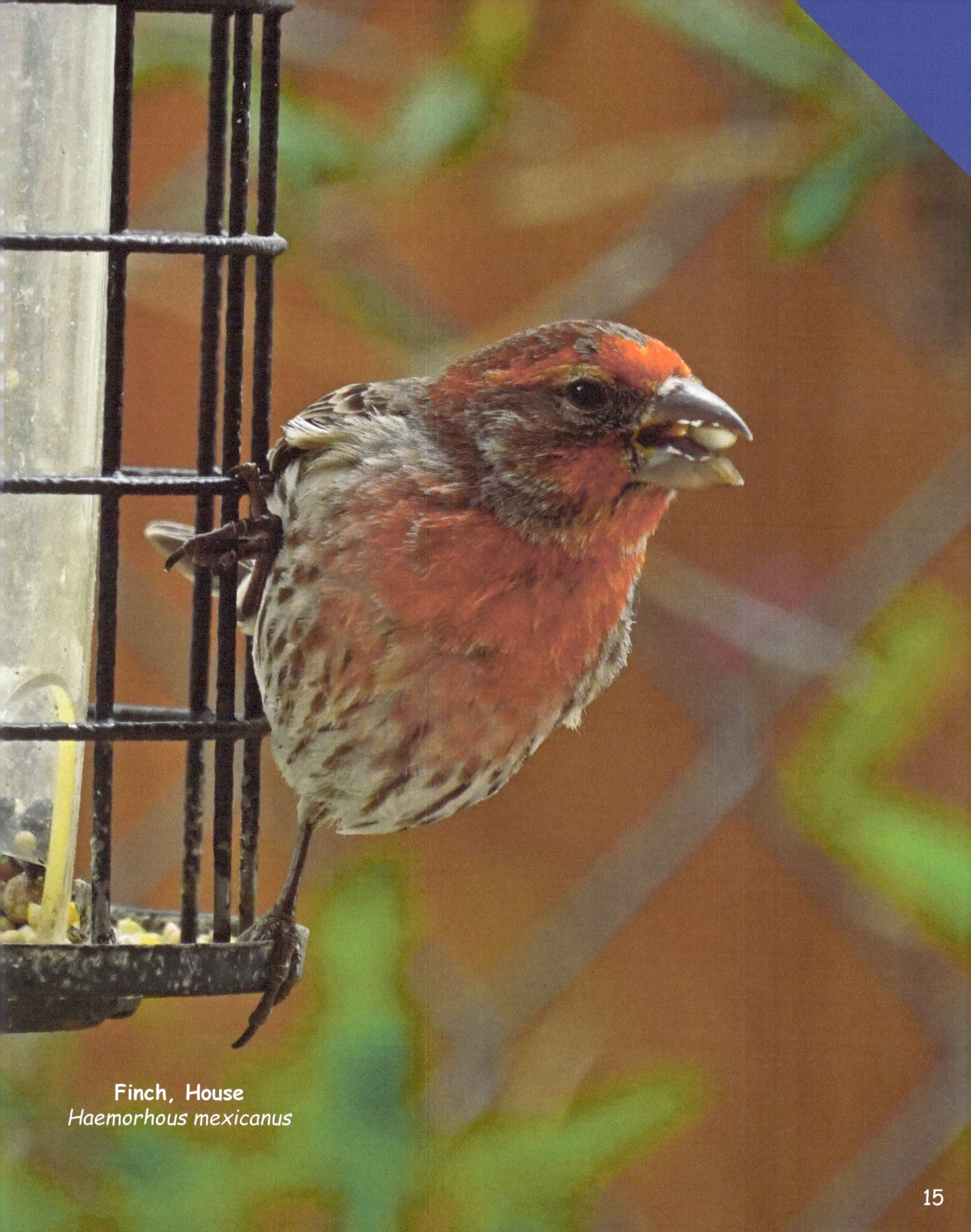

Finch, House
Haemorhous mexicanus

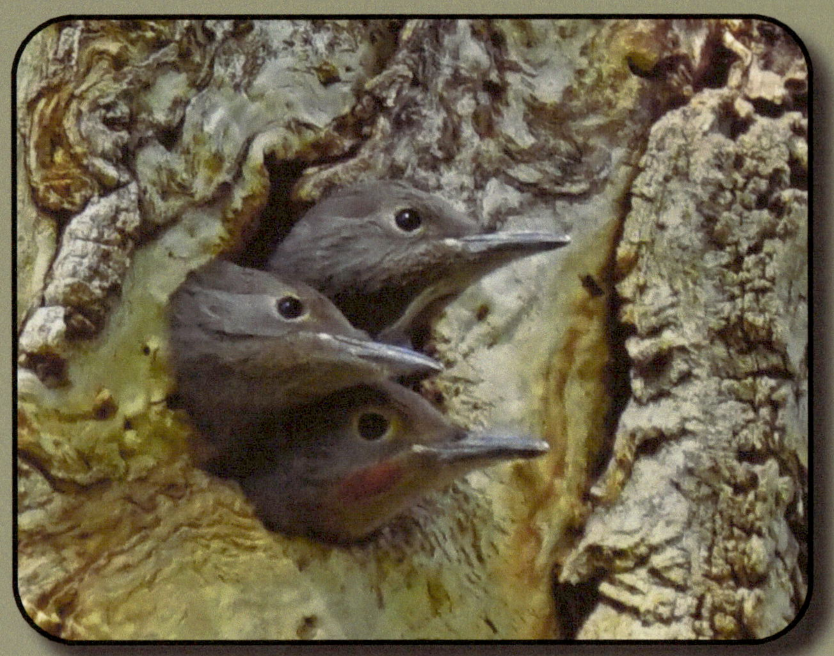

Flicker chicks in their nest

Northern Flickers are plentiful in Parker and are year-round residents. They are a species of woodpecker (fam: Picidae). Unlike other woodpeckers they feed largely on the ground.

Male and female are similar in color except for a distinctive red flash on the cheek of the male.

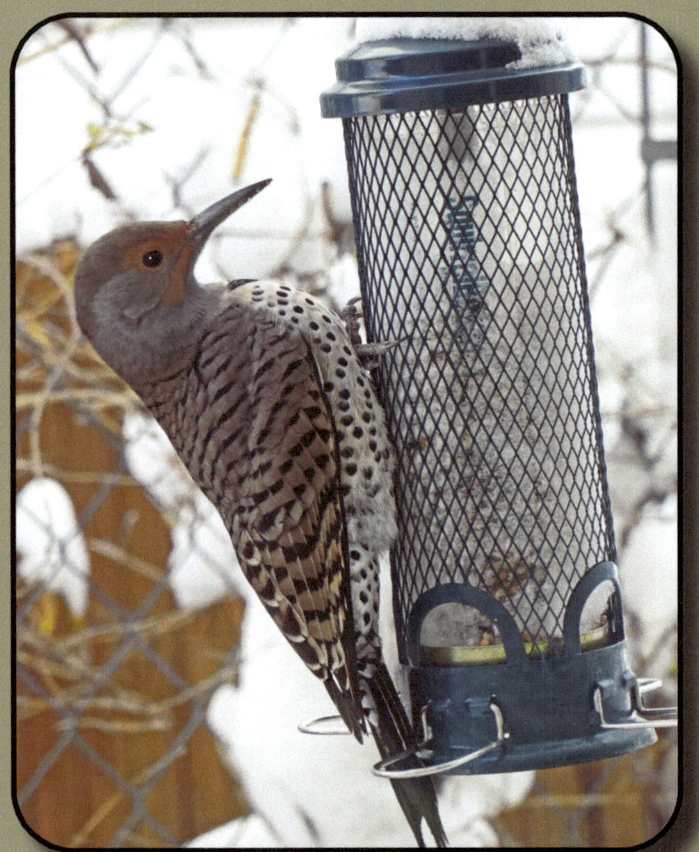

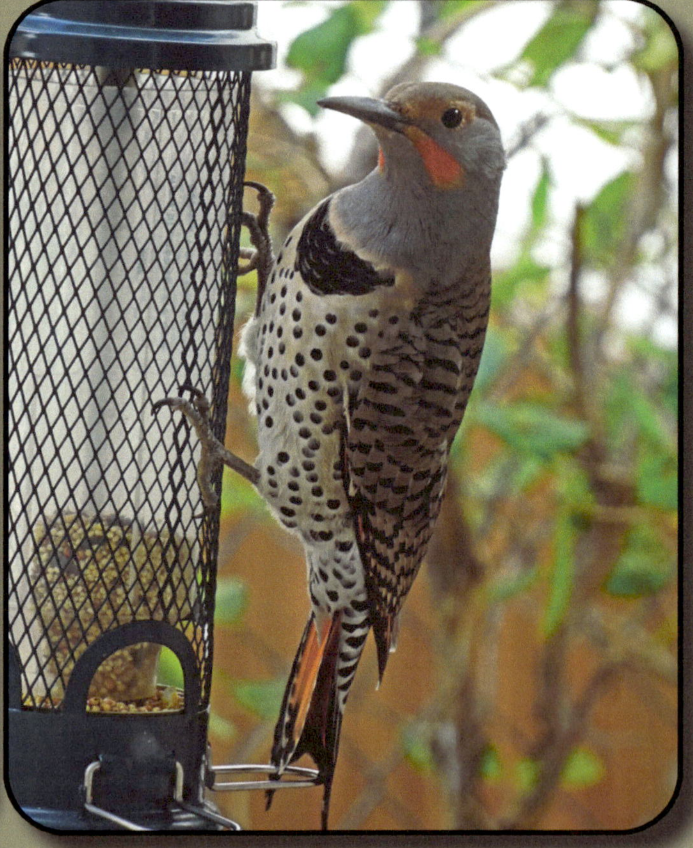

Female Flicker (left) and male (right)

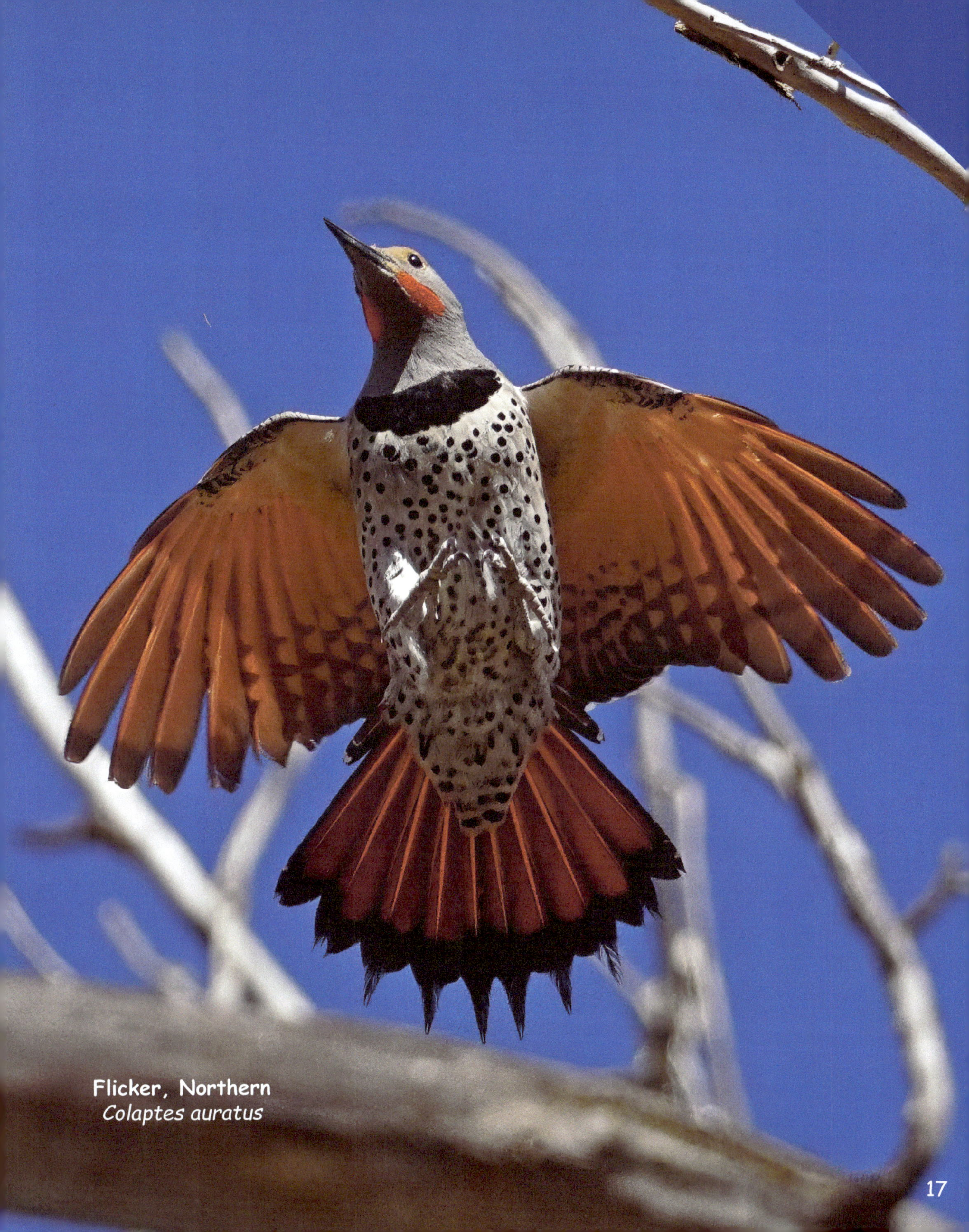

Flicker, Northern
Colaptes auratus

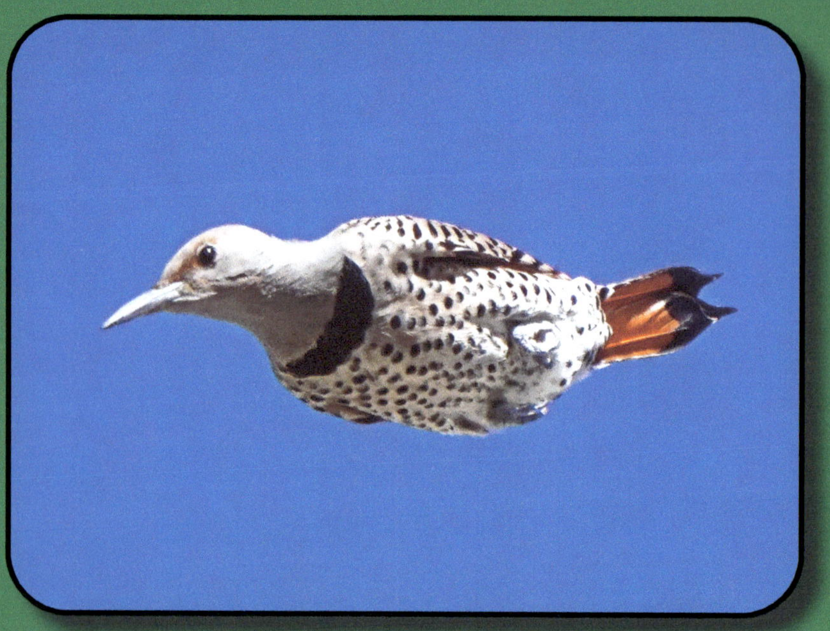

Female Flicker

Flickers make their nests by hollowing out mature trees. They often drum on trees or even metal objects to declare territory.

Right: Cleaning out a nest by "flicking" the wood chips out.

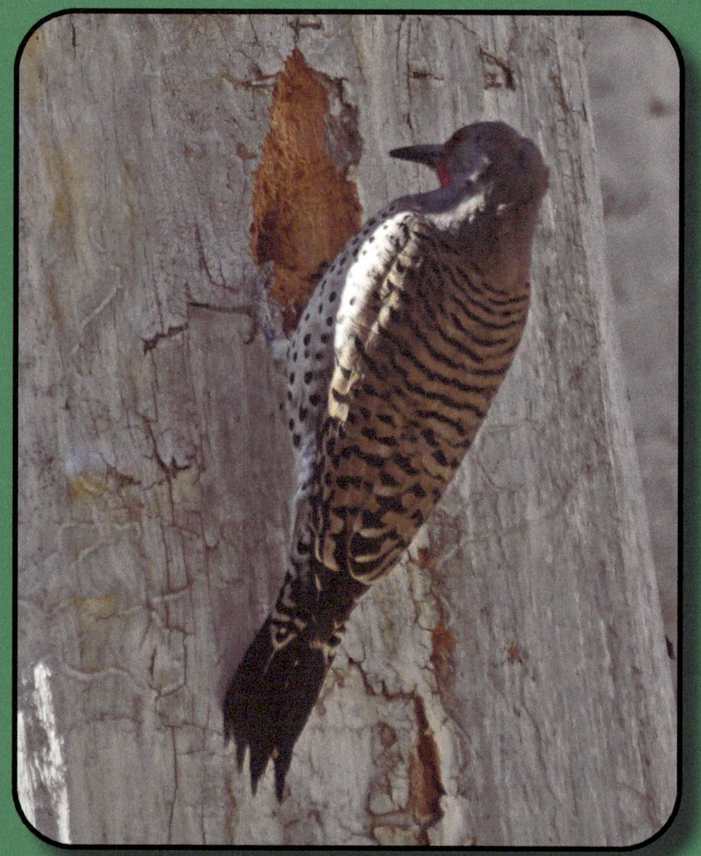

Male Flicker begins nest contruction

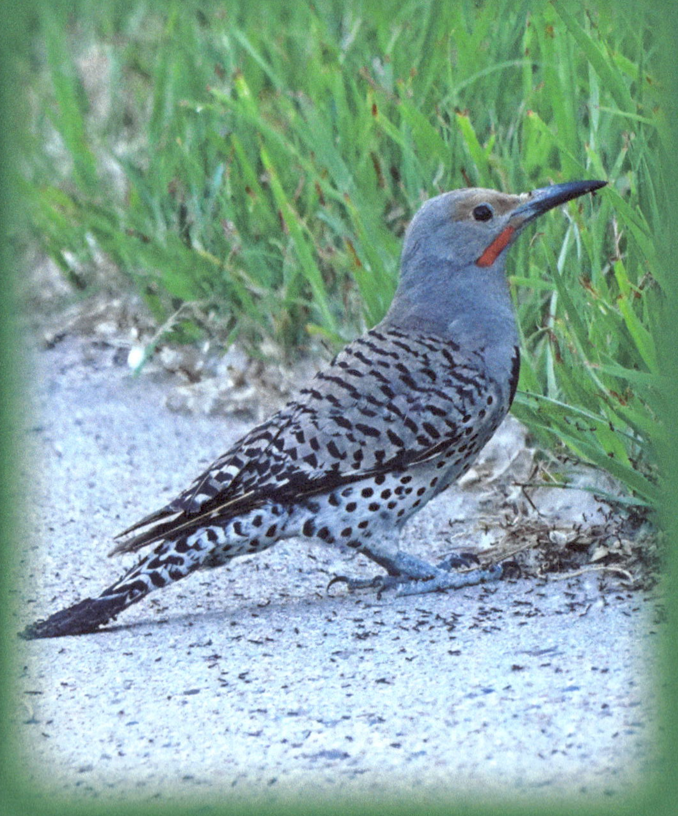

Flickers are ground feeders

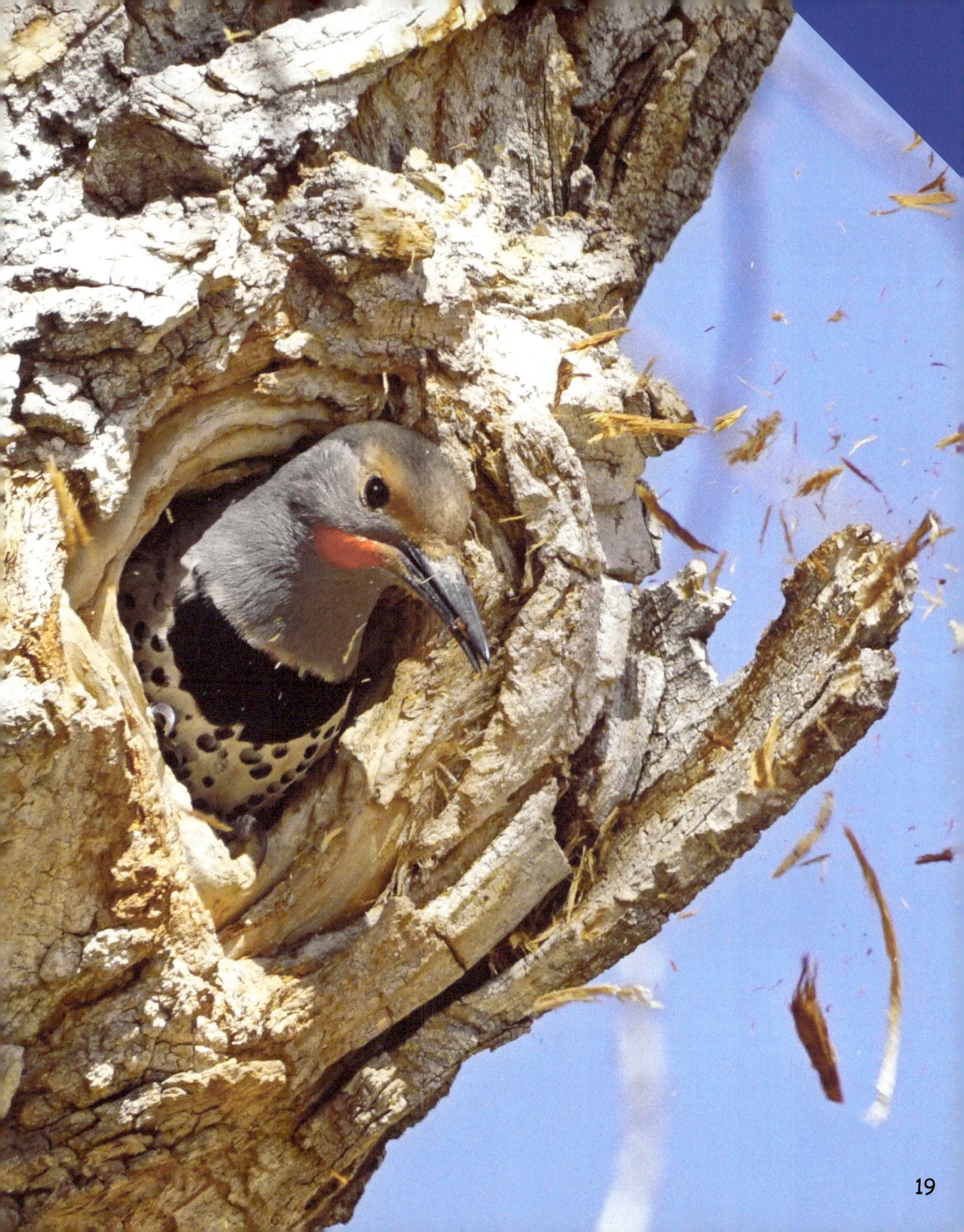

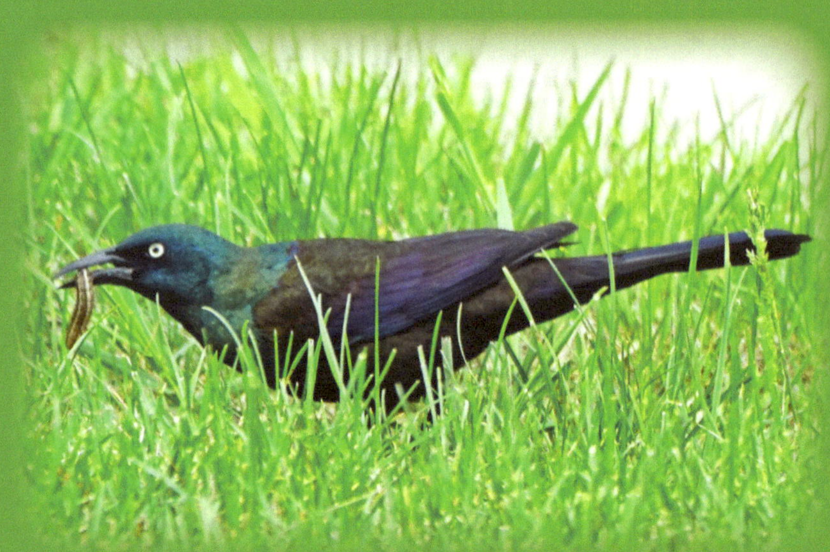

Common Grackles are only in Colorado during the summer months. They nest in trees in suburban neighborhoods, especially in dense evergreens. They forage on the ground, often in large flocks, but occasionally will be seen on bird feeders.

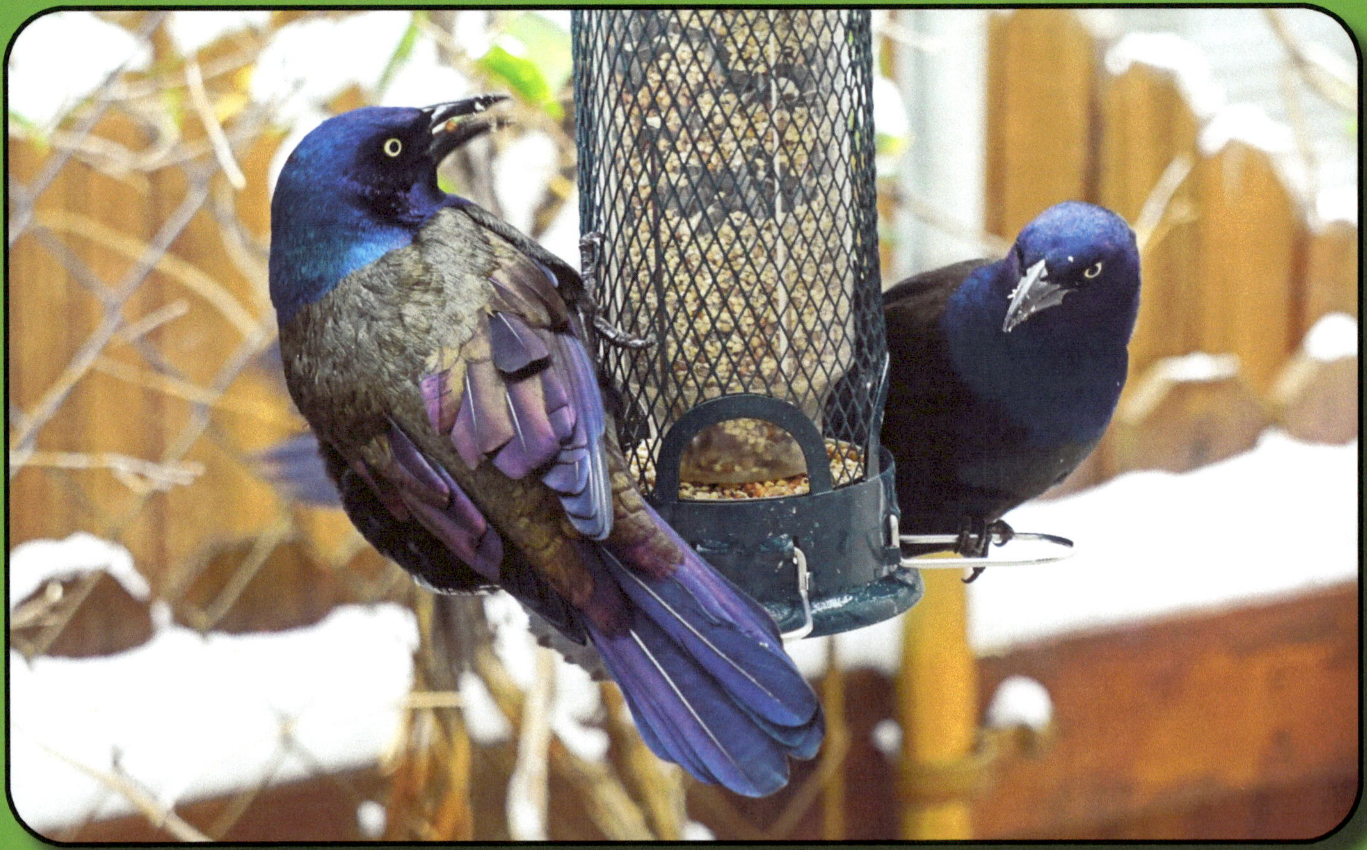

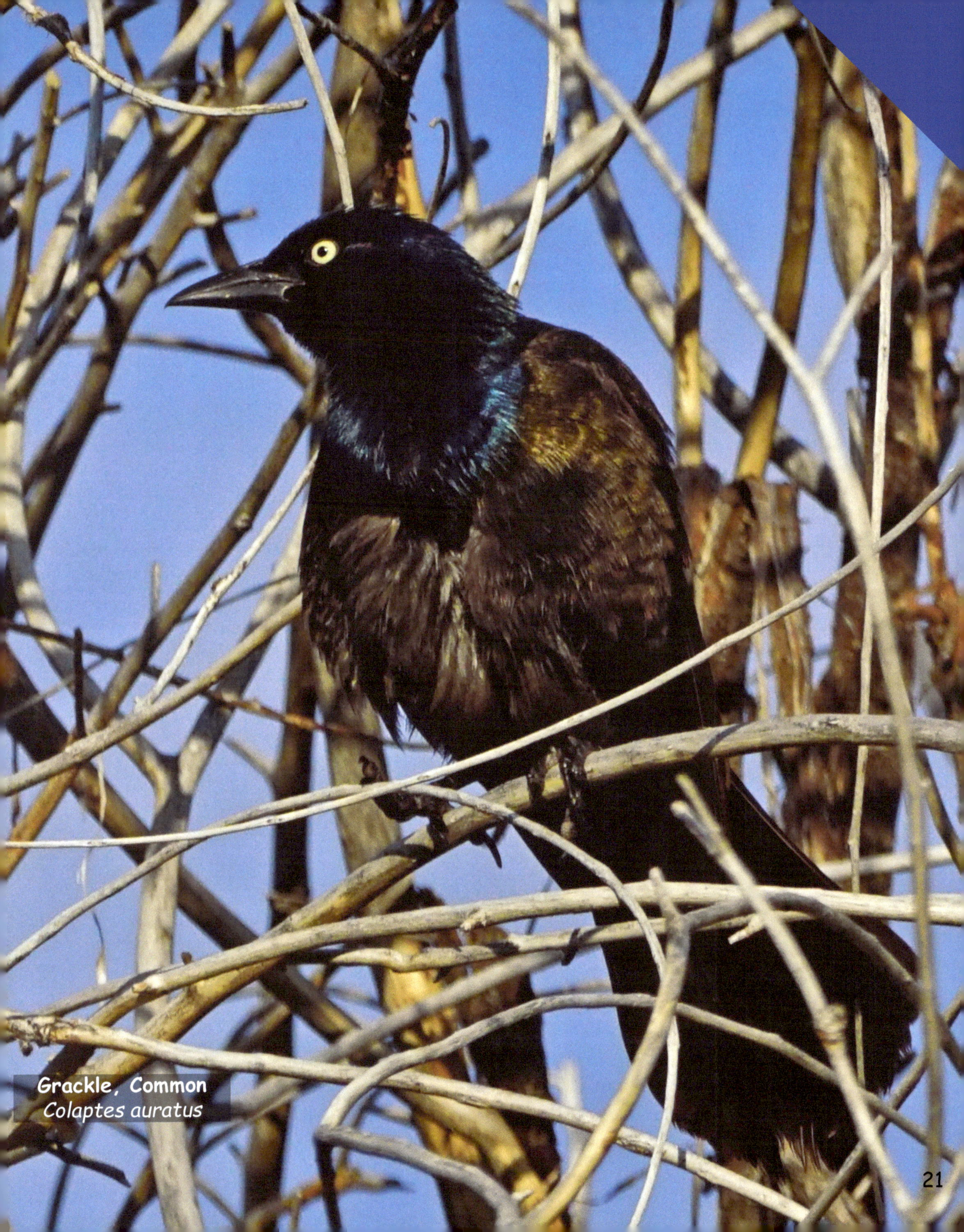

Grackle, Common
Colaptes auratus

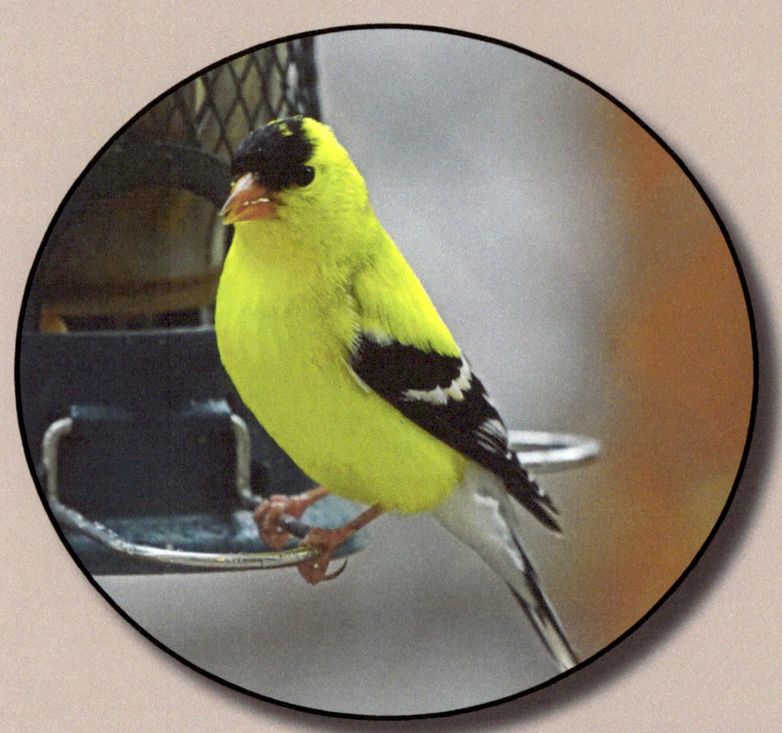

Although not numerous, **American Goldfinches** can be seen year-round in Parker, feeding on tree buds, grass and weed seeds (especially thistles).Occasionally they will be found on bird feeders. Both male and female are bright yellow in color but adult males have a distinctive black forehead.

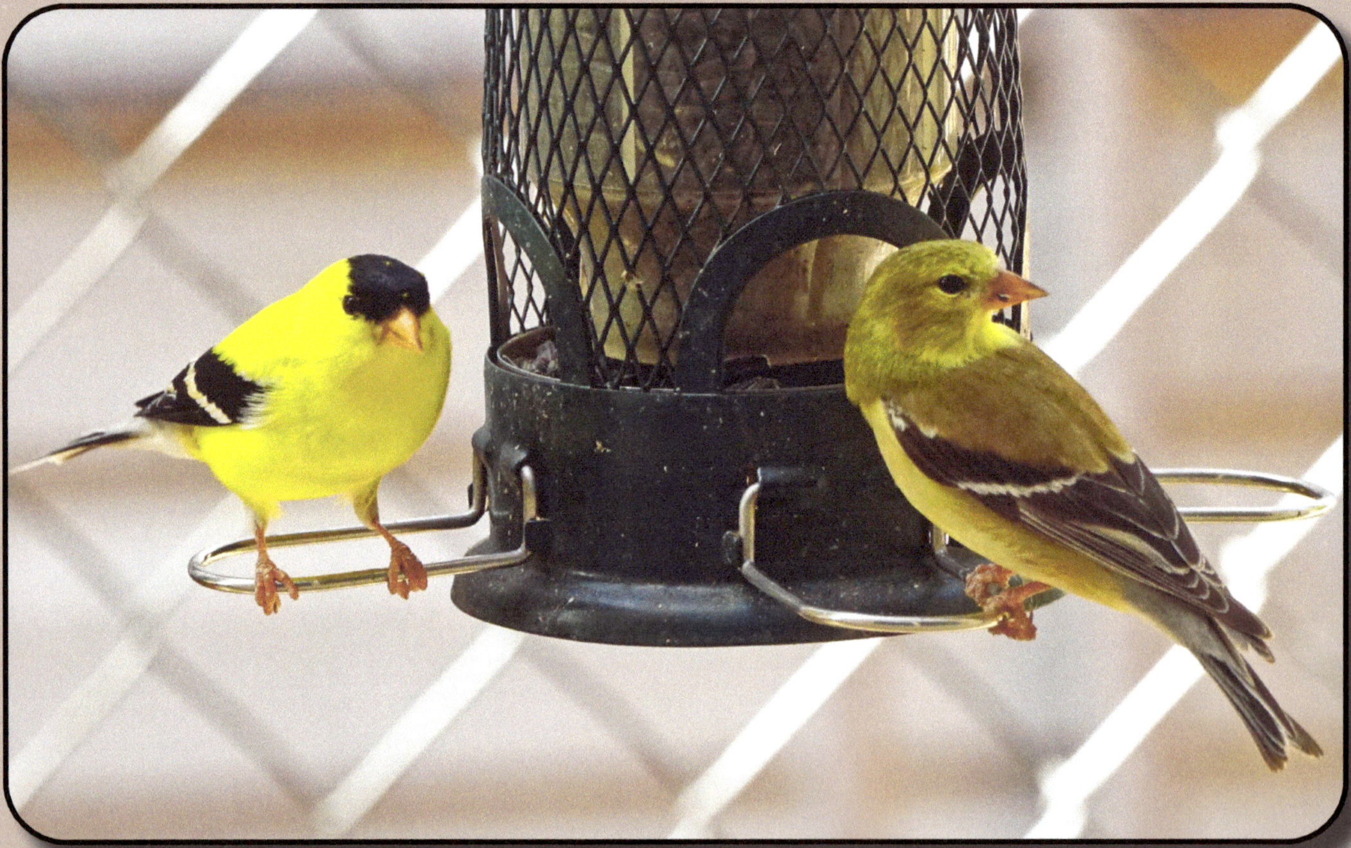

Male American Goldfinch (left) and female (right)

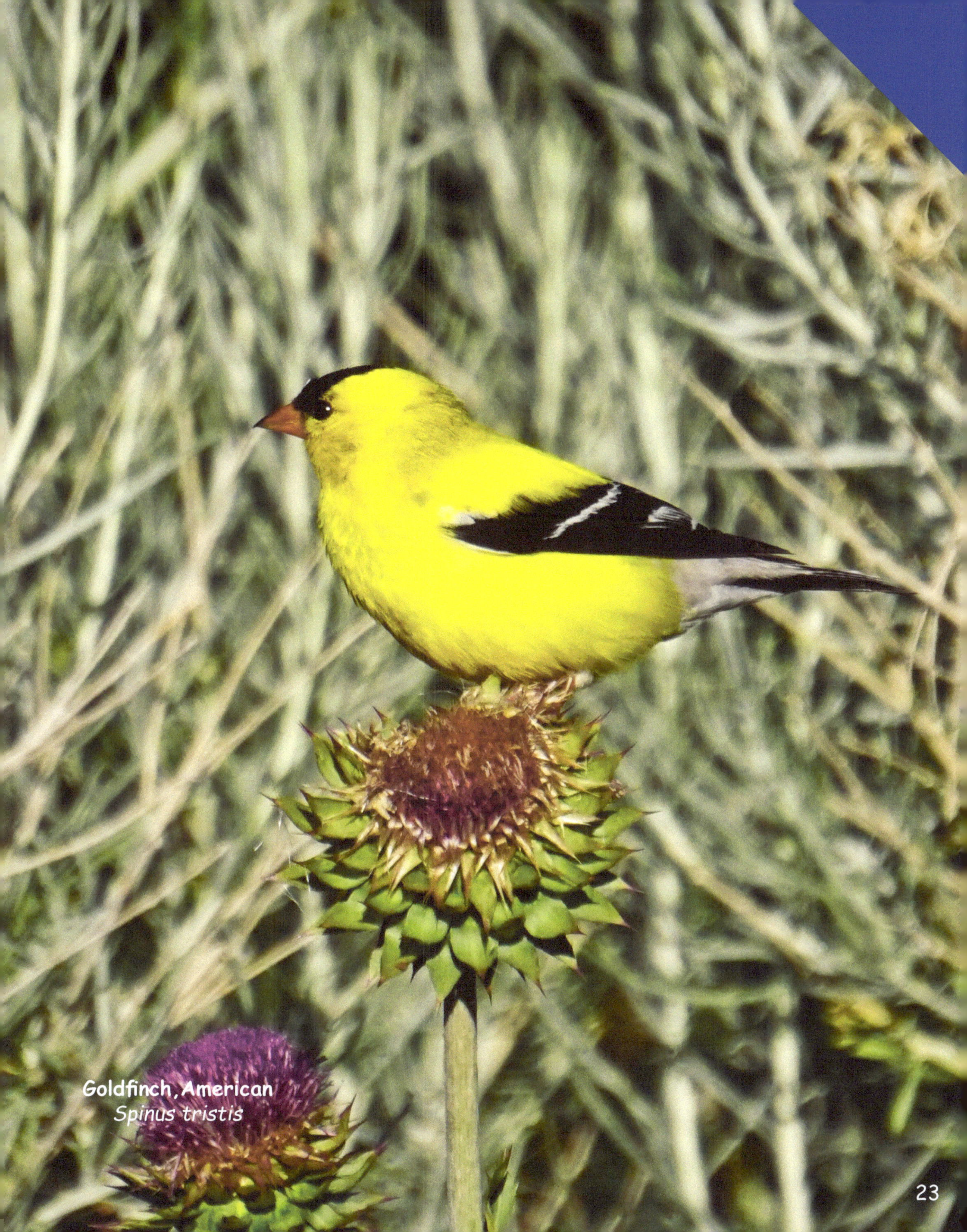

Goldfinch, American
Spinus tristis

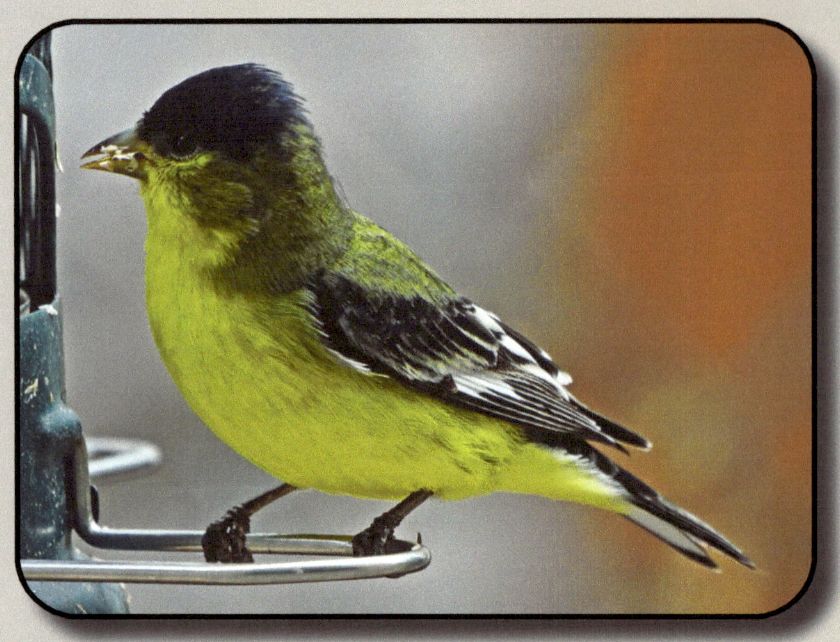

Lesser Goldfinches have similar habits to the American Goldfinch. Occasionally they will be found on bird feeders. Both male and female are bright yellow but adult males have a distinctive black head.

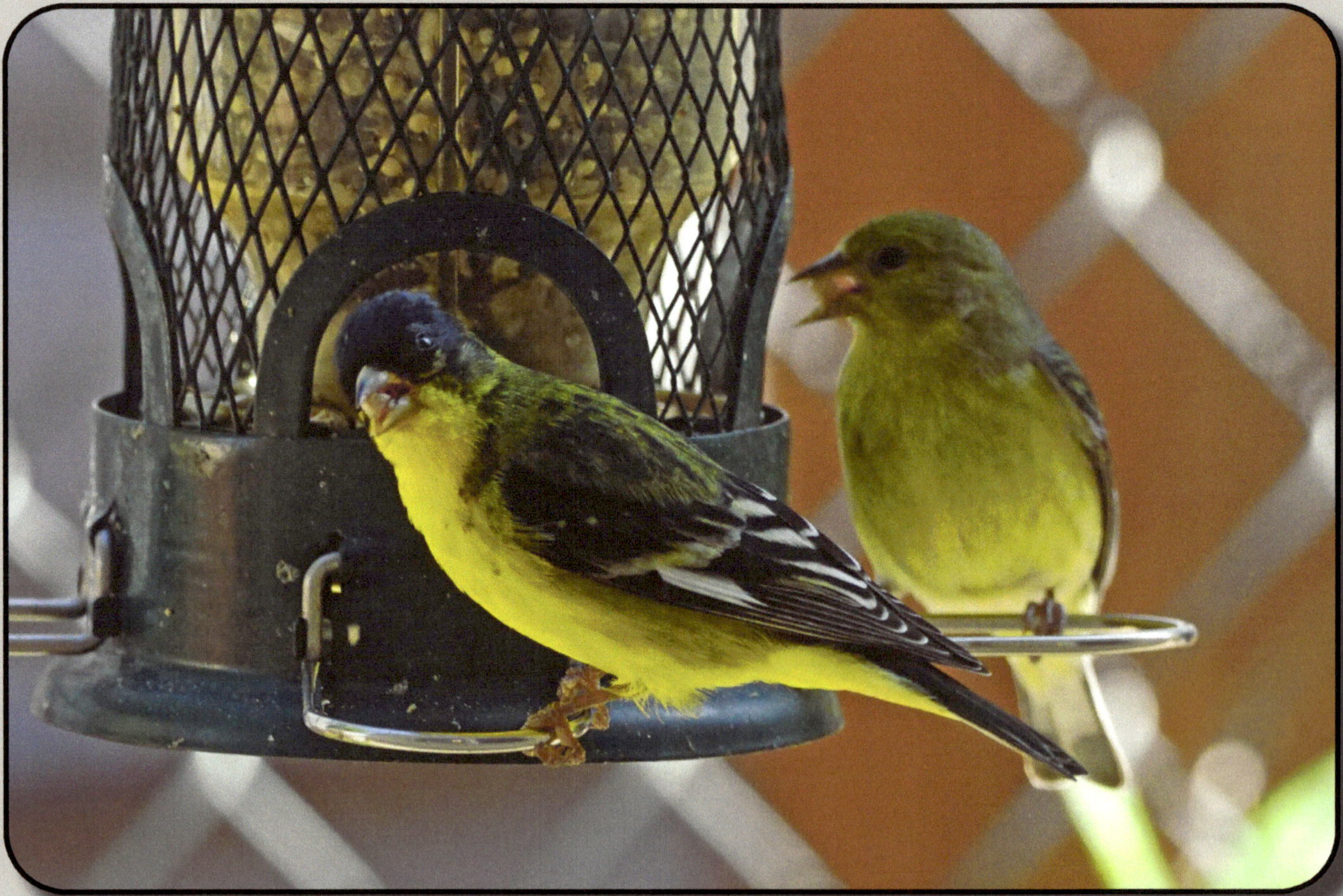

A pair of Lesser Goldfinches, Male (left) and female (right)

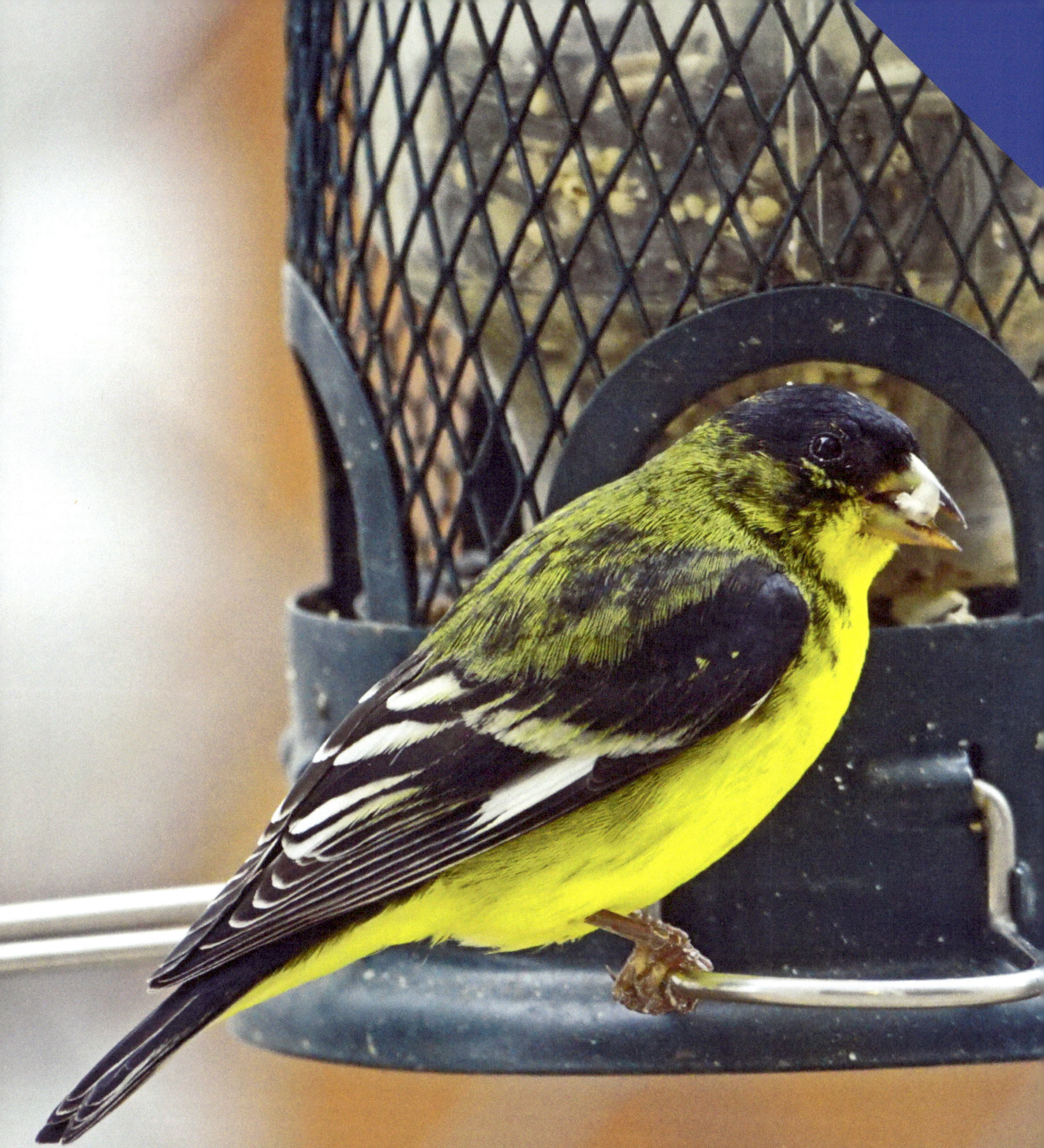

Goldfinch, Lesser
Spinus psaltria

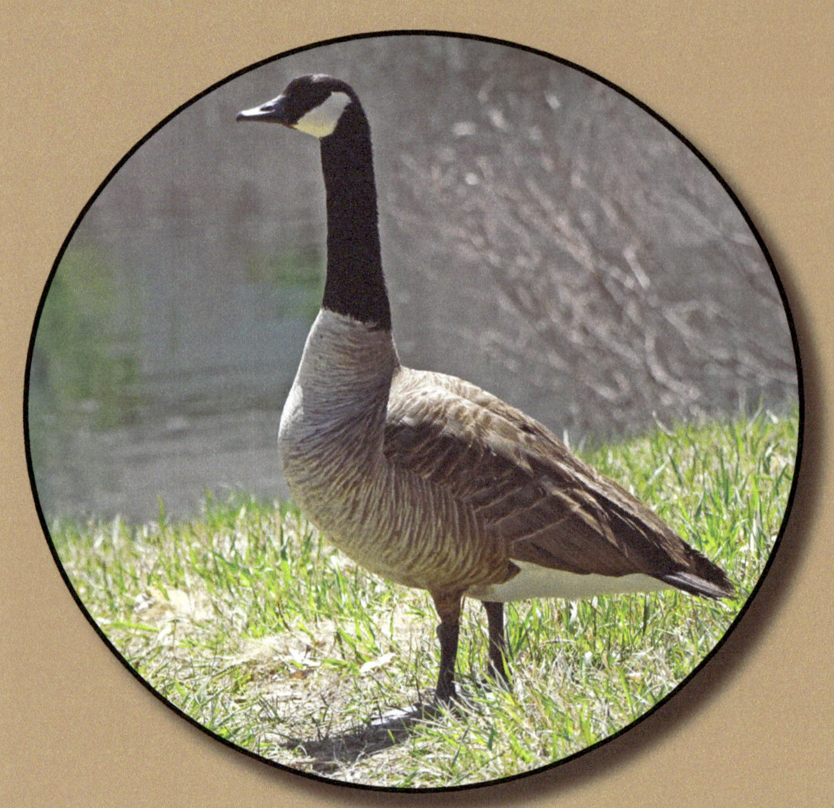

The **Canada Goose** needs no introduction as it is very common and widespread, even through the winter months. They can be found on or near any body of water.

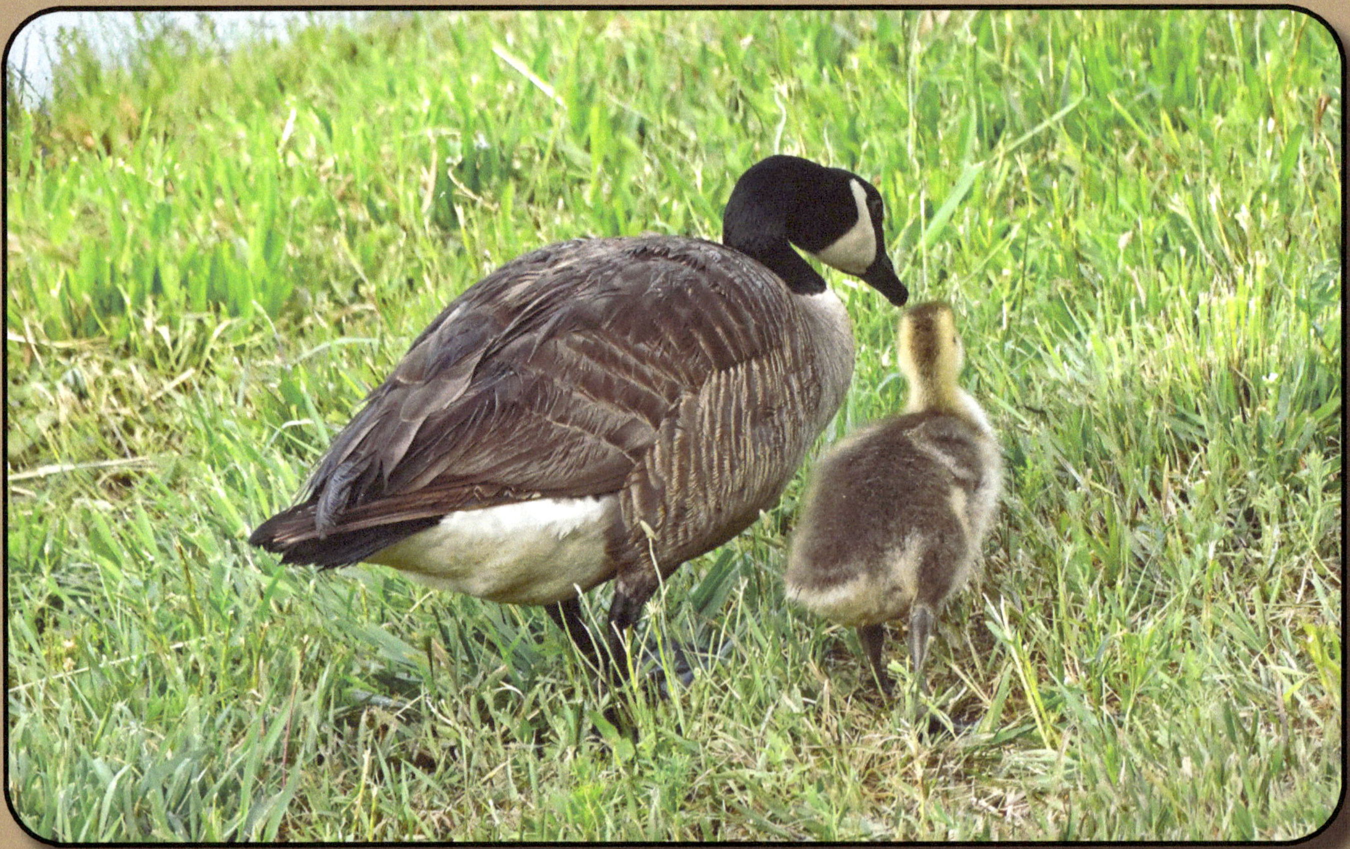

Canada Goose adult and gosling

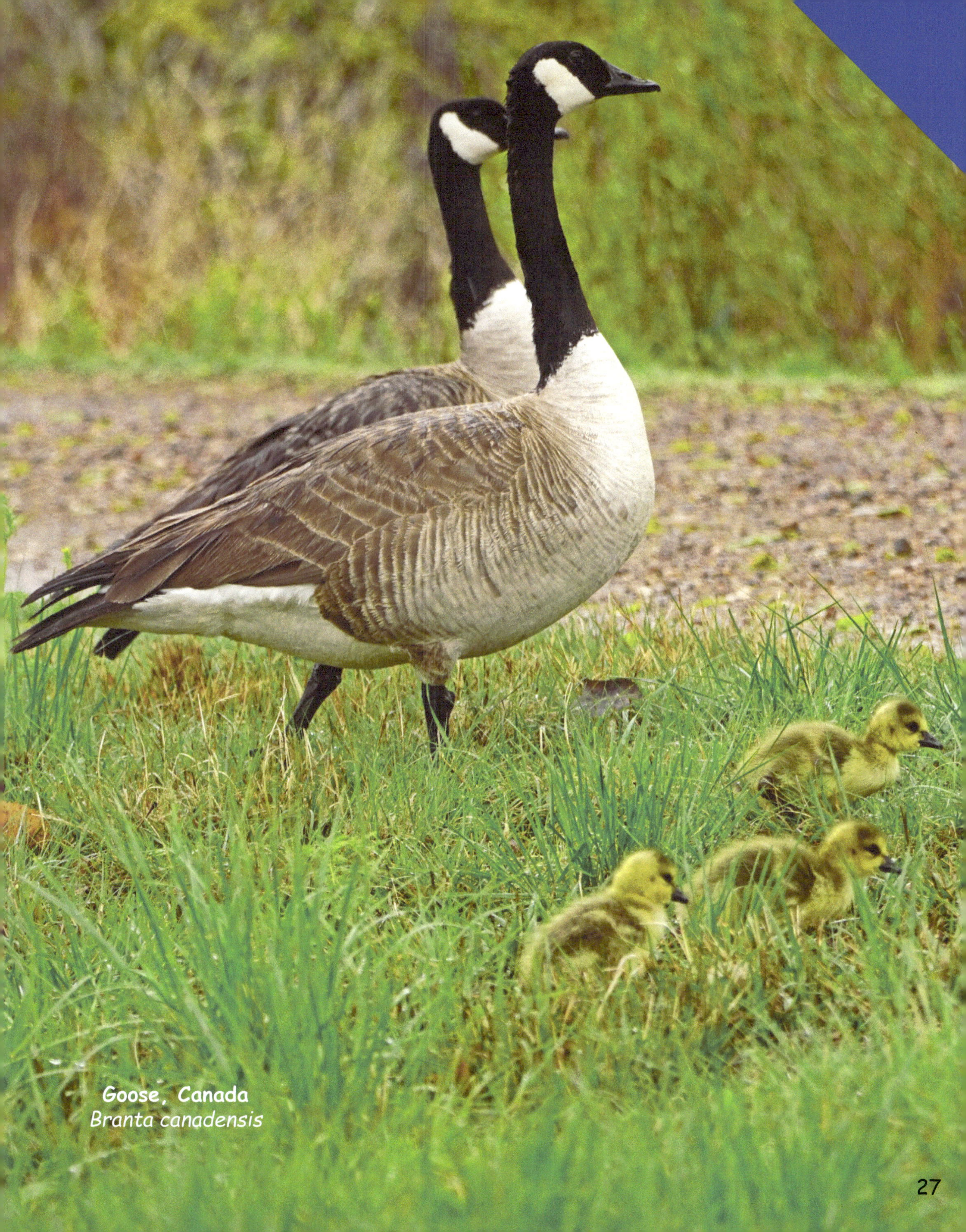

Goose, Canada
Branta canadensis

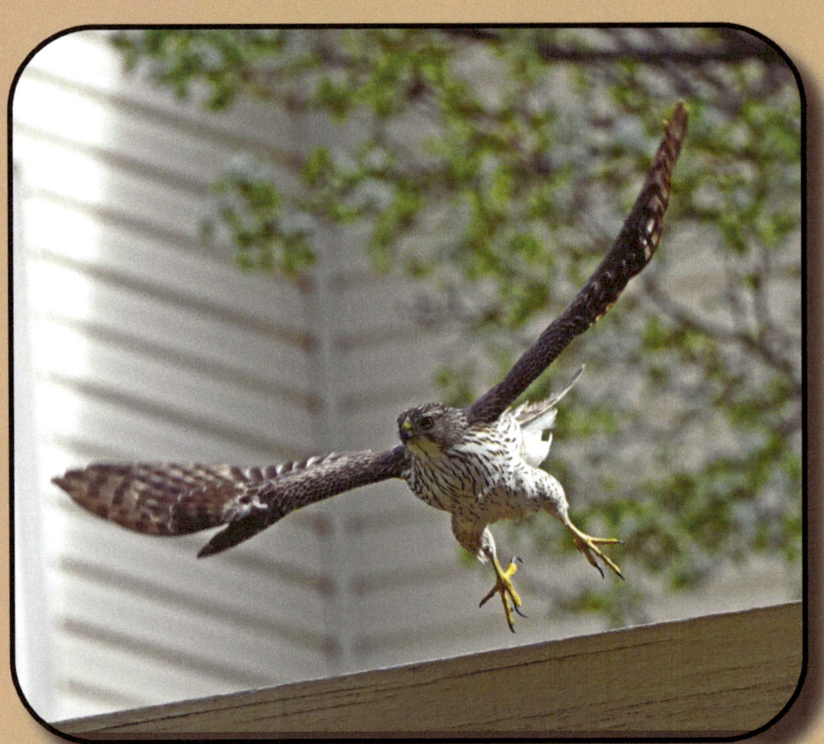

Cooper's Hawks nest in the Parker area each summer and can be seen building their nest of sticks beginning in early April.

They hunt small birds and rodents can often be seen perched near bird feeders hoping for a meal.

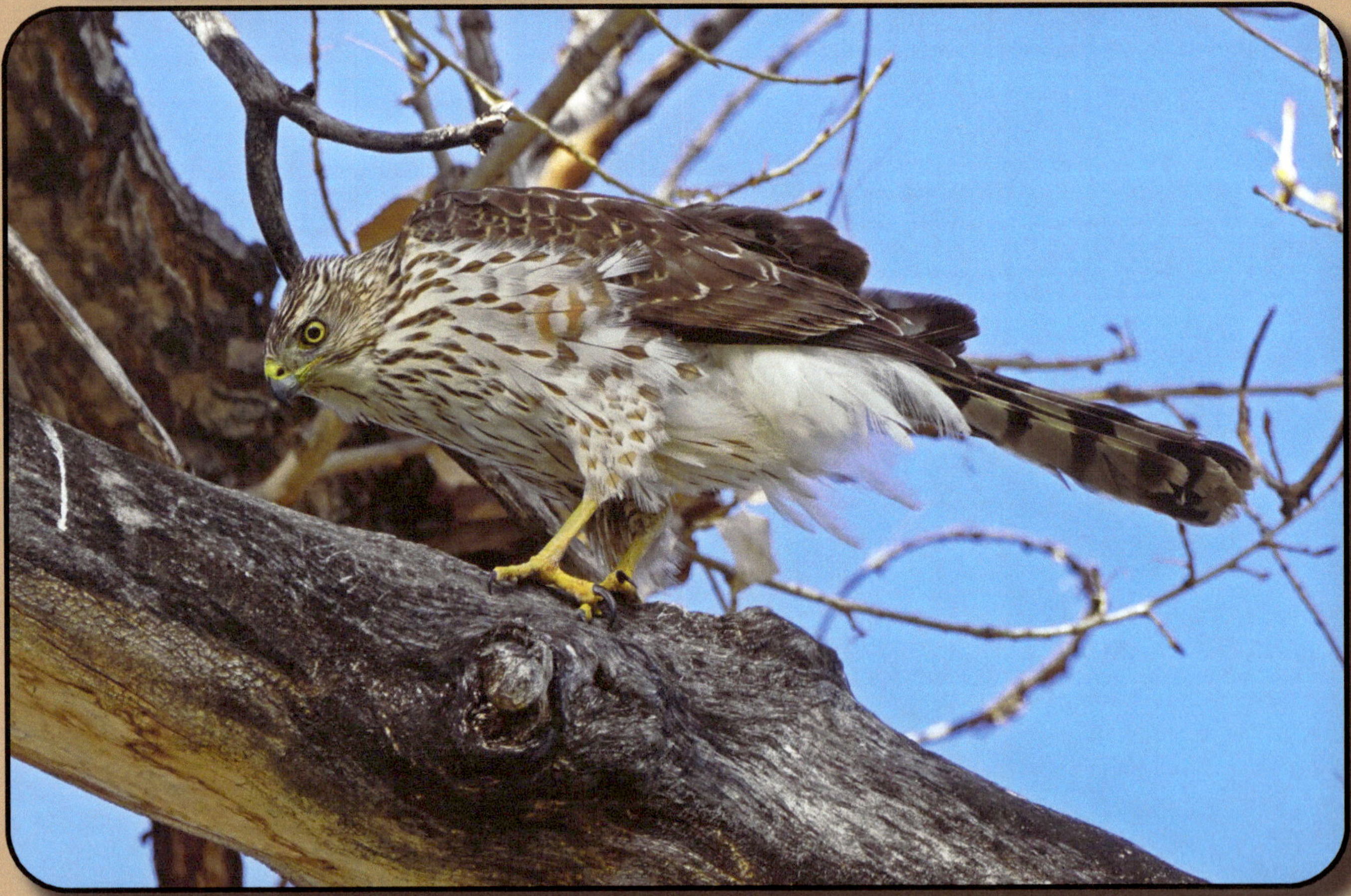

Juvenile (1st year) Cooper's Hawk

28

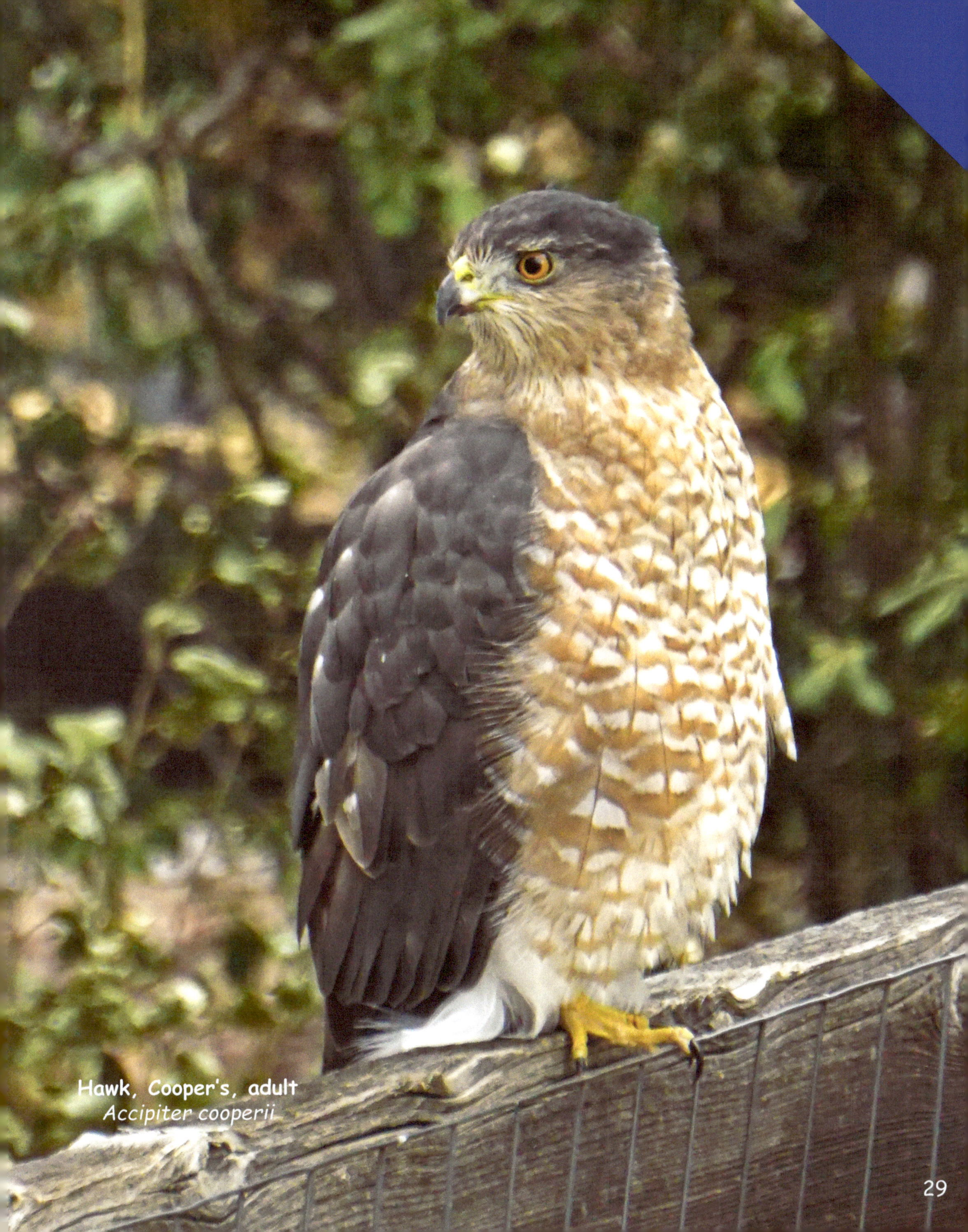

Hawk, Cooper's, adult
Accipiter cooperii

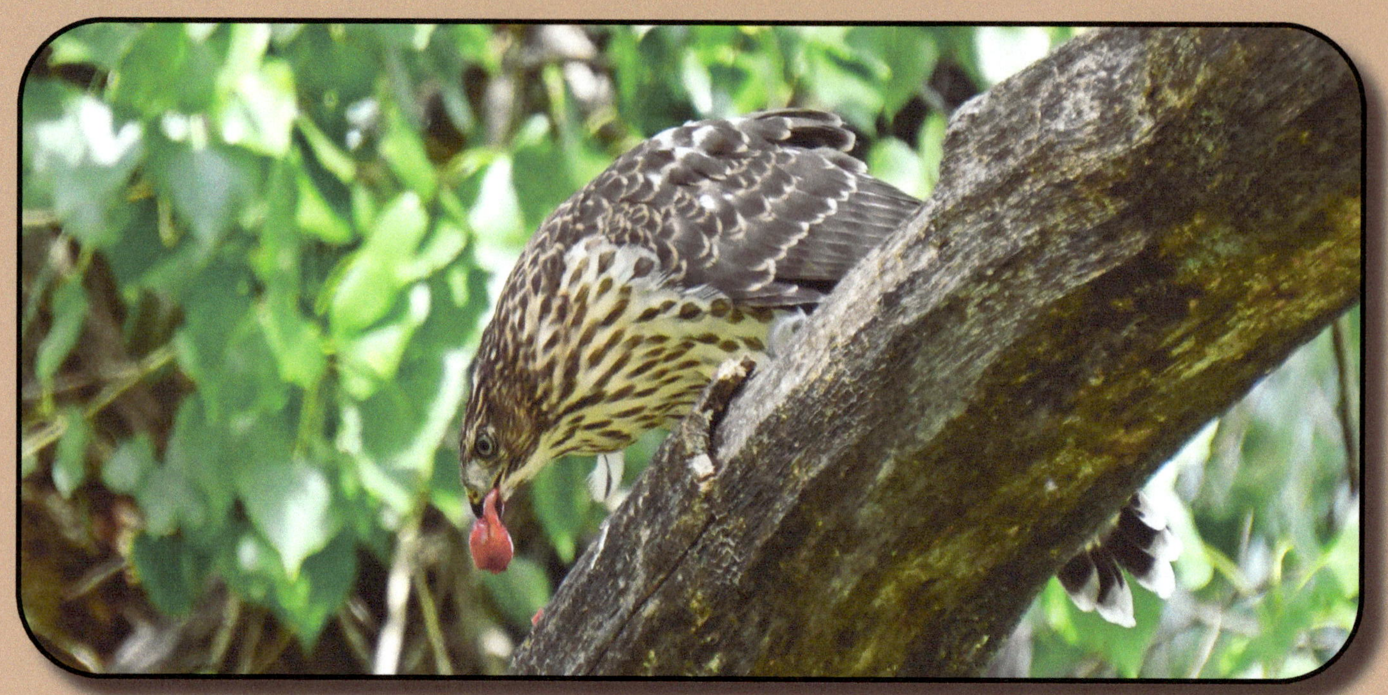

Cooper's Hawk feeding

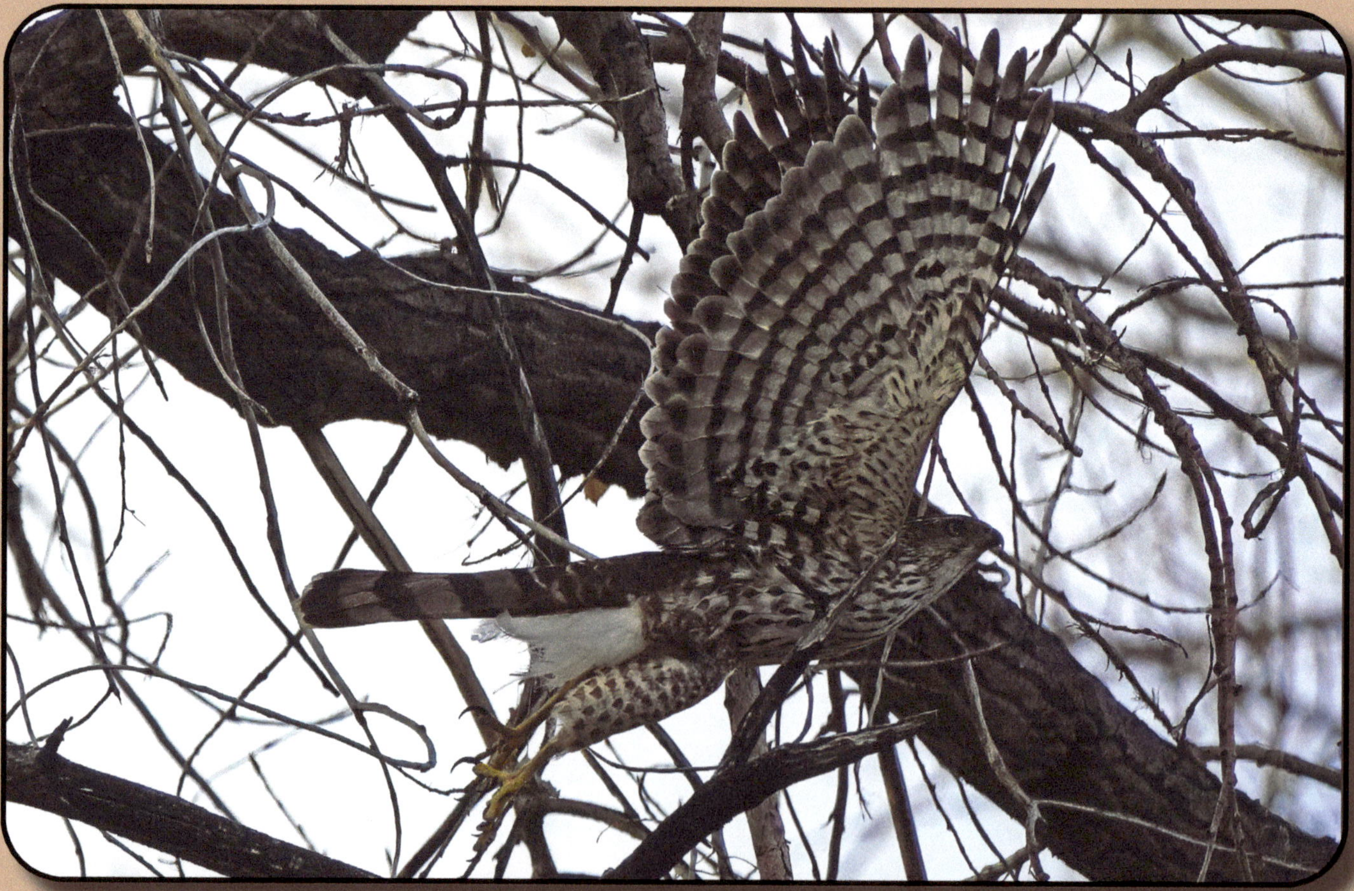

Cooper's Hawk taking off

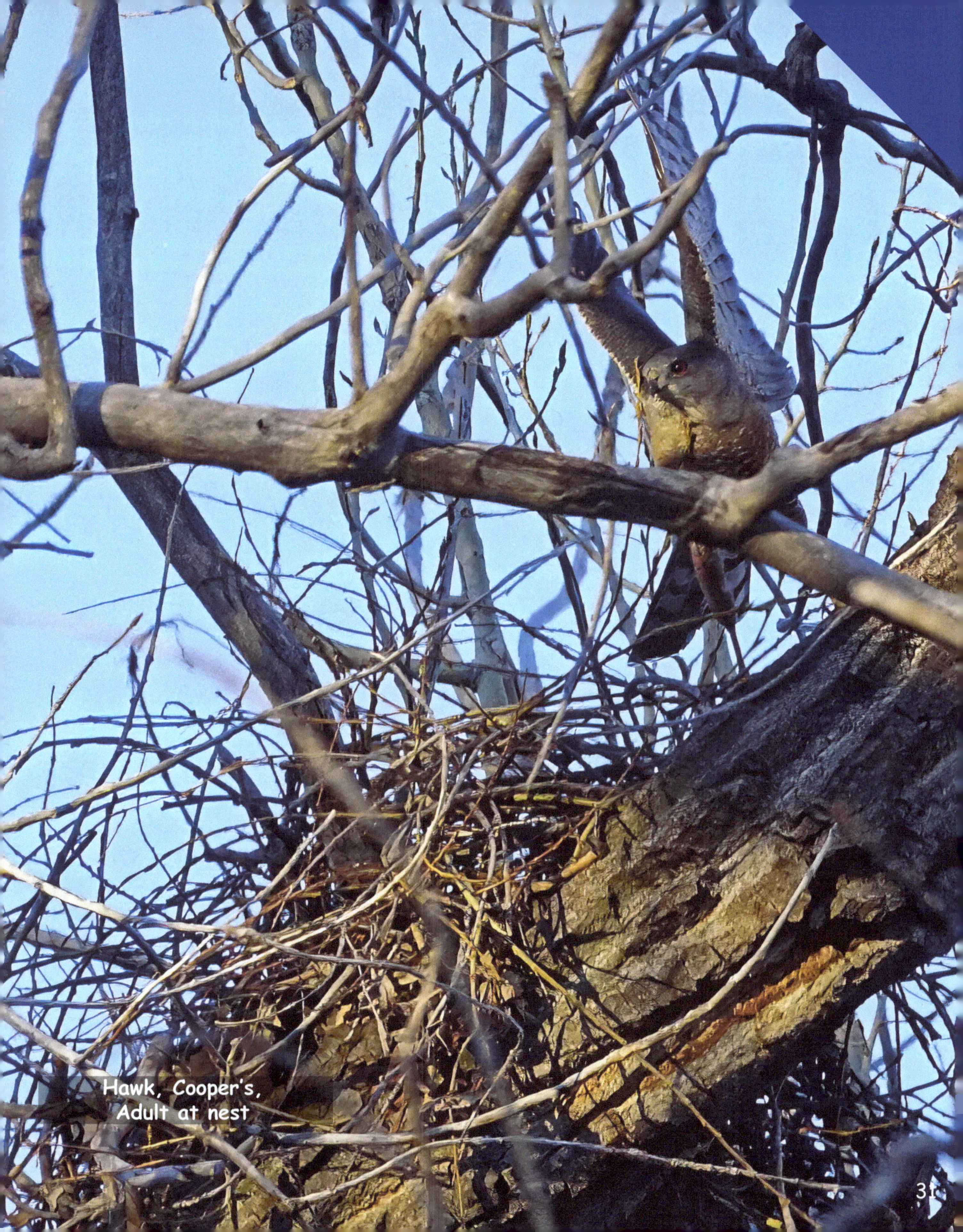

31

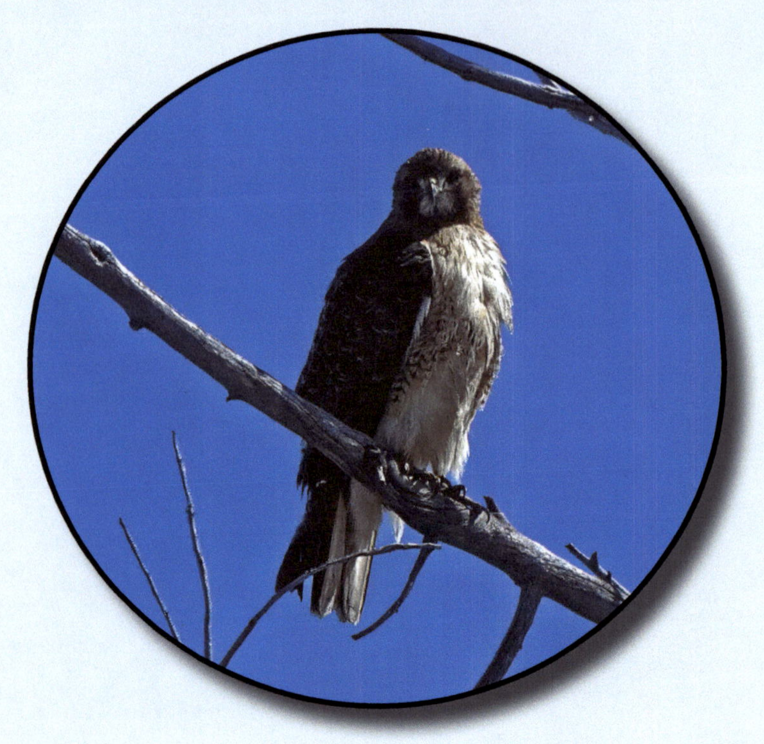

Red-tailed Hawks can be seen year-round in Parker. The red tail of the adult is conspicuous. They are often perched on posts along roadsides or in open fields.

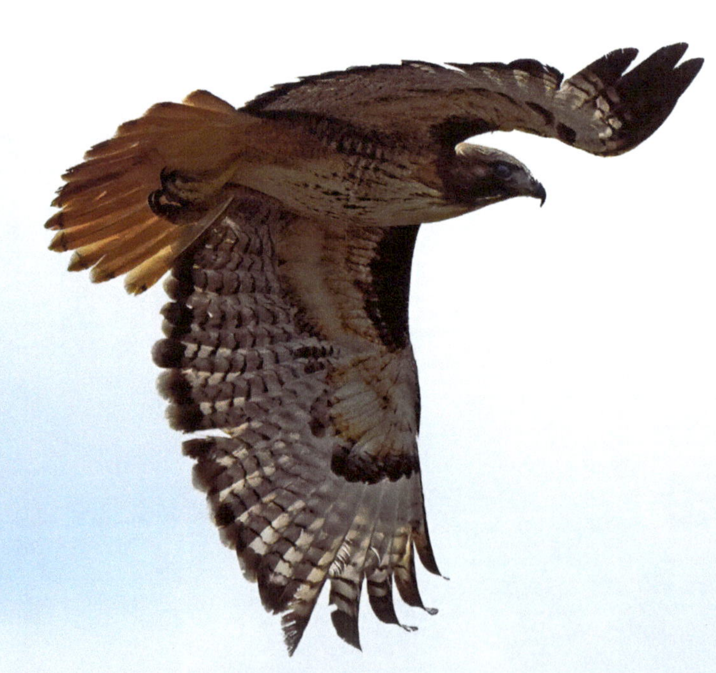

The distinctive tail of the Red-tailed Hawk

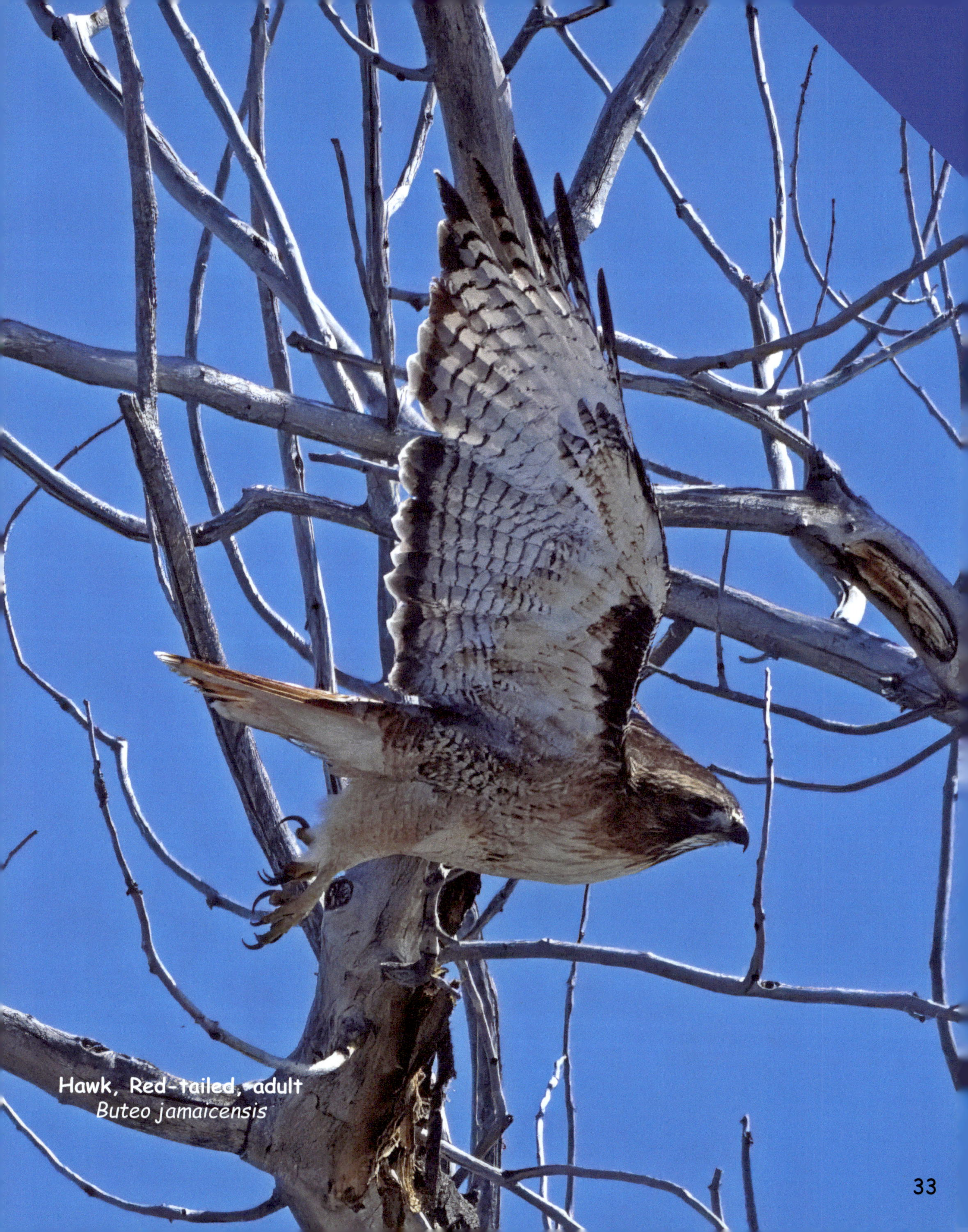

Hawk, Red-tailed, adult
Buteo jamaicensis

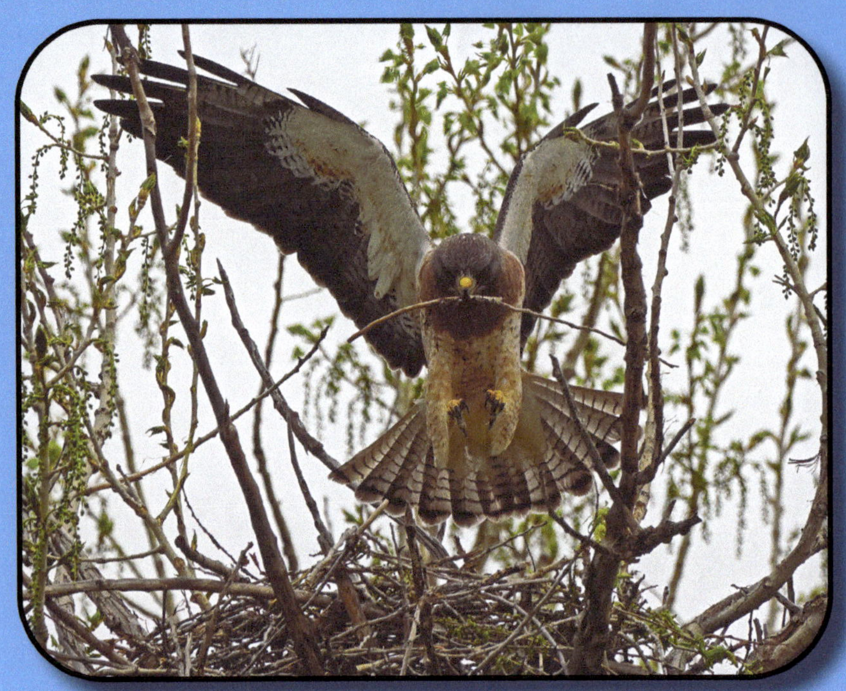

Building a nest

A pair of **Swainson's Hawks** have returned to the same area along Tallman Gulch Trail, in Parker, in late Apri/early May for several years to build their nest.

Adults are recogizable by the uniform brown feathers on their chests. Unlike the Red-tailed Hawk, they migrate south in late August.

Typically two chicks are hatched.

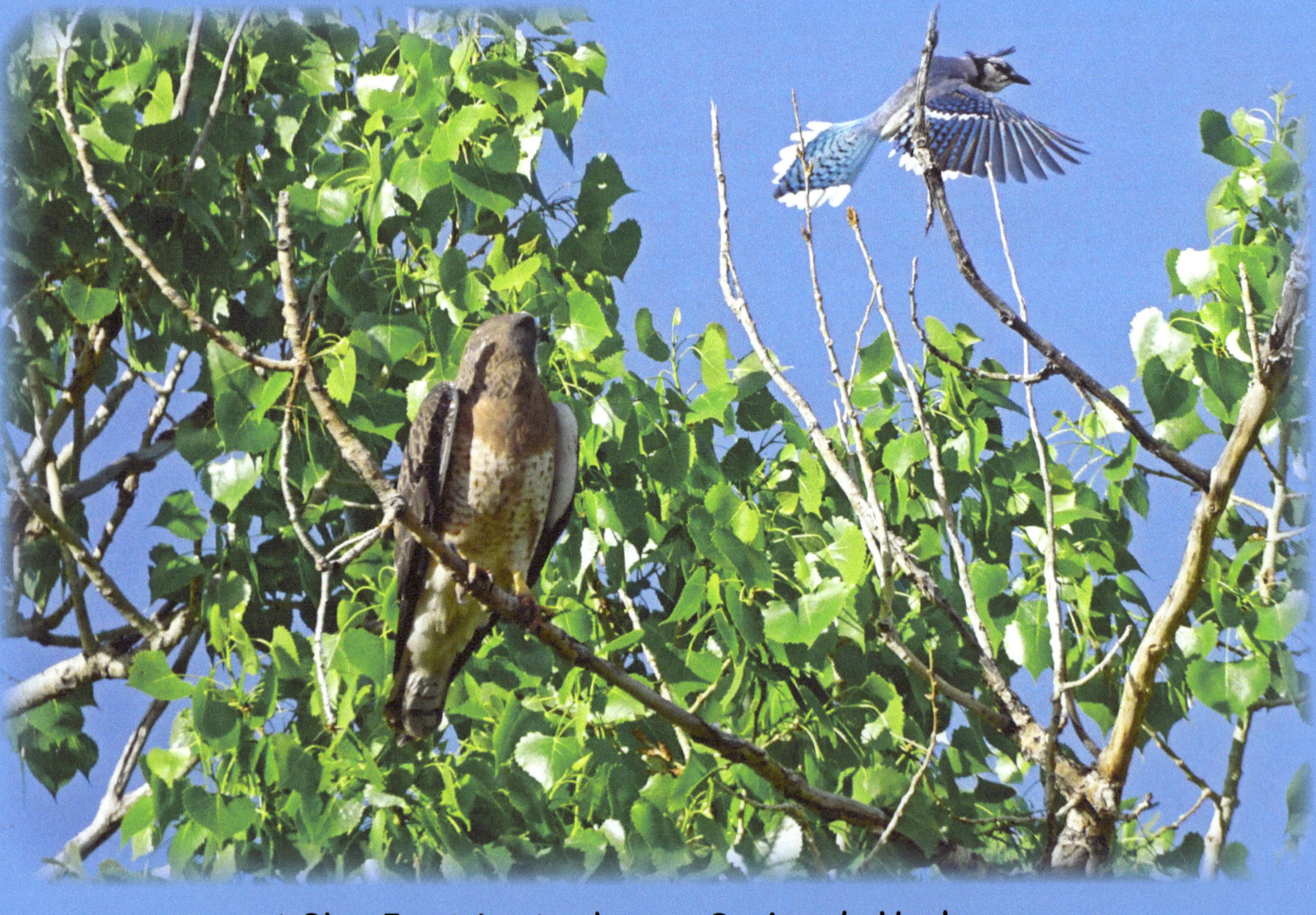

A Blue Jay tries to chase a Swainson's Hawk away

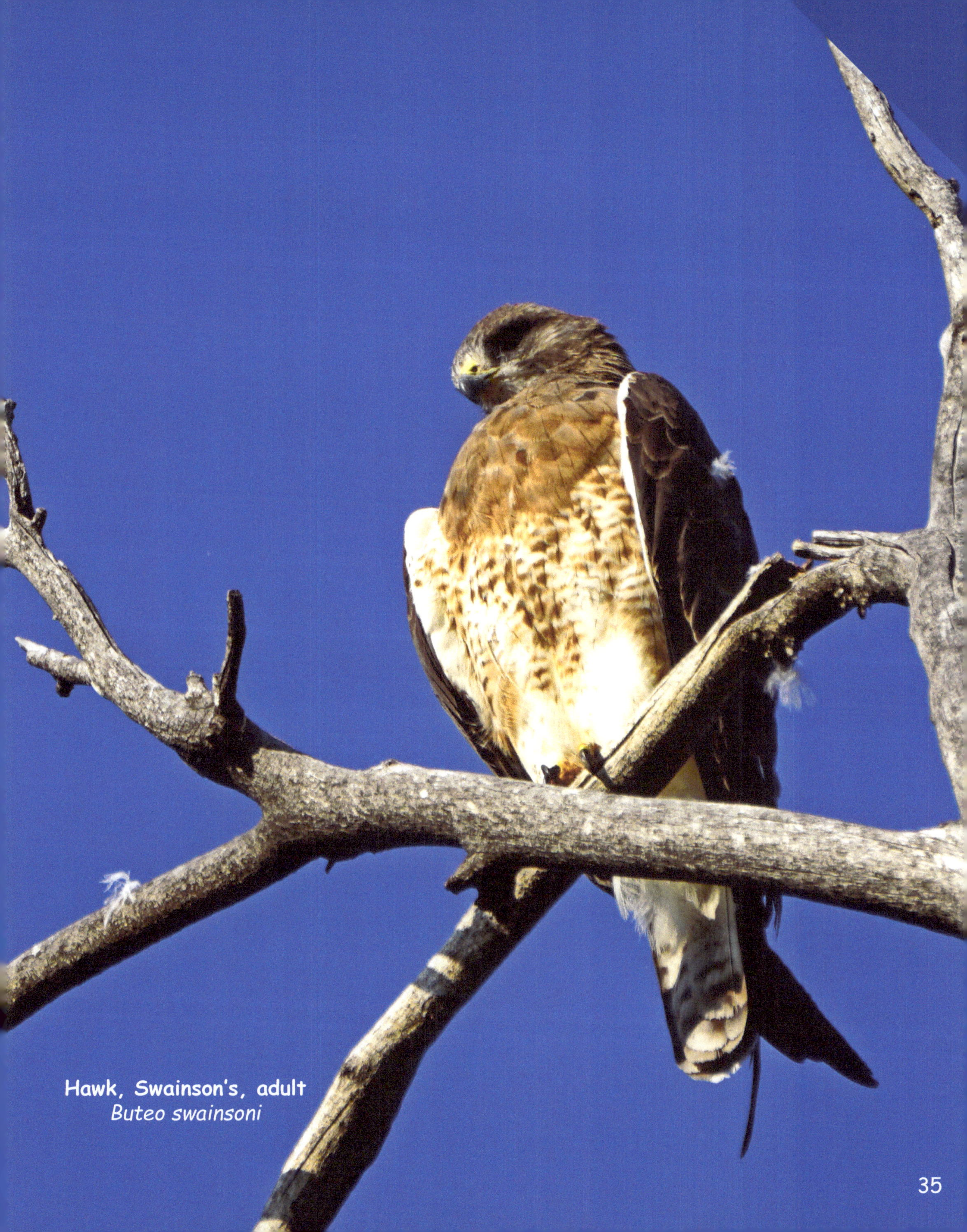

Hawk, Swainson's, adult
Buteo swainsoni

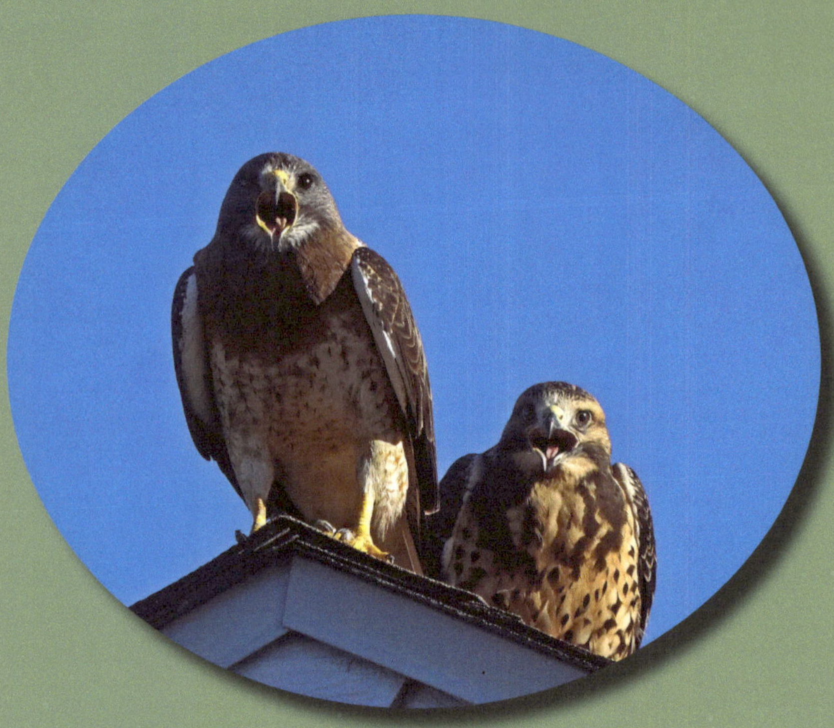

Swainson's Hawk adult with a juvenile

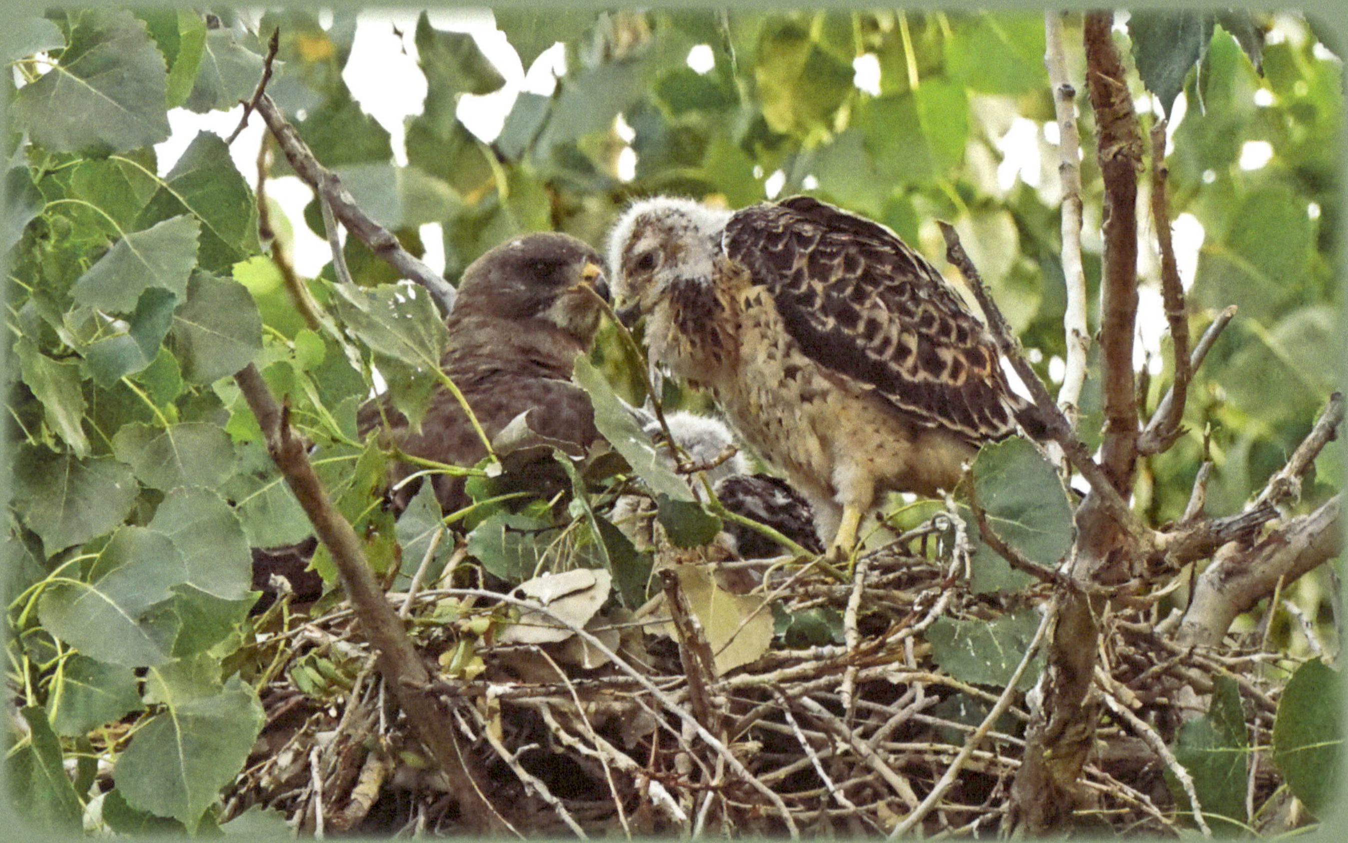

Swainson's Hawks feed on small mammals and reptiles in summer and grasshoppers and other invertebrates for the rest of the year.

They feed the juveniles for several weeks after they fledge and leave the nest, until they can hunt for themselves.

They will often perch on rooftops near the nest site during August.

Swainson's Hawk adult with two chicks in the nest

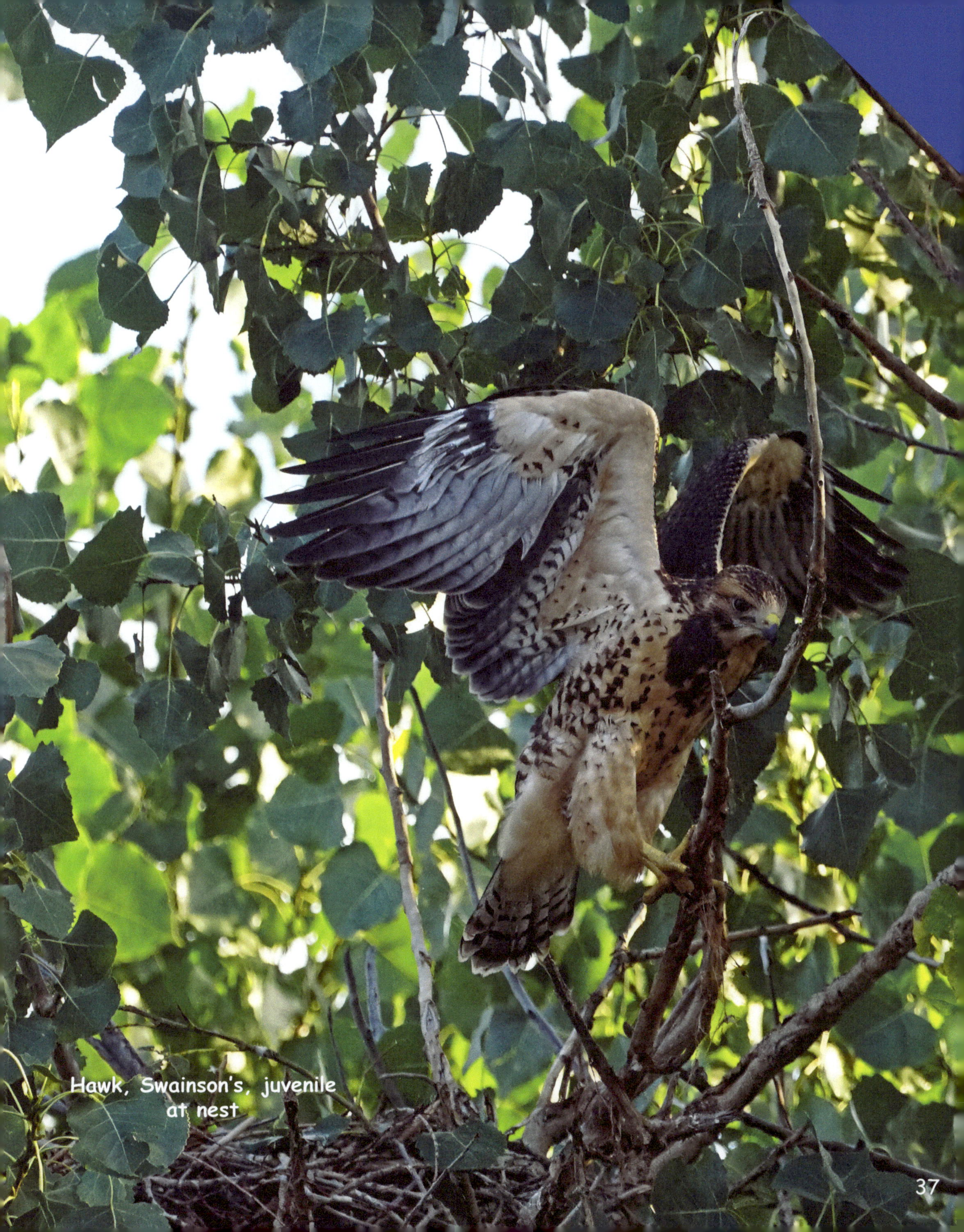

Hawk, Swainson's, juvenile
at nest

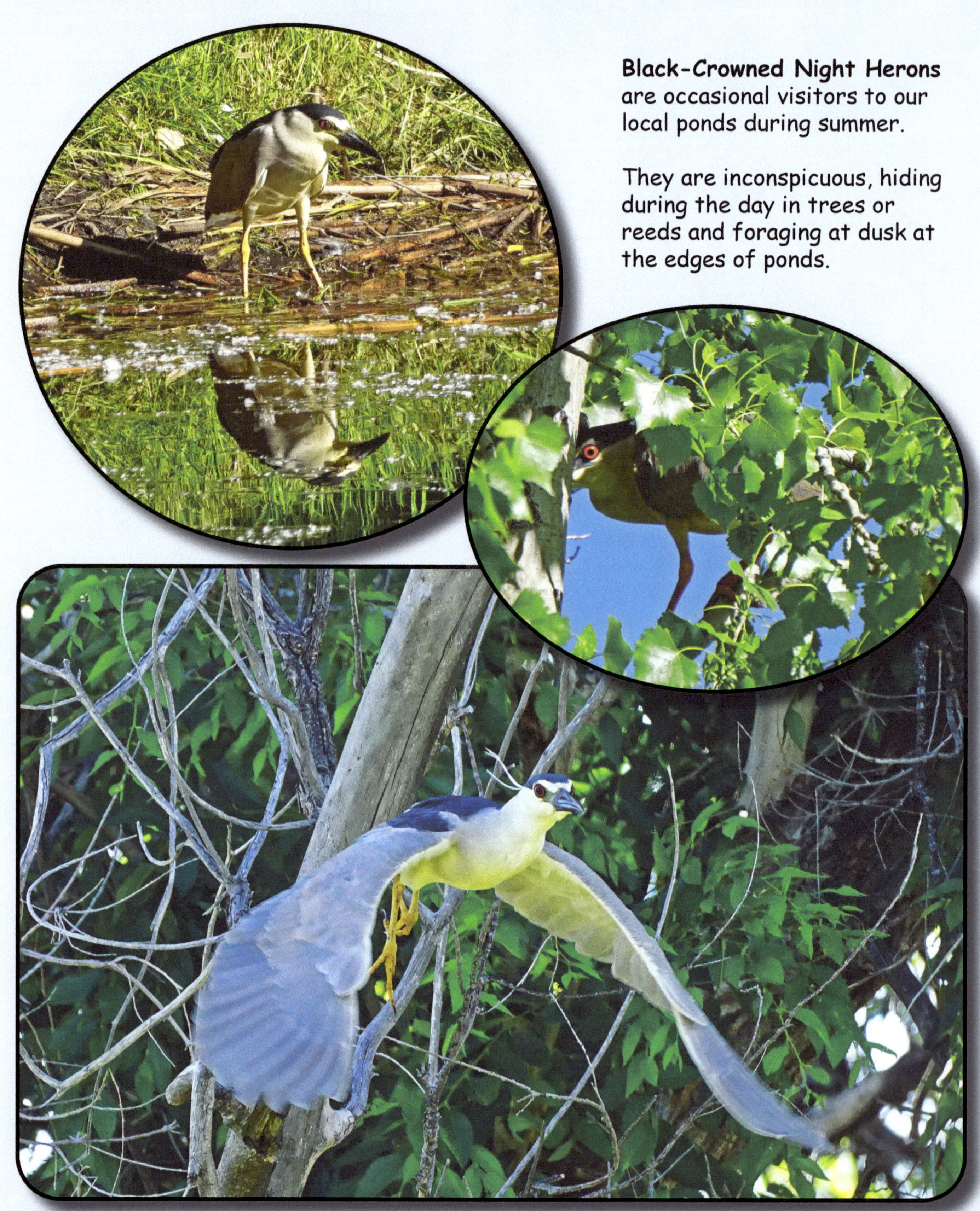

Black-Crowned Night Herons are occasional visitors to our local ponds during summer.

They are inconspicuous, hiding during the day in trees or reeds and foraging at dusk at the edges of ponds.

Black-crowned Night Heron

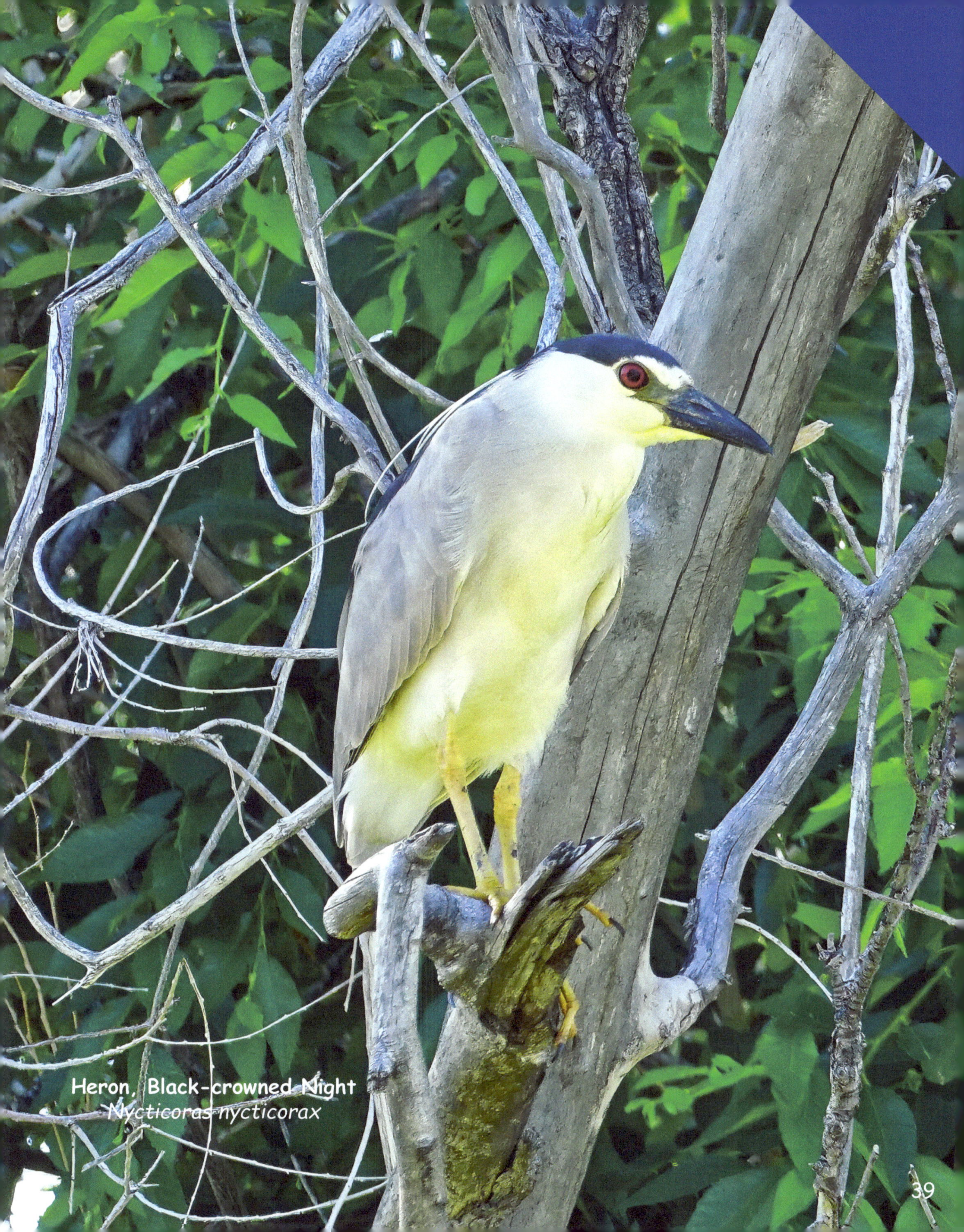
Heron, Black-crowned Night
Nycticoras nycticorax

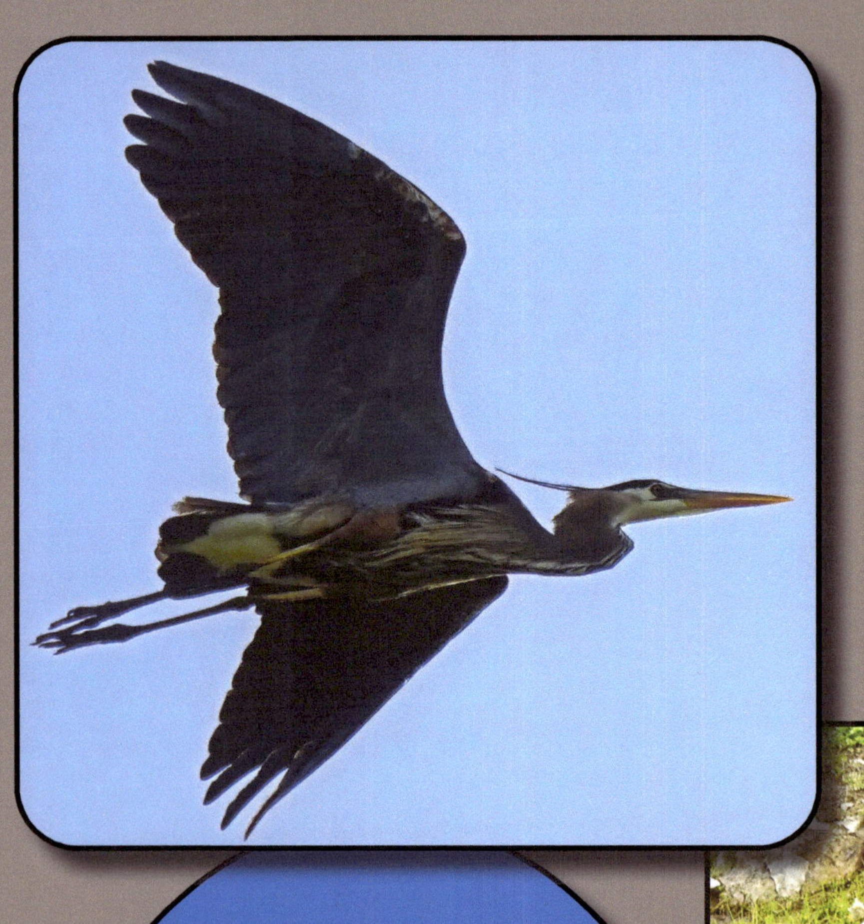

Great Blue Herons are common, nesting in colonies along Cherry Creek in the Parker area during the summer months.

They are ccasionally seen in ponds along the local recreational trails.

They are the largest and heaviest heron, standing up to 72in (1.84M) tall.

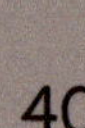

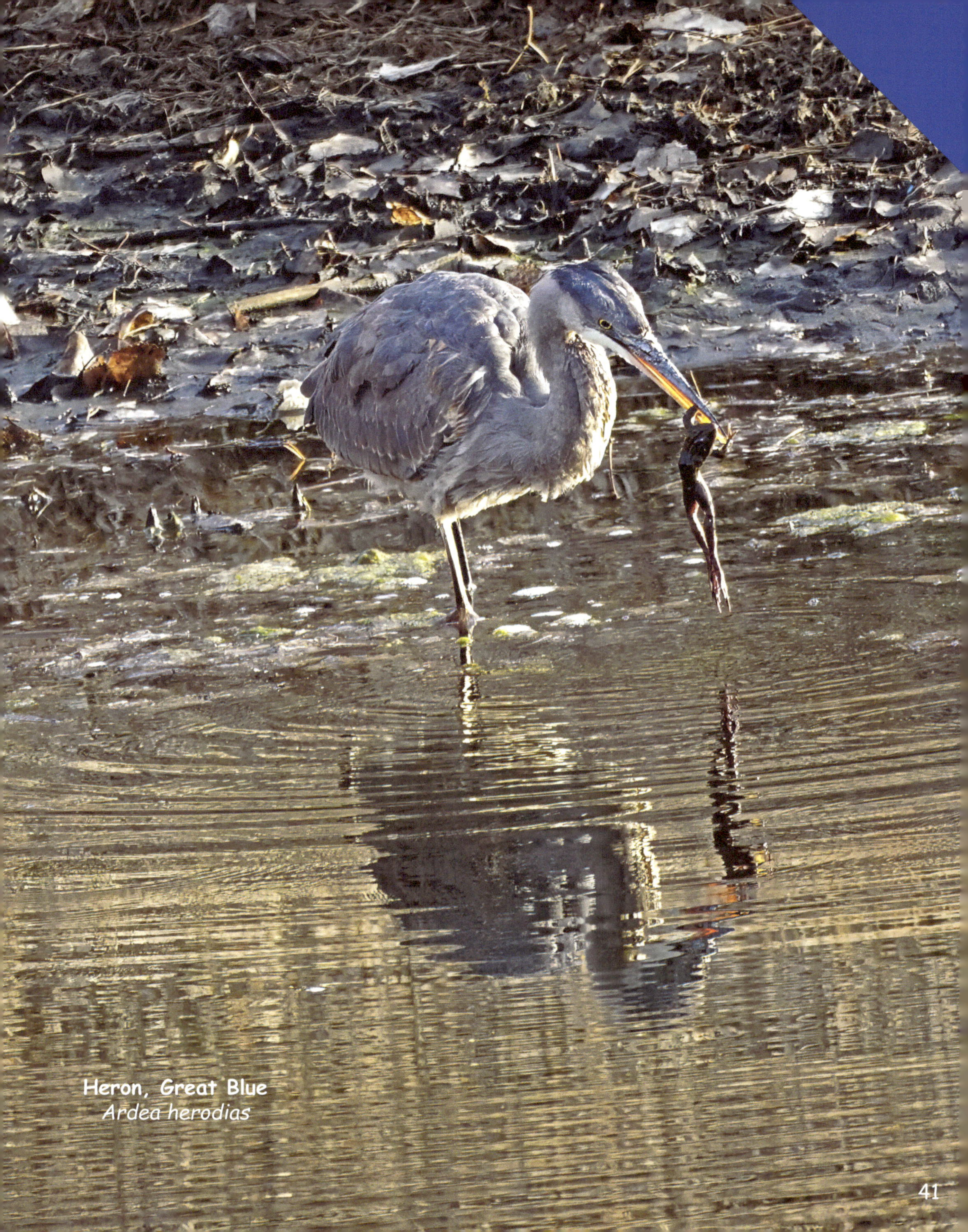

Heron, Great Blue
Ardea herodias

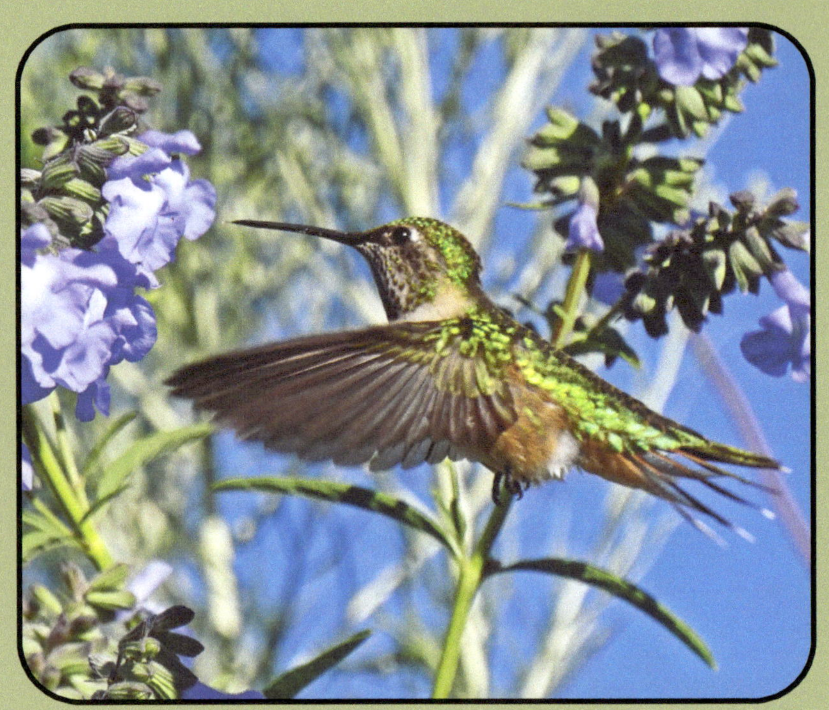

Broad-tailed Hummingbirds migrate from Central and South America, arriving in May, and will breed and nest here before returning south in October.

We can look for them along the local trails and at Hummingbird feeders put out by many residents.

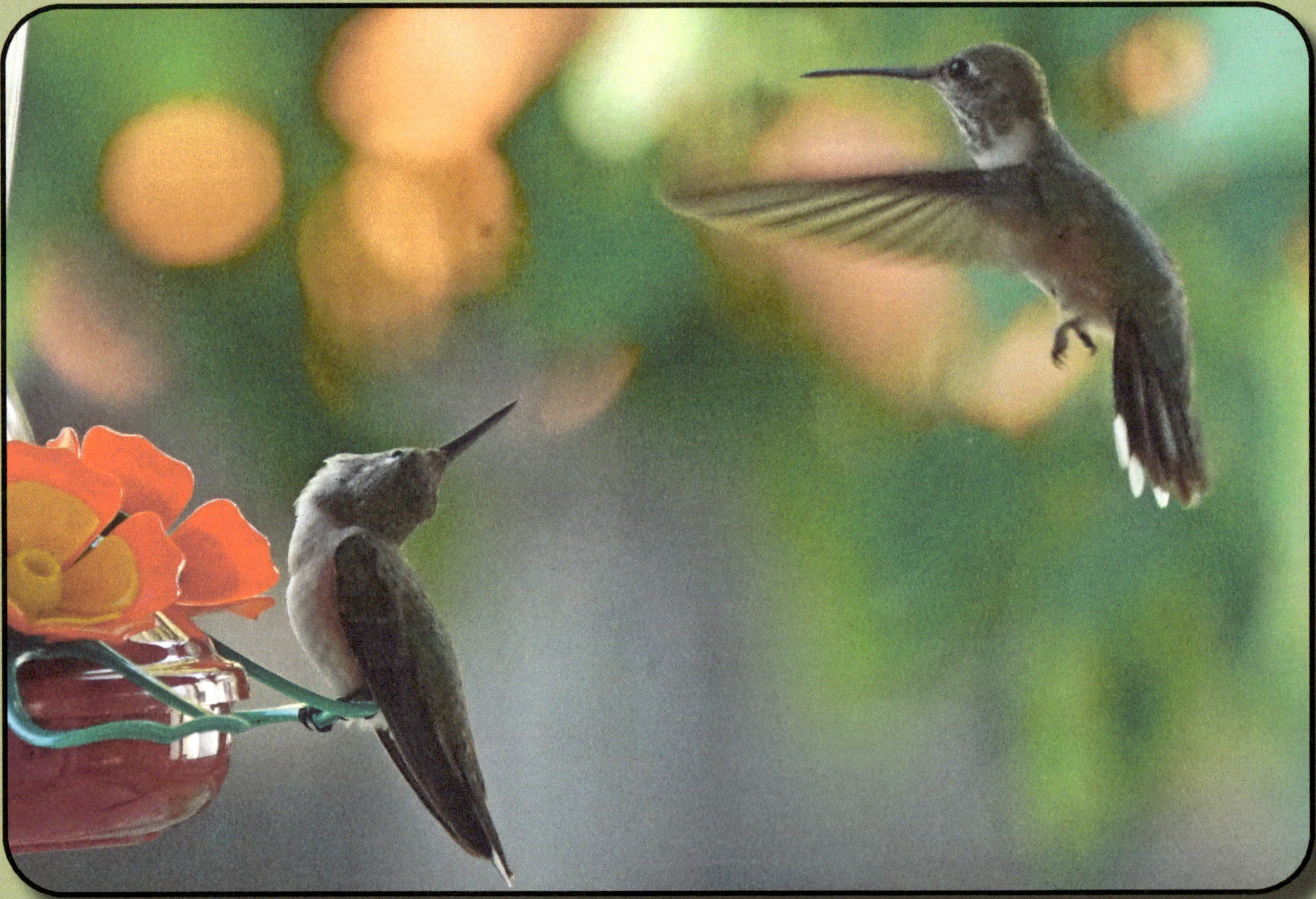

Broad-tailed Hummingbirds at a feeder

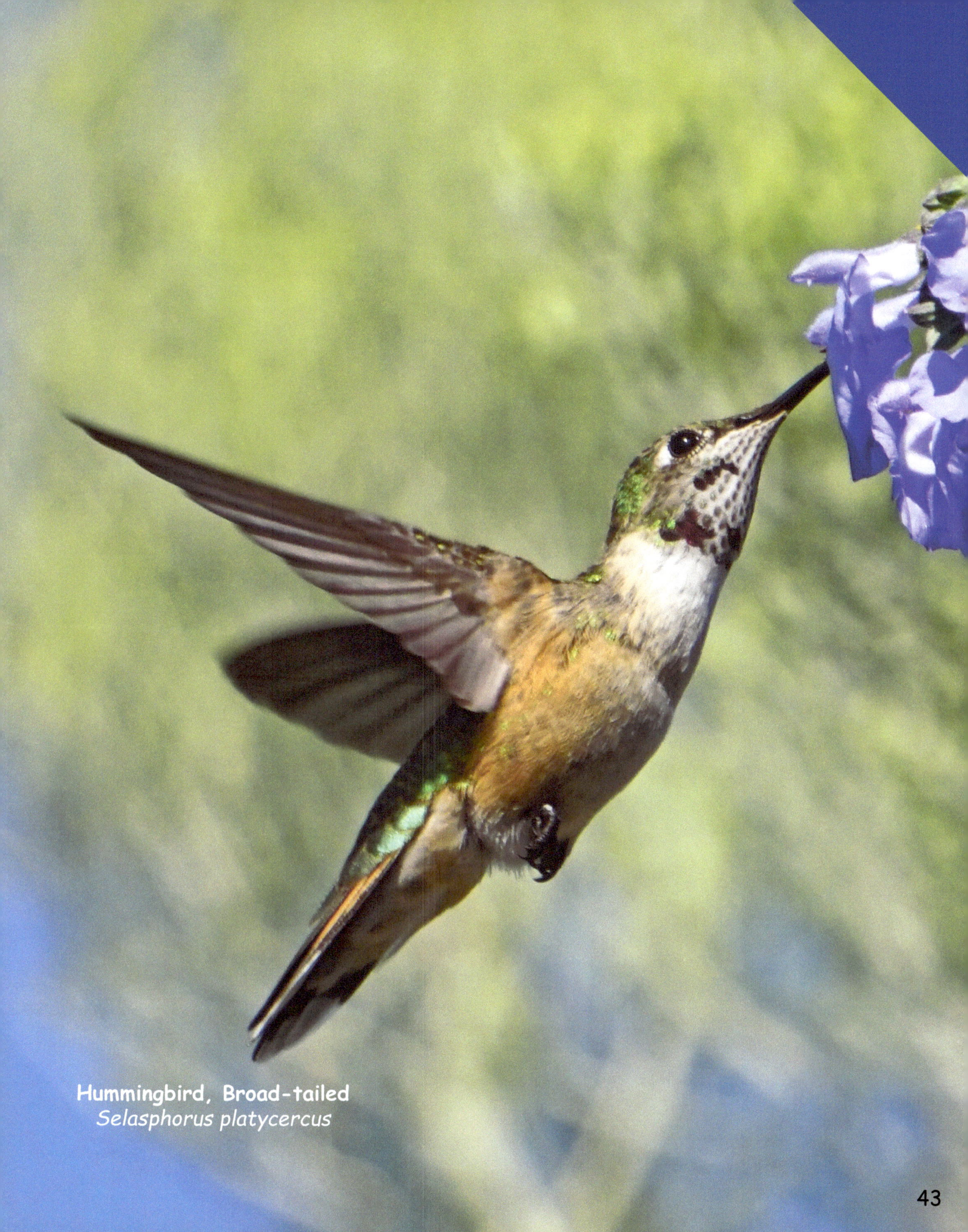

Hummingbird, Broad-tailed
Selasphorus platycercus

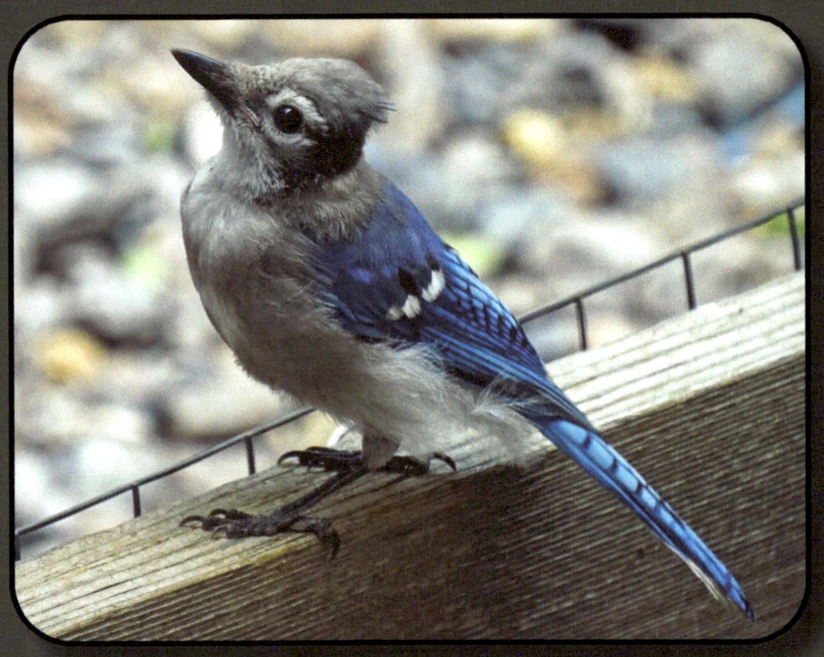

Juvenile Blue Jay

Blue Jays are year-round residents from Eastern Colorado to the Atlantic coast in the USA. Occasionally we will see one at our bird feeder.

Male and female are similar in color.

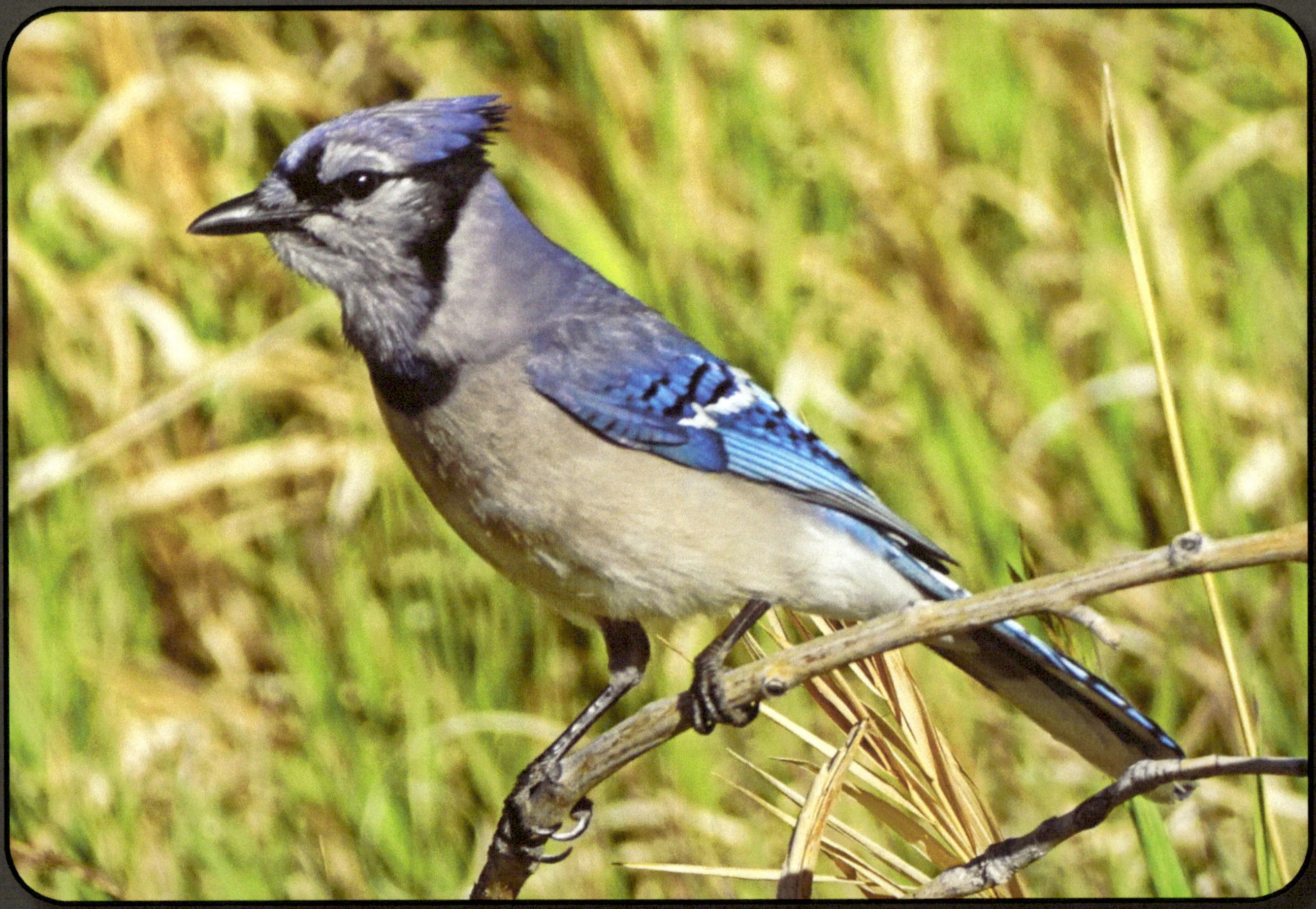

Adult Blue Jay

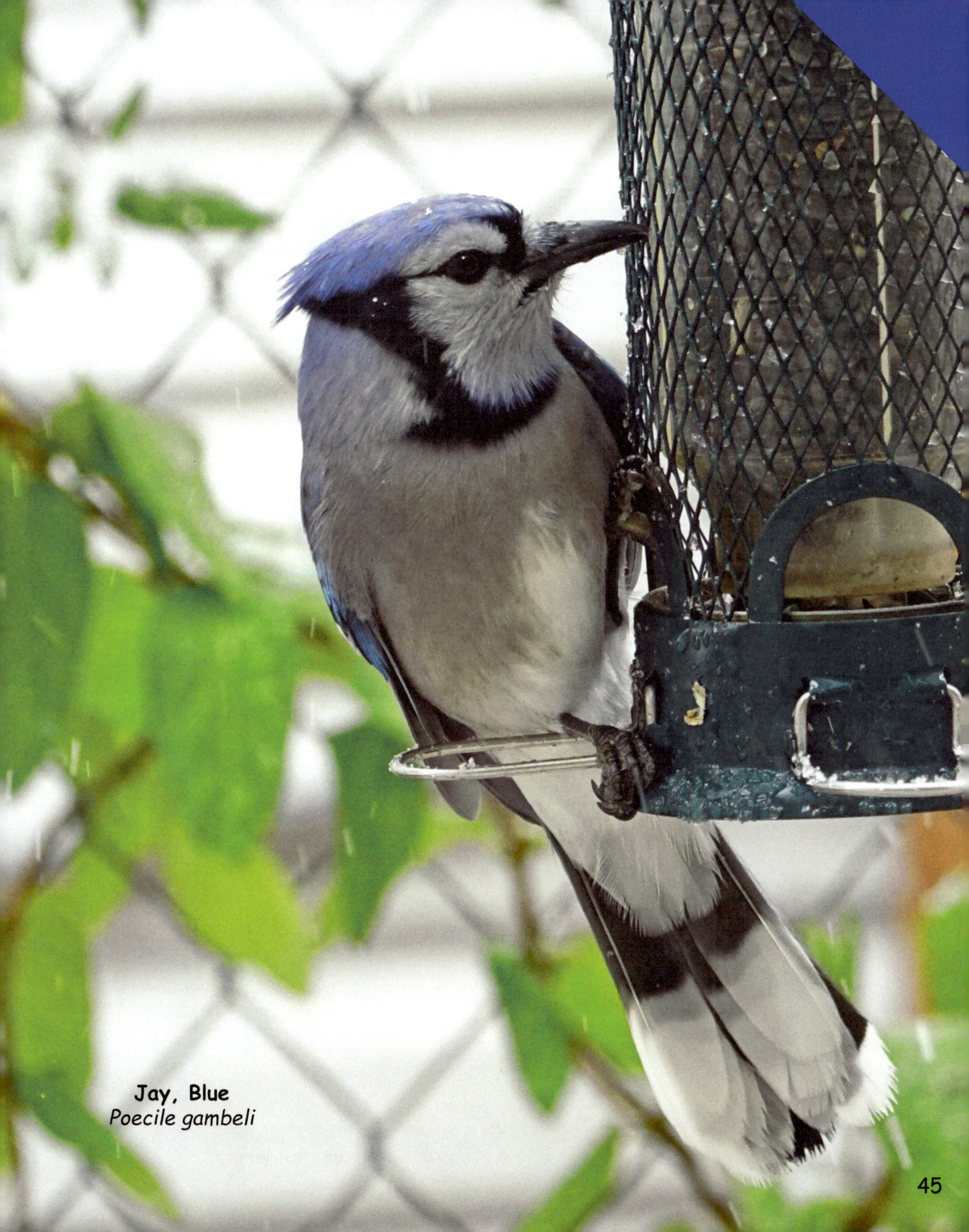

Jay, Blue
Poecile gambeli

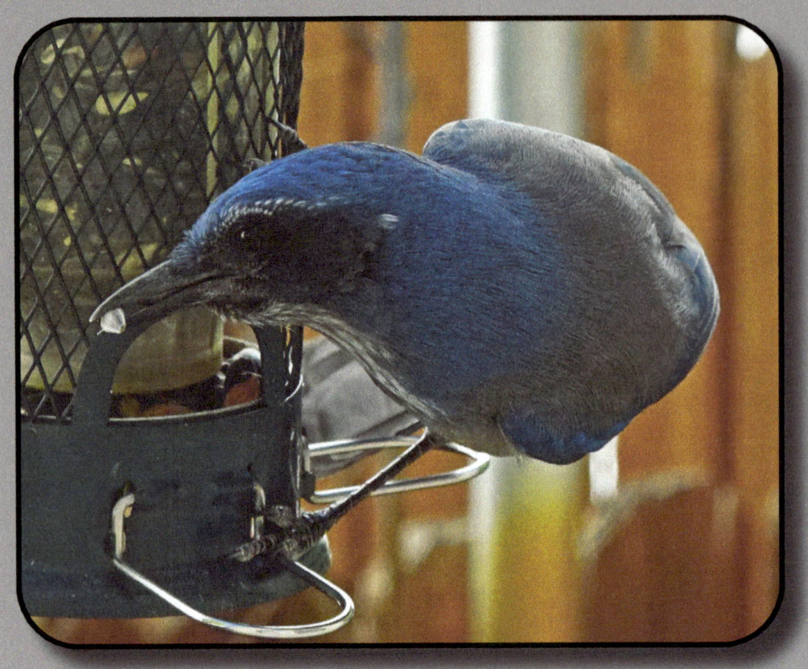

Woodhouse's Scrub Jay is native to the western United States. It is nonmigratory and can be found in urban areas, where it can become tame and come to bird feeders. They feed on small animals, such as frogs and lizards, eggs and young of other birds, insects, and (particularly in winter) grains, nuts, and berries. Research has suggested that Woodhouse's Scrub Jays are among the most intelligent of animals. They store food in scattered caches within their territories.

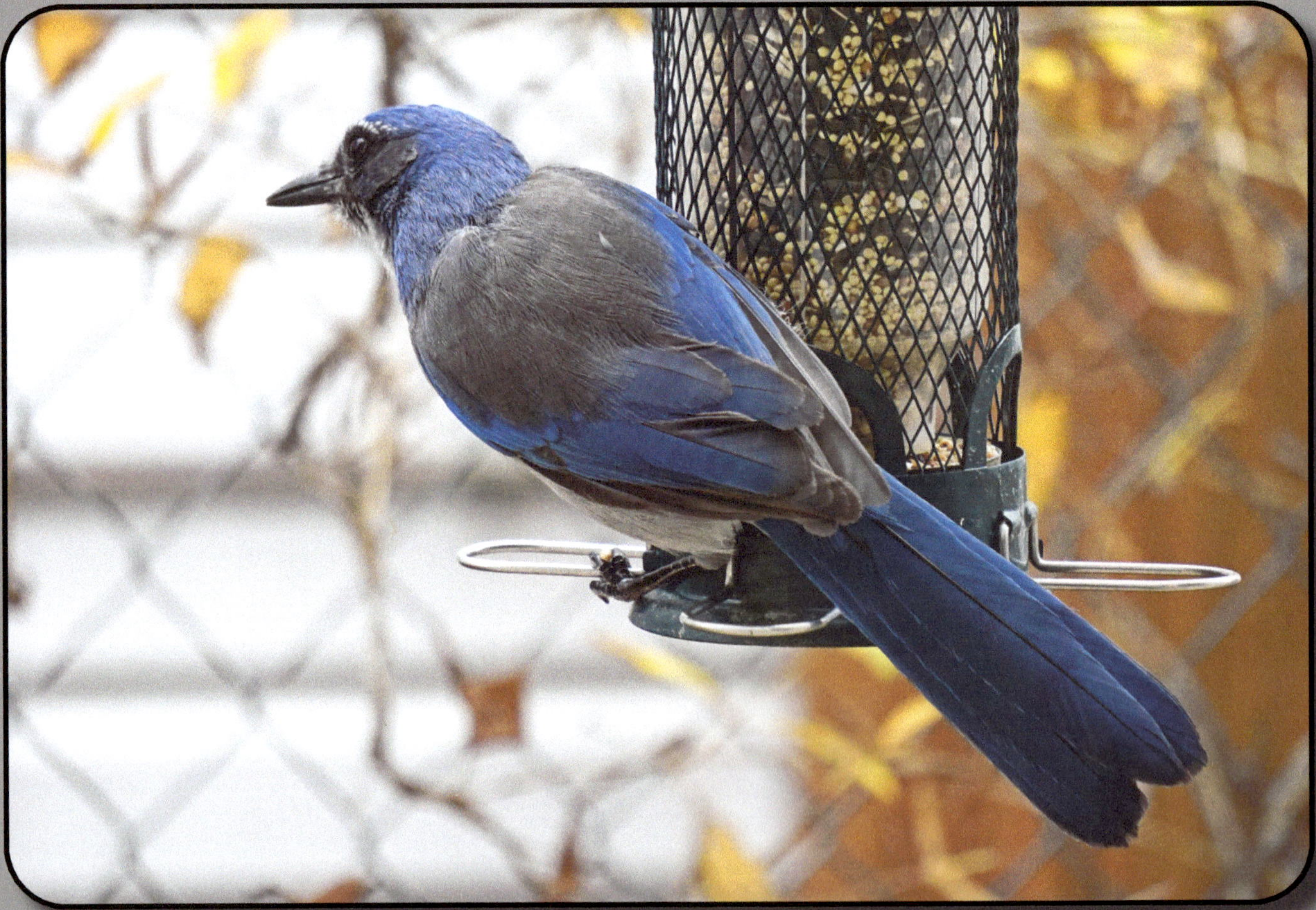

Woodhouse's Scrub Jays can be seen on feeders

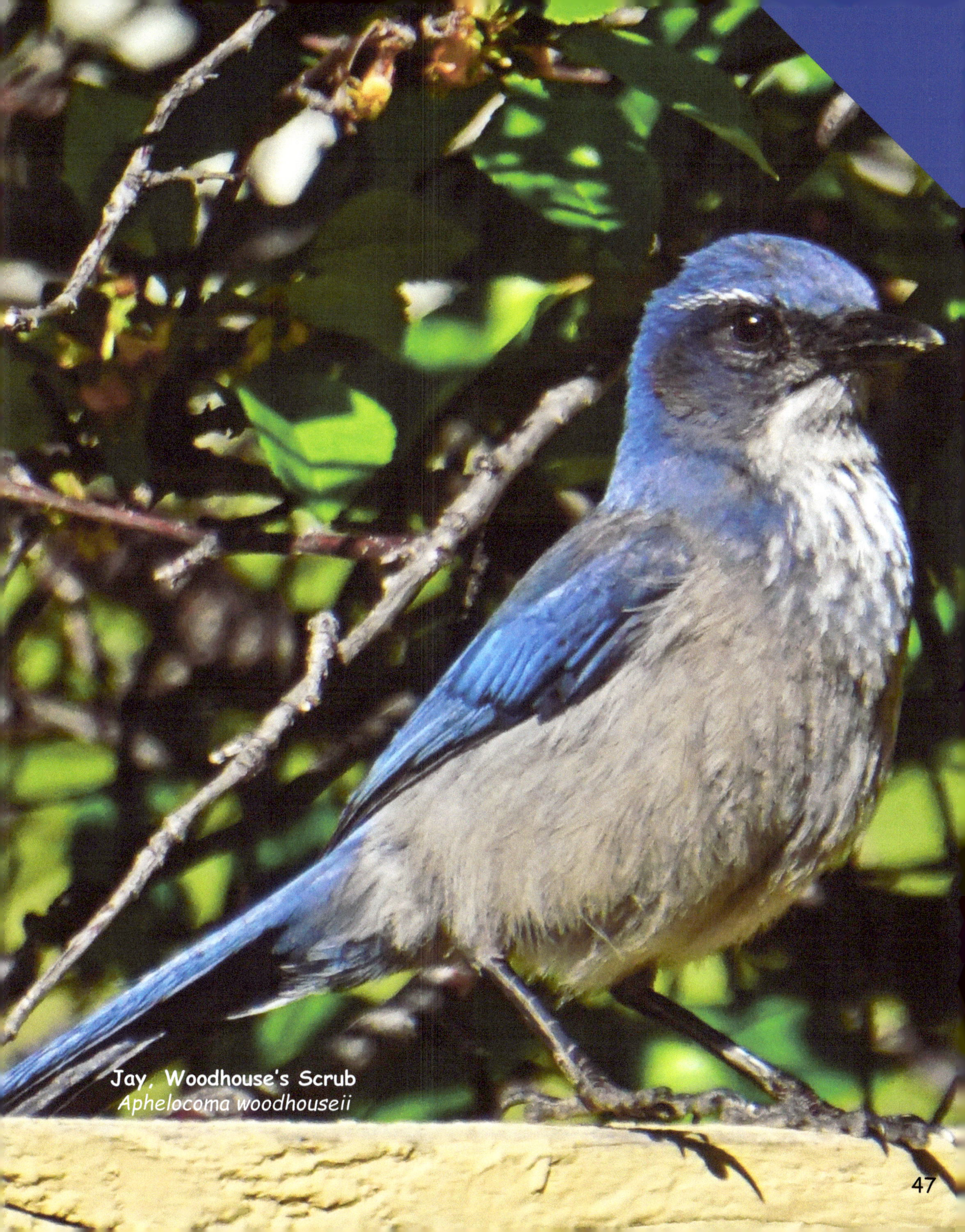

Jay, Woodhouse's Scrub
Aphelocoma woodhouseii

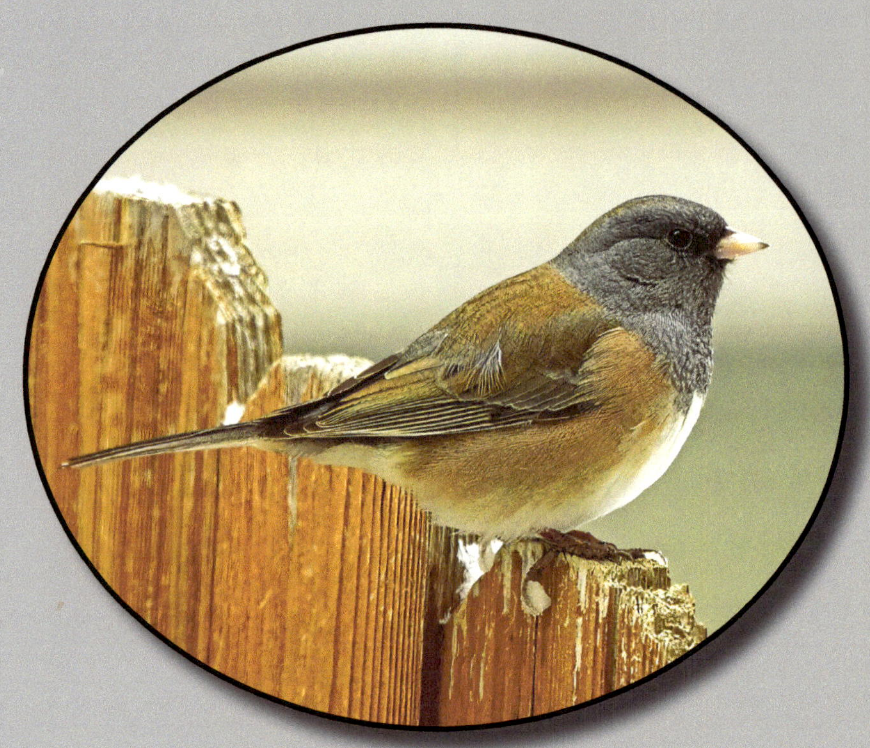

Dark-eyed Juncos are familiar winter visitors to our bird feeders. There are six regional populations across the country, each with slightly different color patterns.

Dark-eyed Junco female

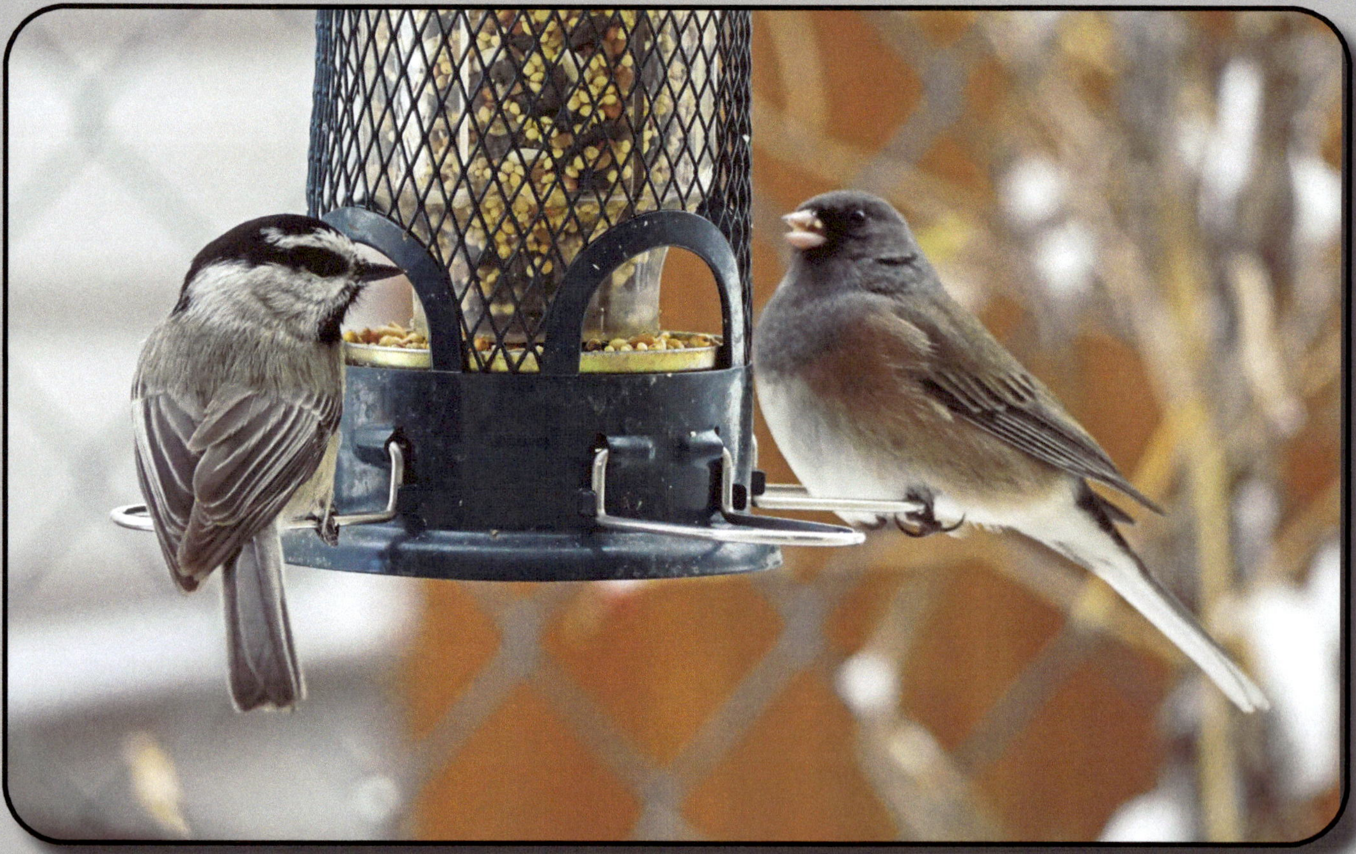

Dark-eyed Junco (right) and Mountain Chickadee

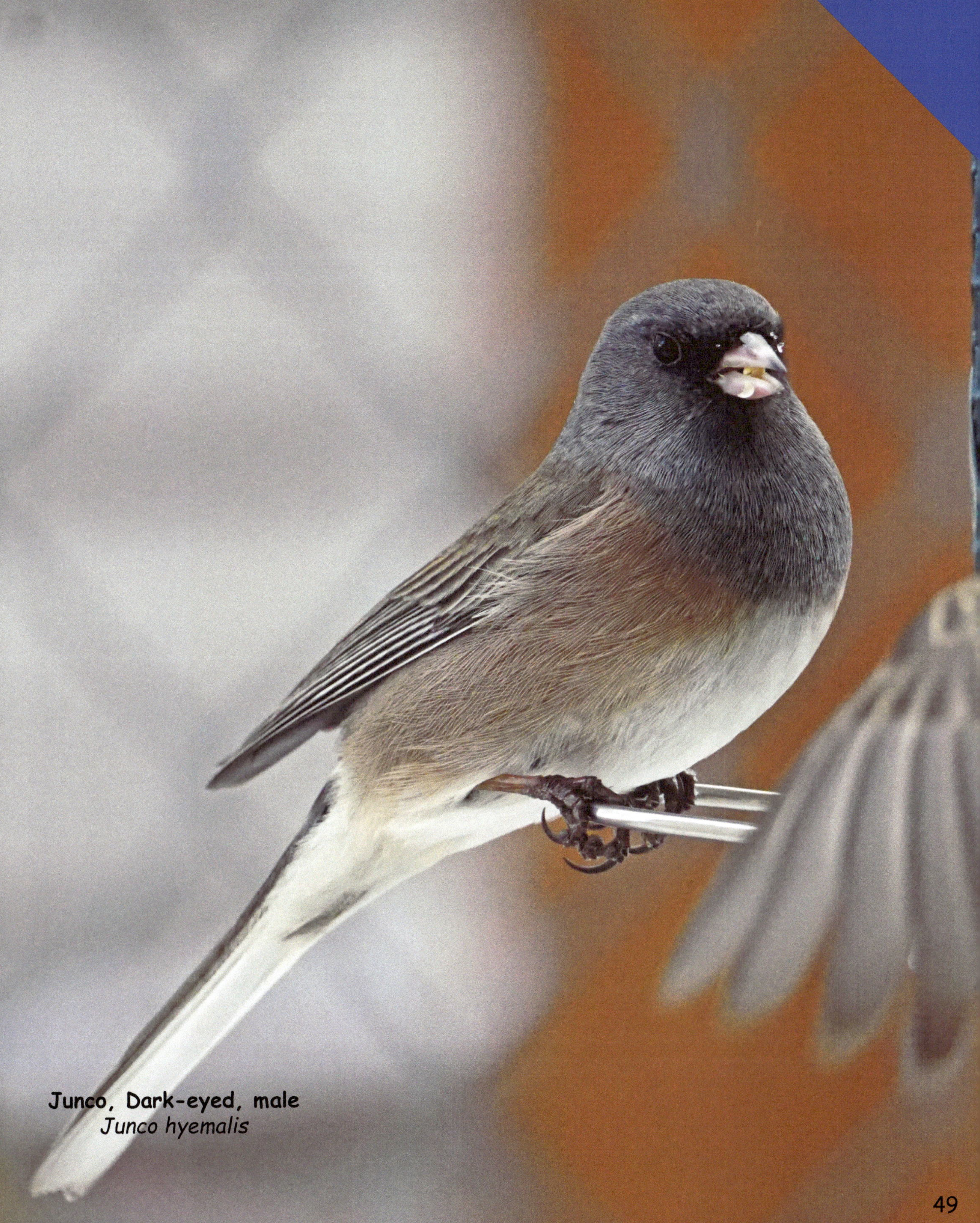

Junco, Dark-eyed, male
Junco hyemalis

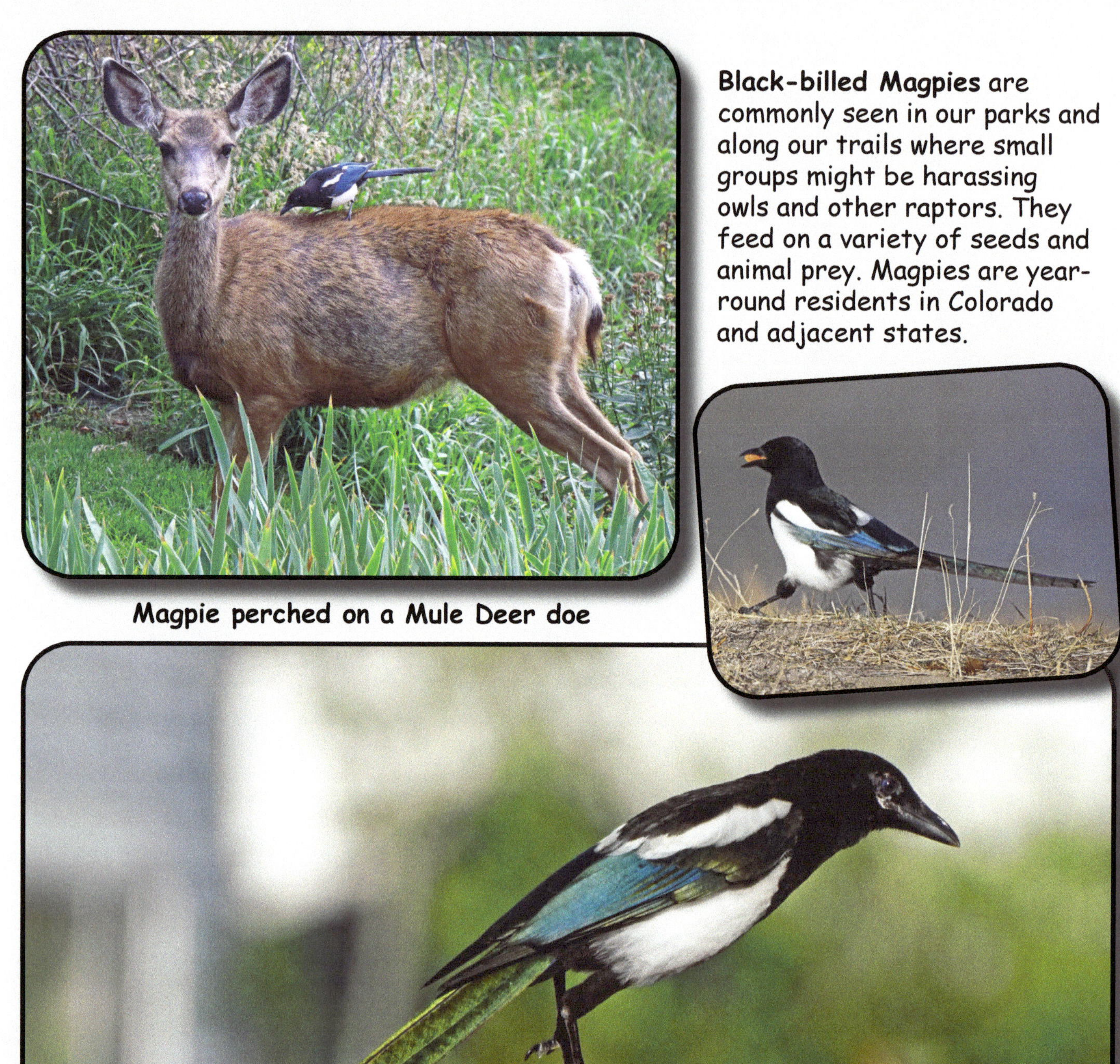

Black-billed Magpies are commonly seen in our parks and along our trails where small groups might be harassing owls and other raptors. They feed on a variety of seeds and animal prey. Magpies are year-round residents in Colorado and adjacent states.

Magpie perched on a Mule Deer doe

The iridescent colors of Magpie feathers

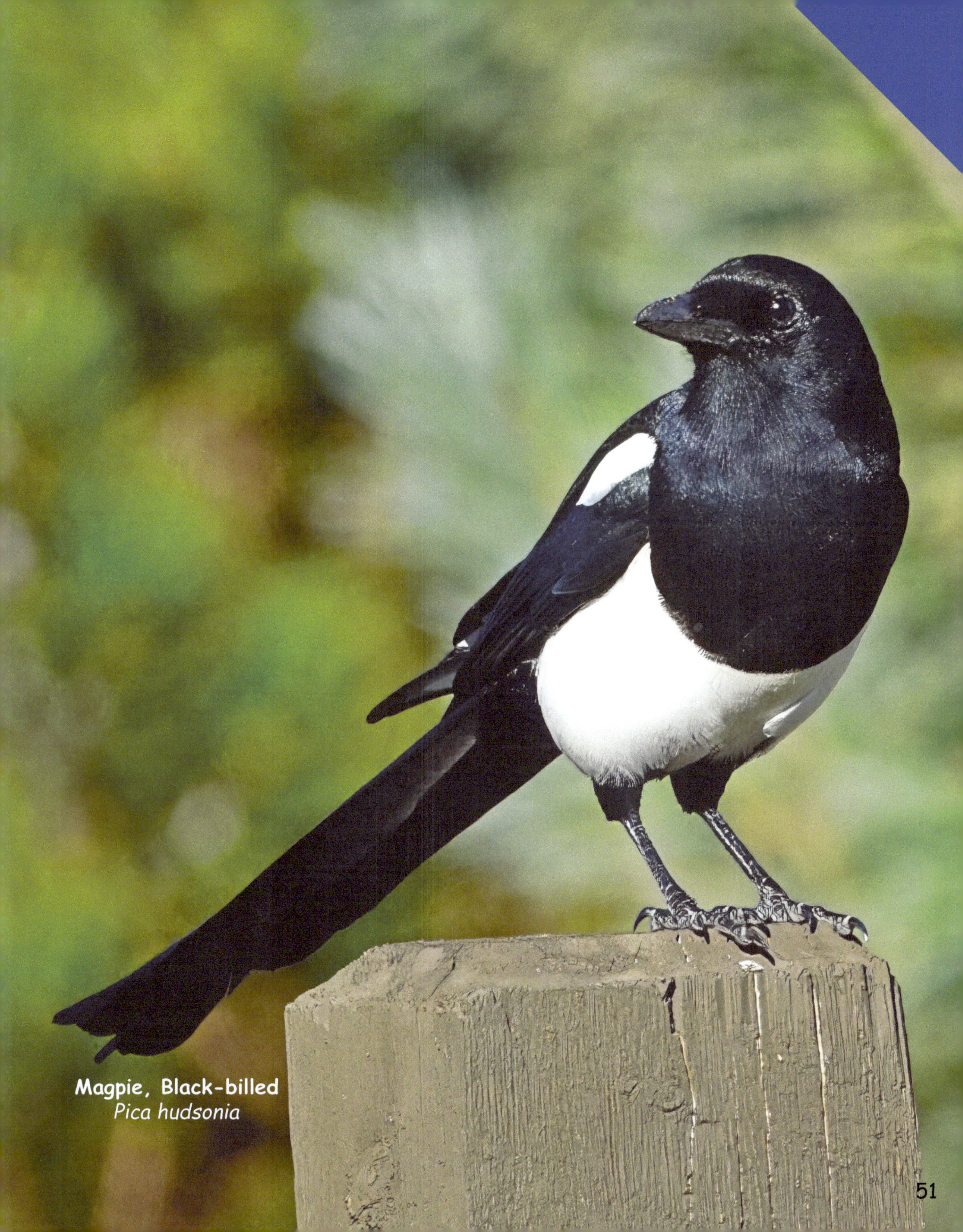

Magpie, Black-billed
Pica hudsonia

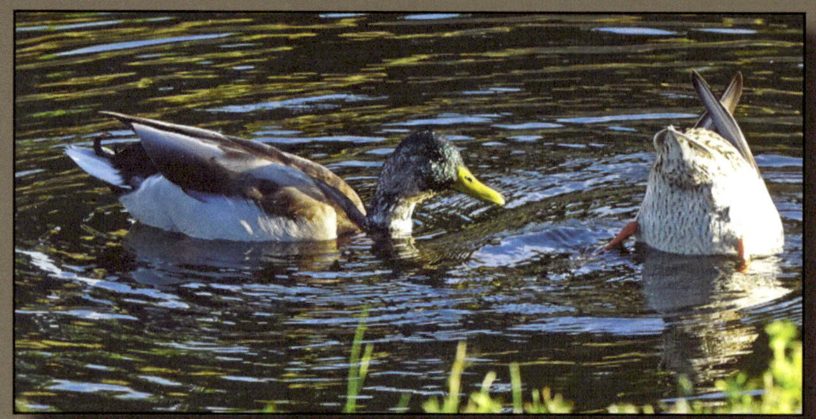

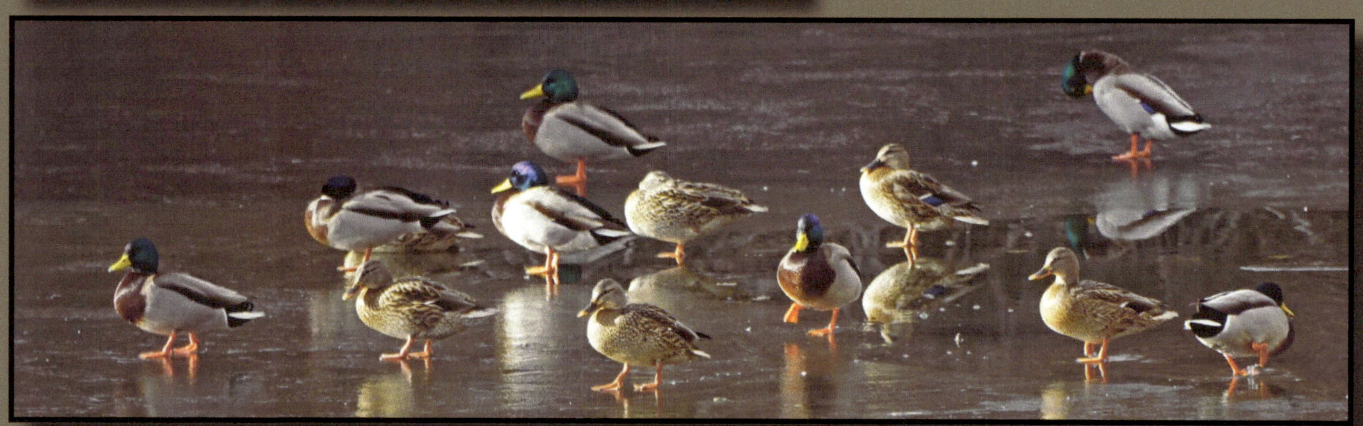

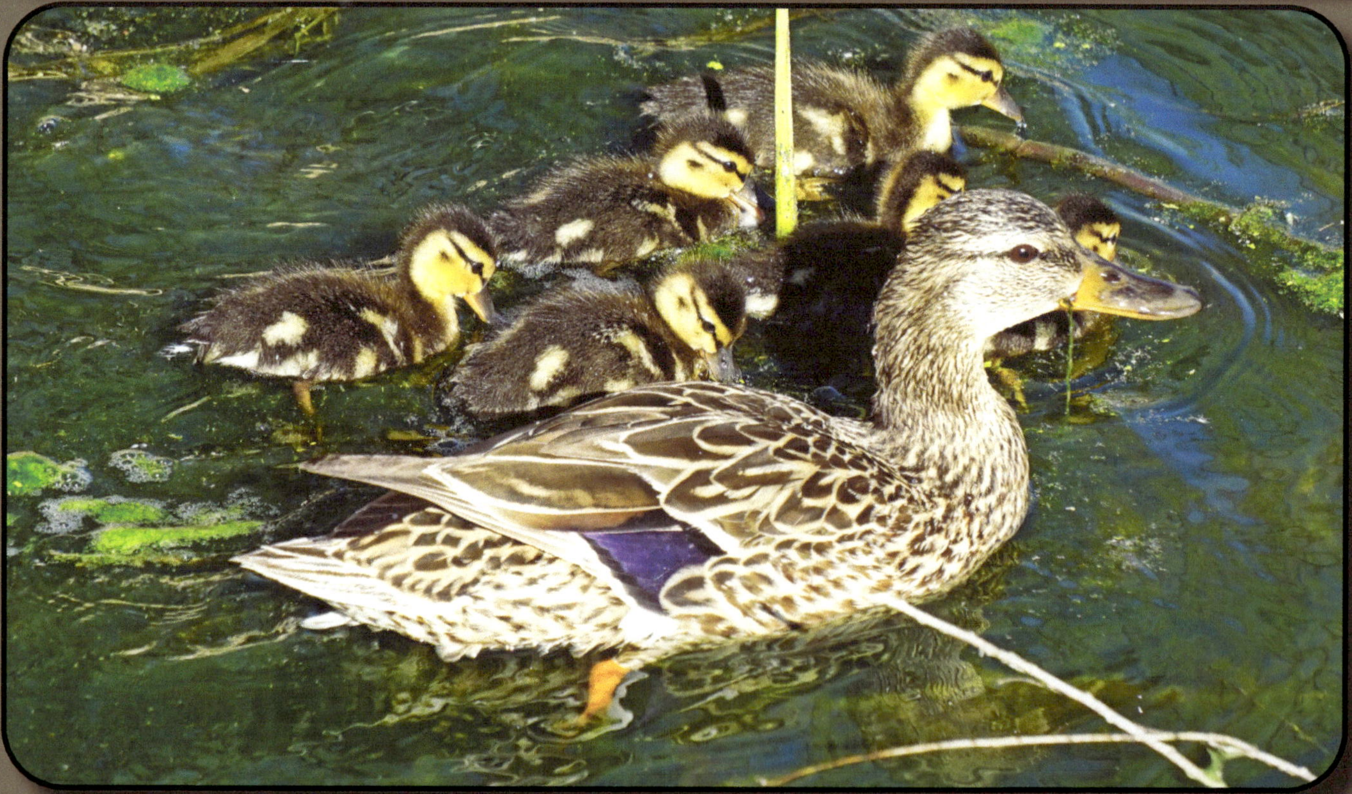

Mallard hen and ducklings - typically hatch in Apr/May

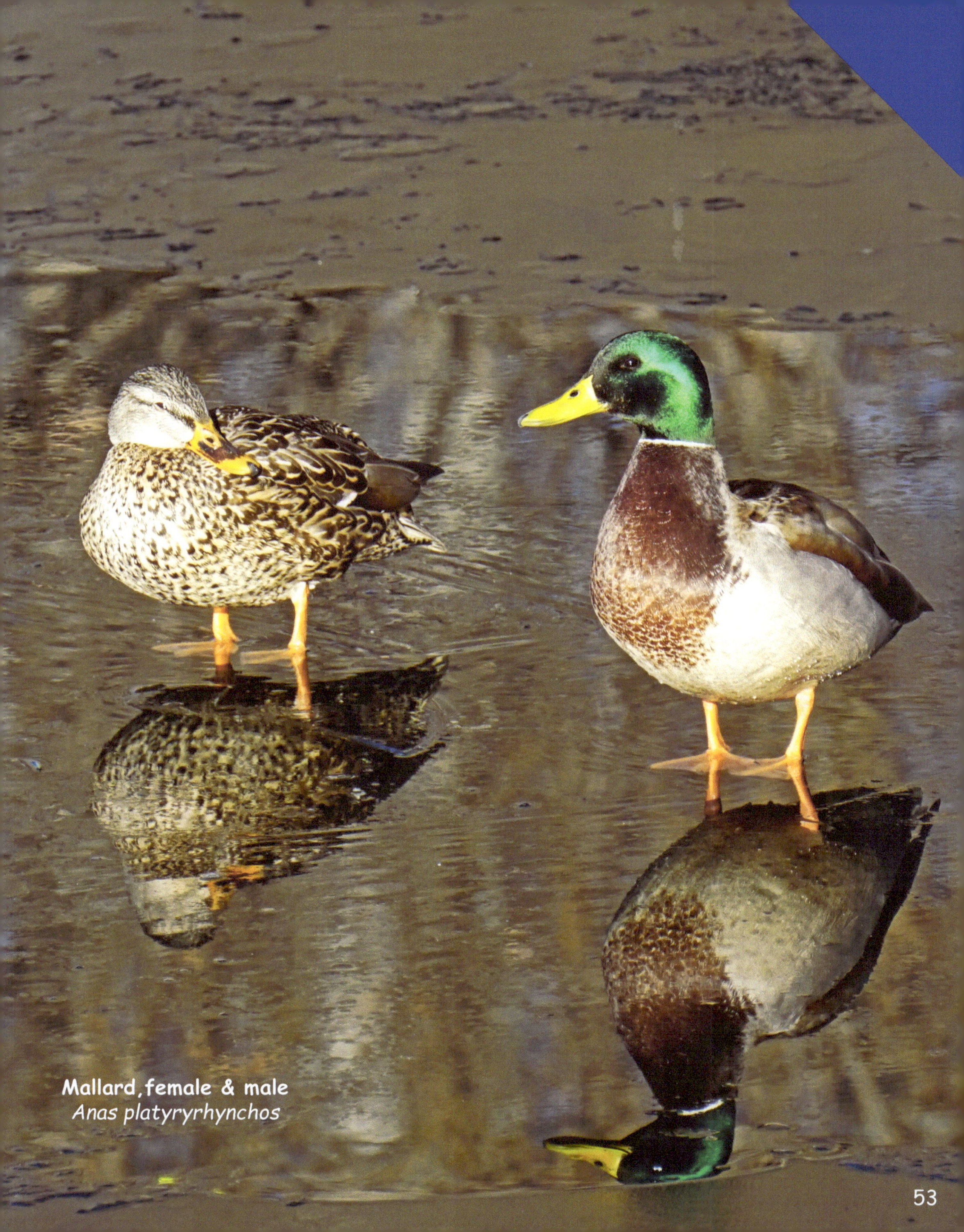

Mallard, female & male
Anas platyryrhynchos

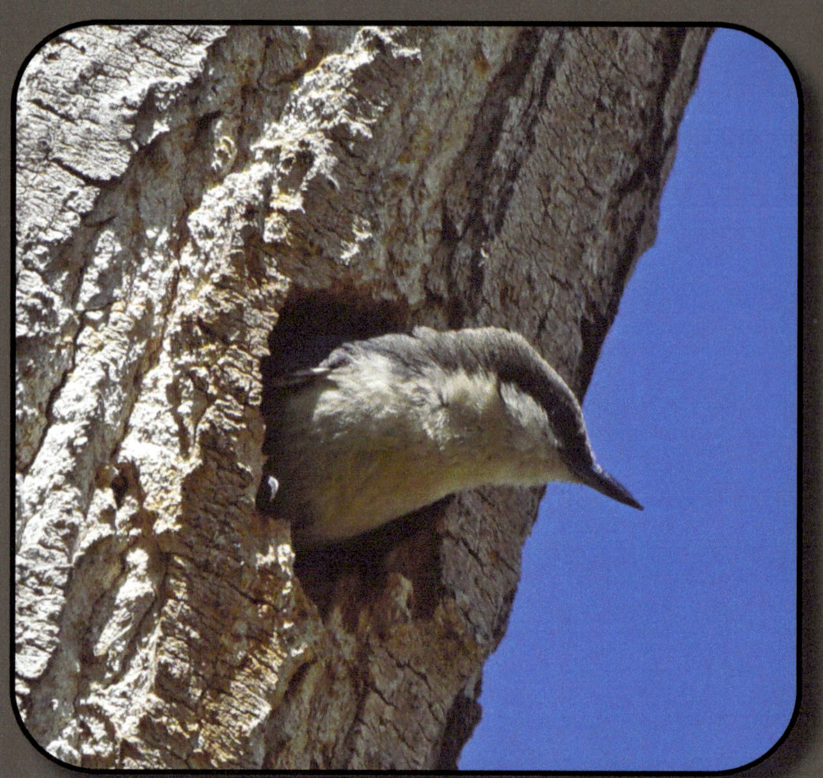

The **Pygmy Nuthatch** is one of three nuthatches found in this area year-round.

Those shown here are nesting in hollows in old cottonwood trees. They feed on insects and seeds and are often mixed with other songbirds such as Chickadees.

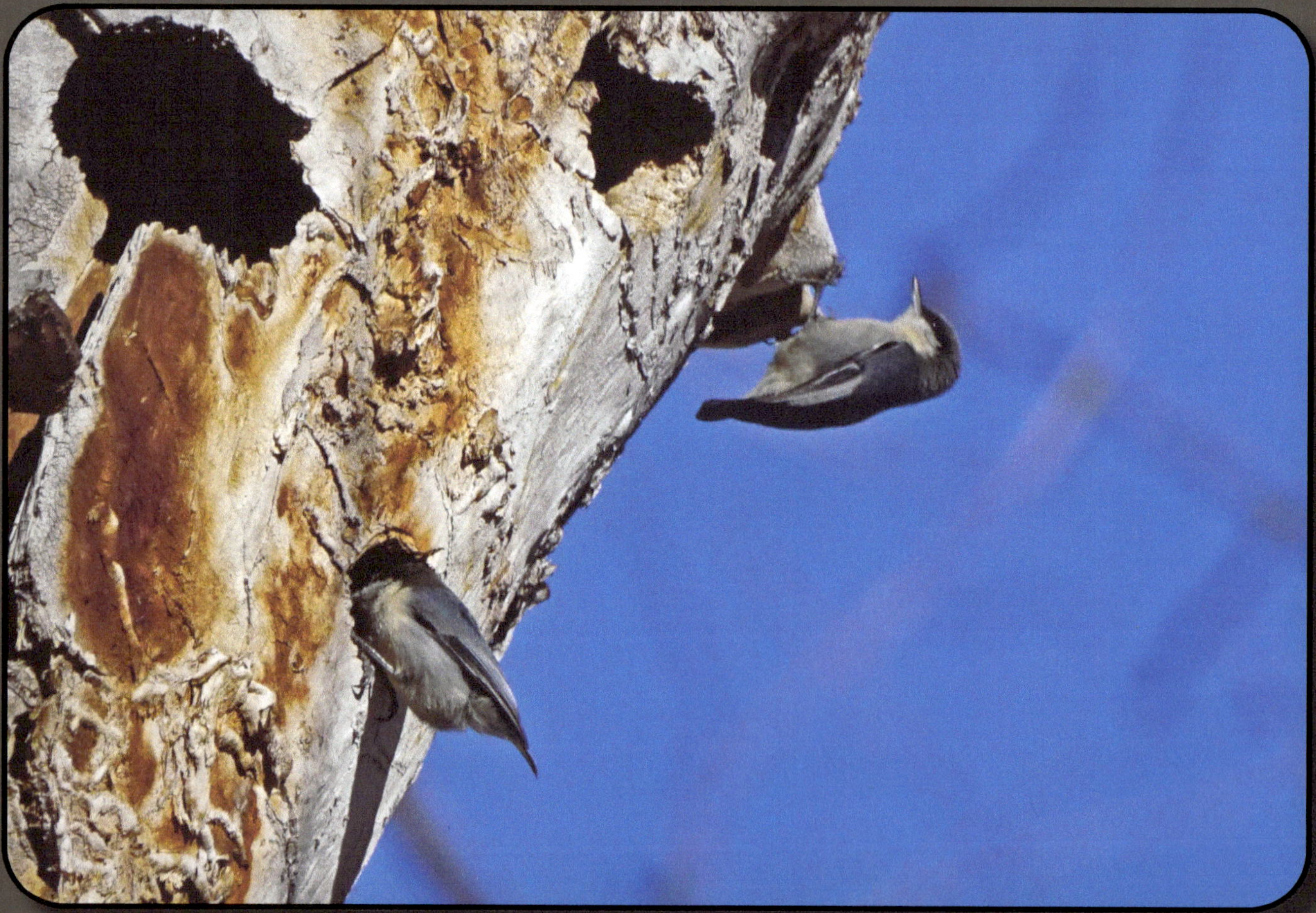

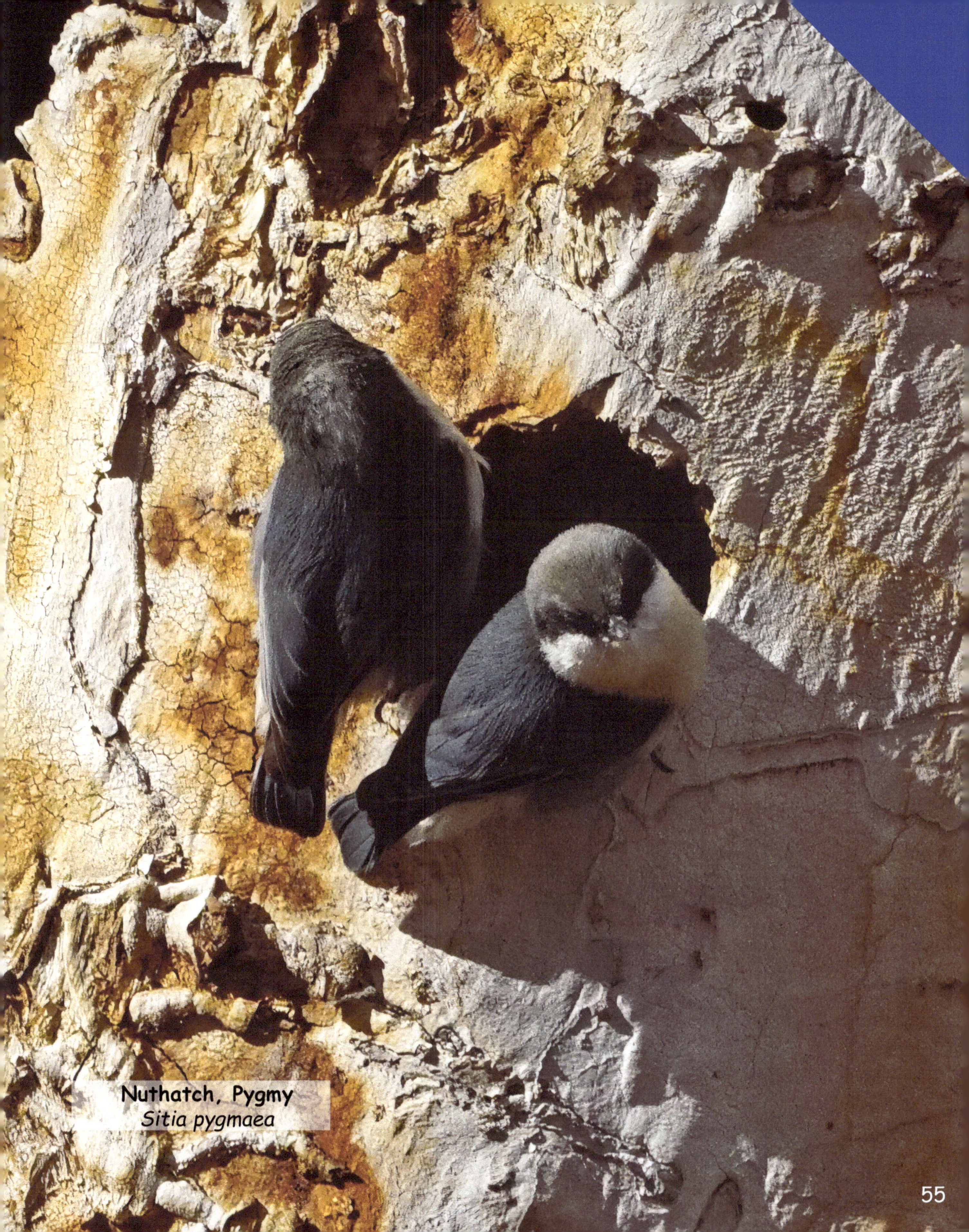

Nuthatch, Pygmy
Sitia pygmaea

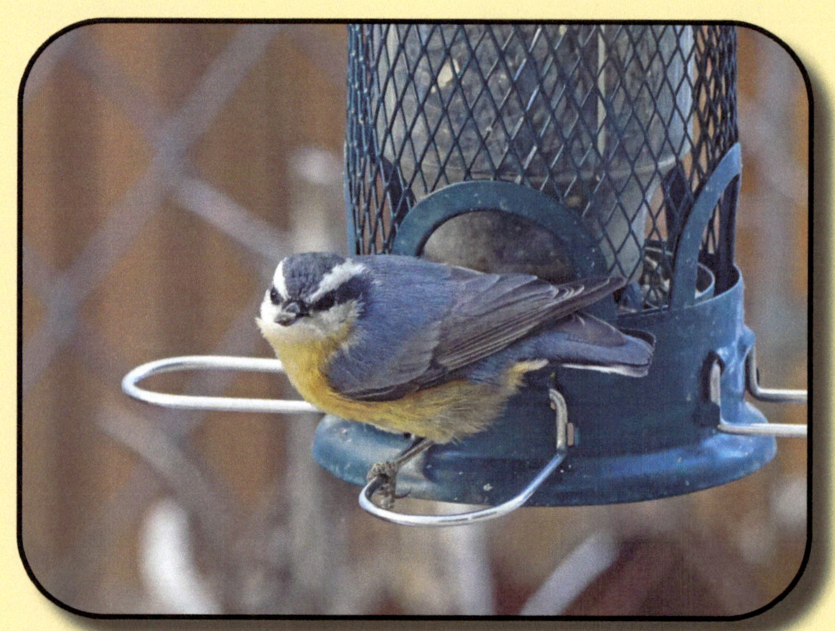

The **Red-breasted Nuthatch** is slightly bigger than the Pygmy Nuthatch. It is generally solitary but may be associated with mixed flocks of small songbirds. It often visits bird feeders. It is also found here year-round.

It is most often seen clinging head-down on tree trunks or feeders.

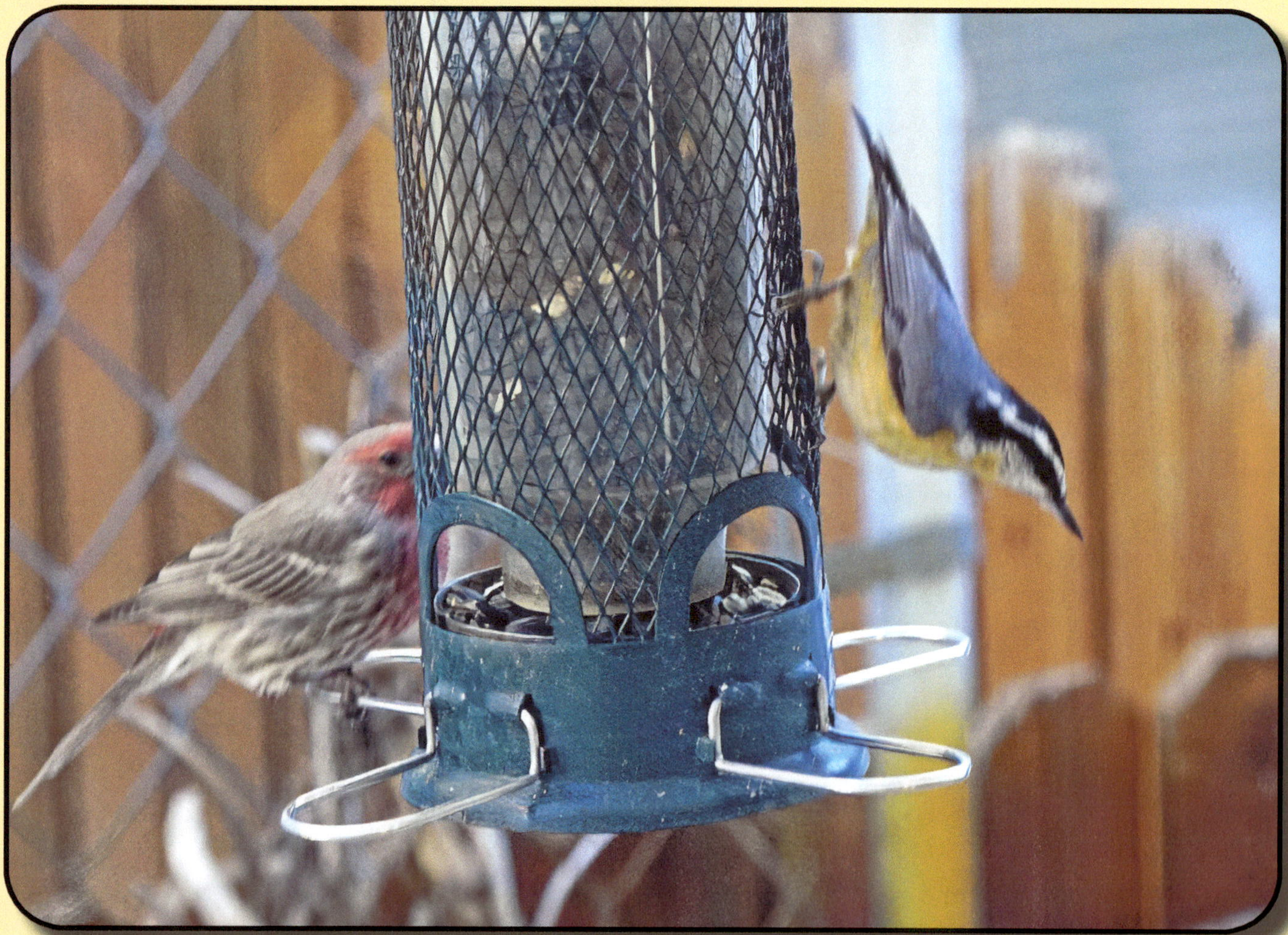

Red-breasted Nuthatch at the feeder with a House Finch

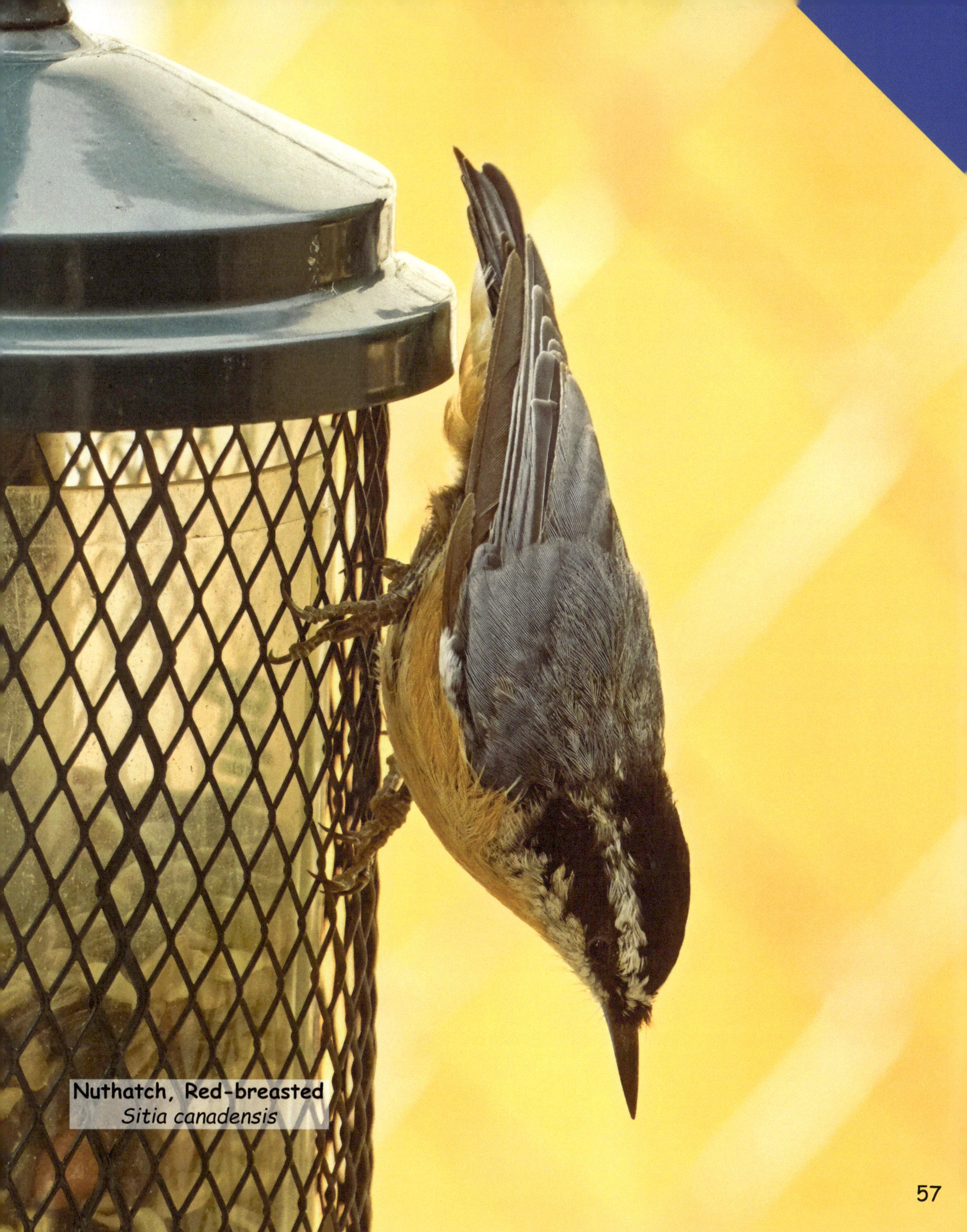

Nuthatch, Red-breasted
Sitia canadensis

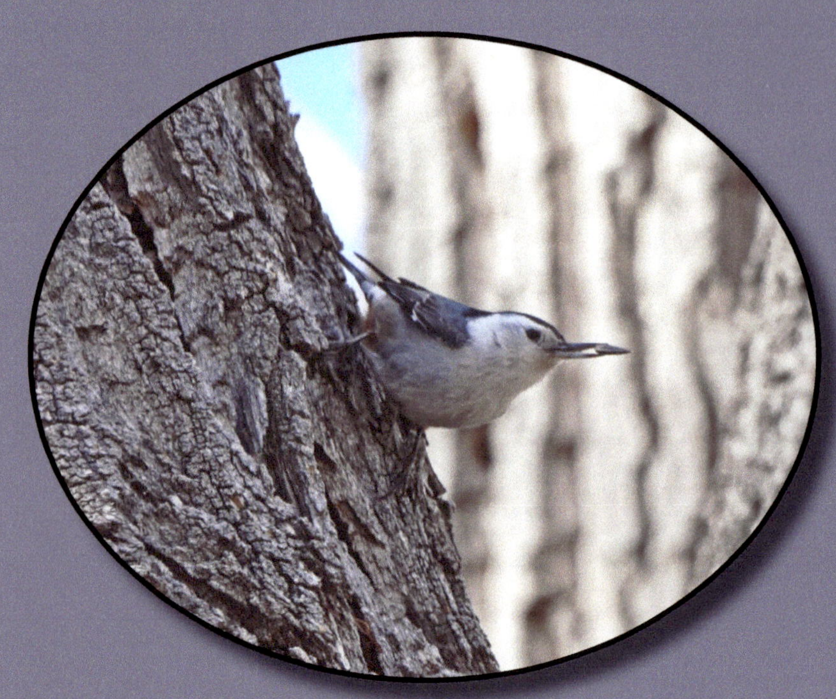

The **White-breasted Nuthatch** is our largest nuthatch. It is solitary or may be in pairs and often visits bird feeders.

It has a distinctive white face with a narrow dark crown. It too is most often seen clinging head-down on tree trunks or feeders.

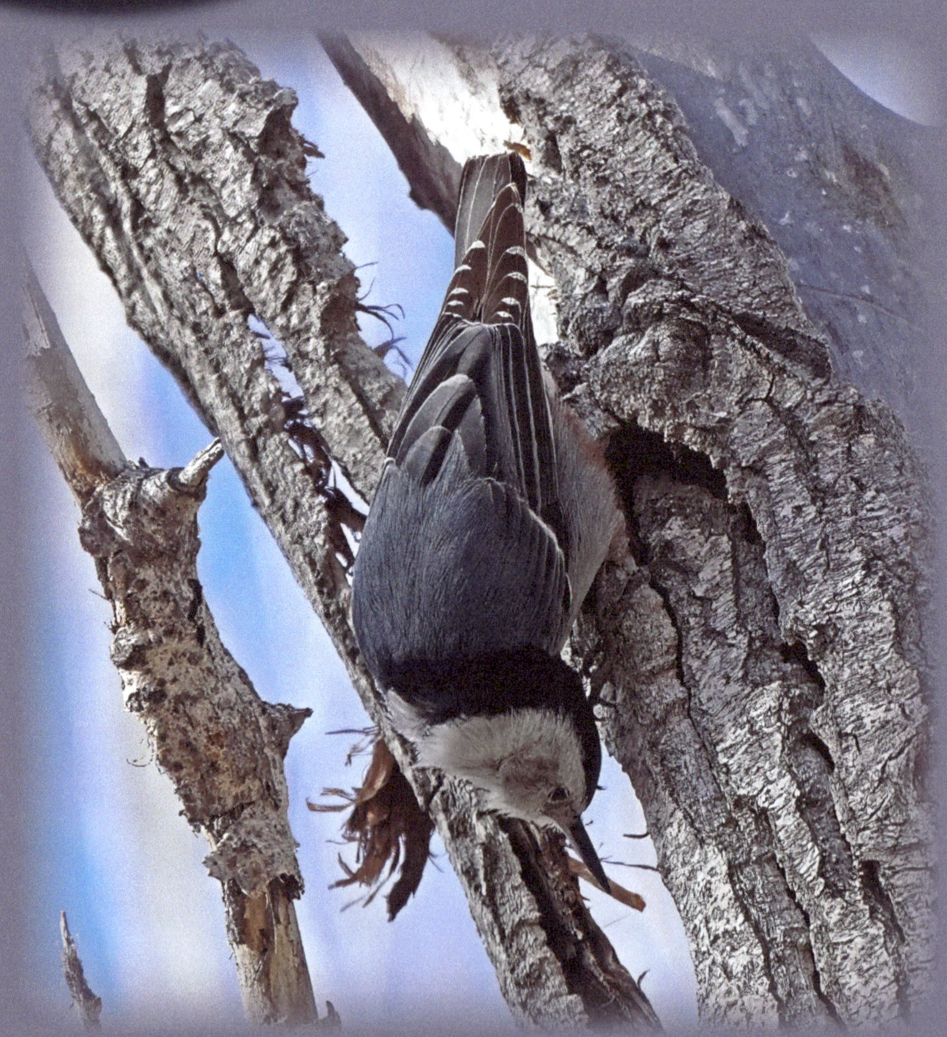

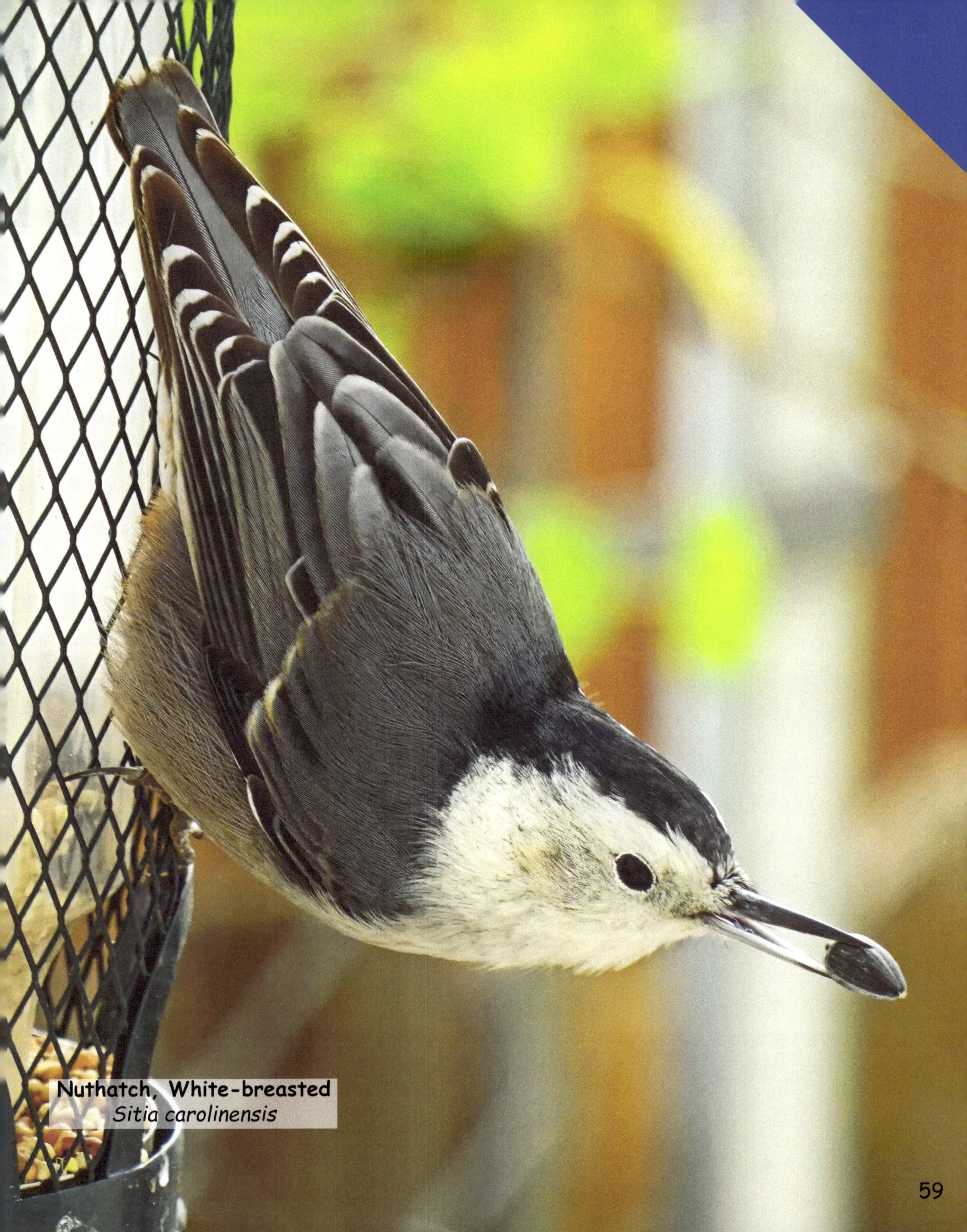

59

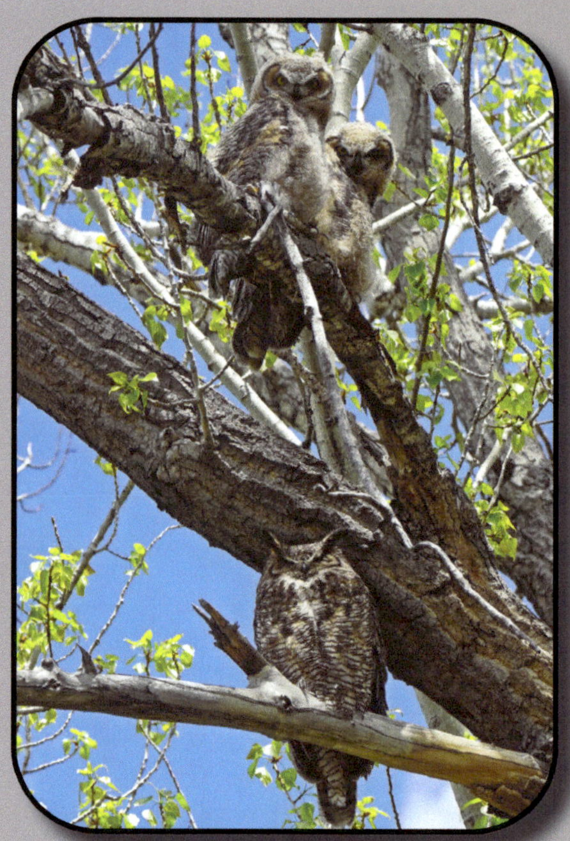

Great Horned Owls (GHO) roost during the day and forage at night for mammals as large as rabbits. Their noctural "hooting" calls are often heard in the Parker area, They mate and lay eggs much earlier in the year than other raptors. Females can be incubating their (2-5) eggs as early as February. Incubation period is from 28 - 35 days. The female sits on the eggs while the male feeds her at night . . .

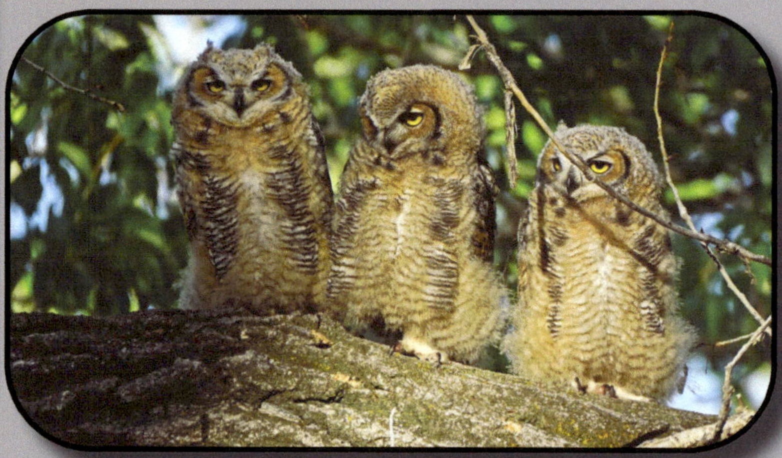

Adult below, owlets above

Triplet owlets, in May

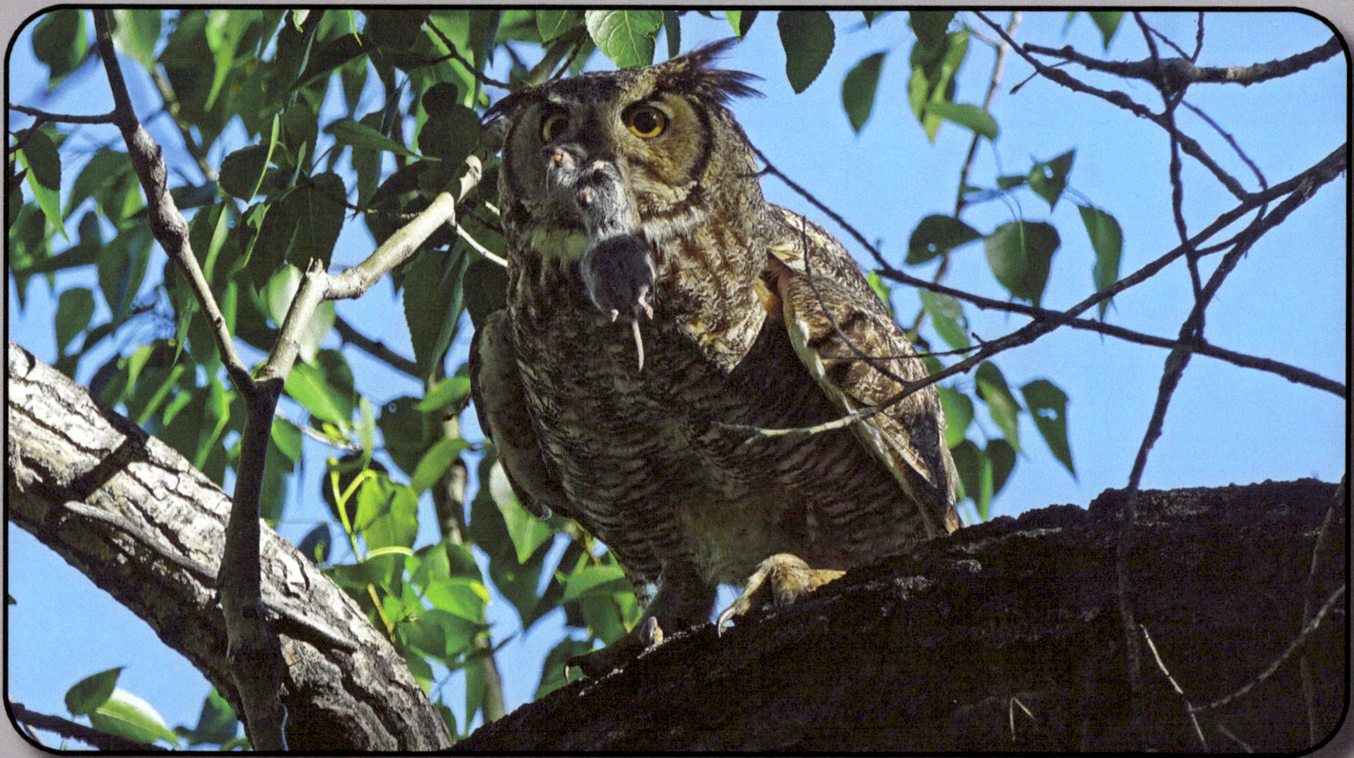

An adult Great Horned Owl brings a meal to her owlets

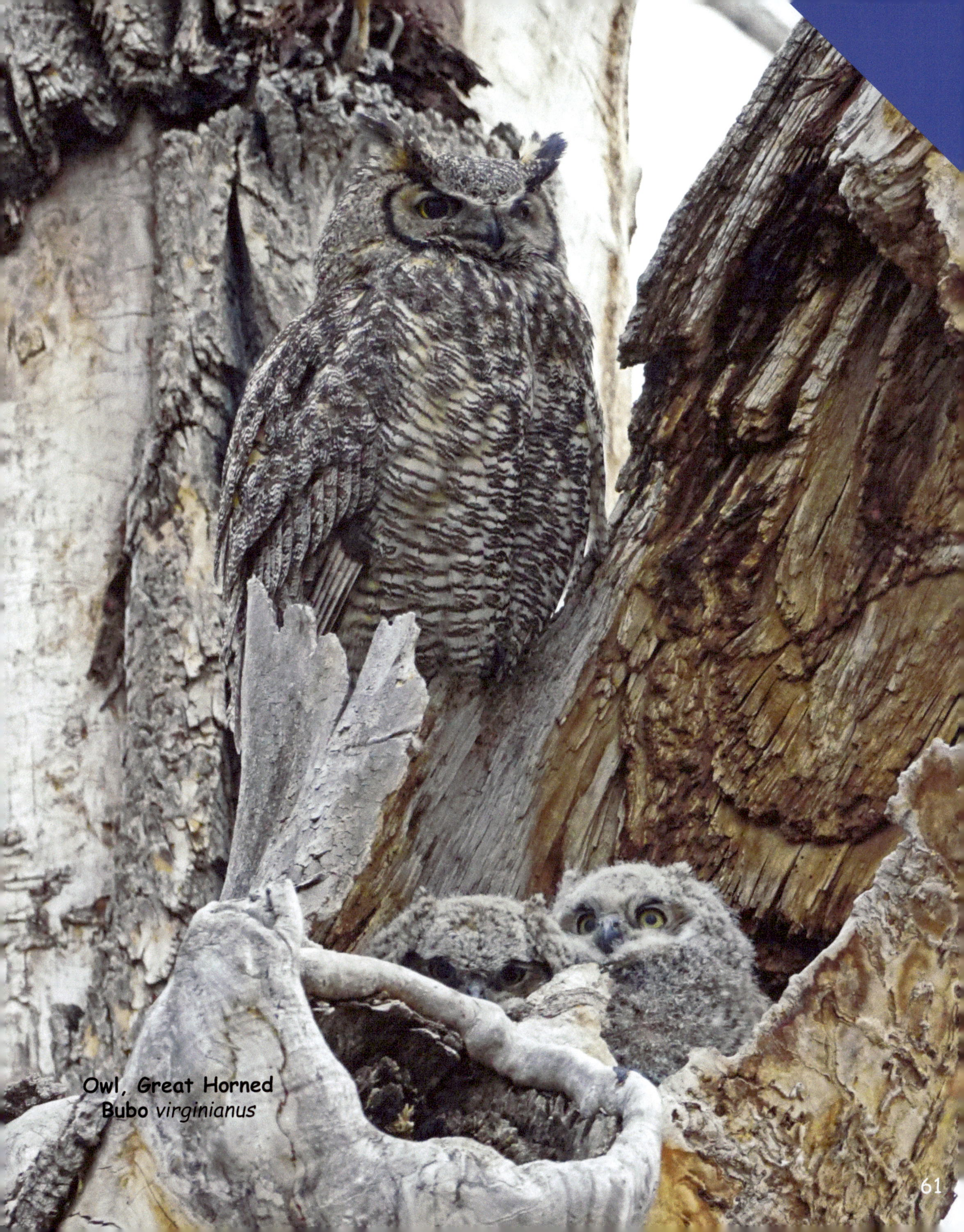

Owl, Great Horned
Bubo virginianus

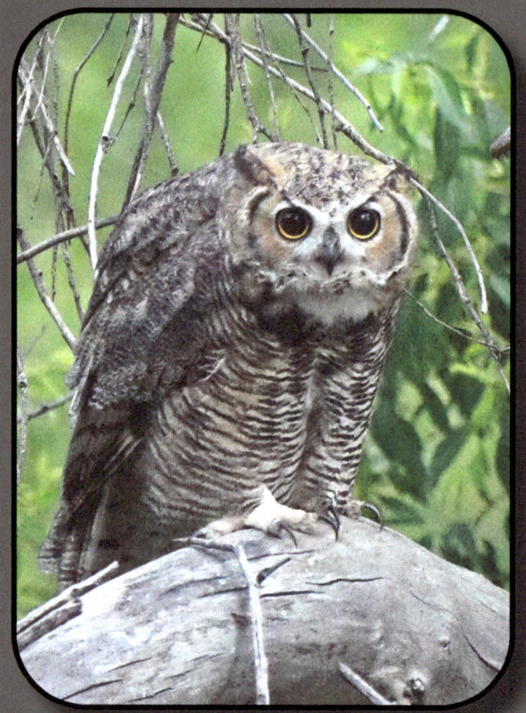

. . . The young are not usually competent fliers until they are about 10 to 12 weeks old. The age at which the young leave the nest varys based on the abundance of food. GHOs in the wild may live for 25 years or more.

The eyebrow-like "horns" are not ears but tufts of feathers called "**plumicorns.**"

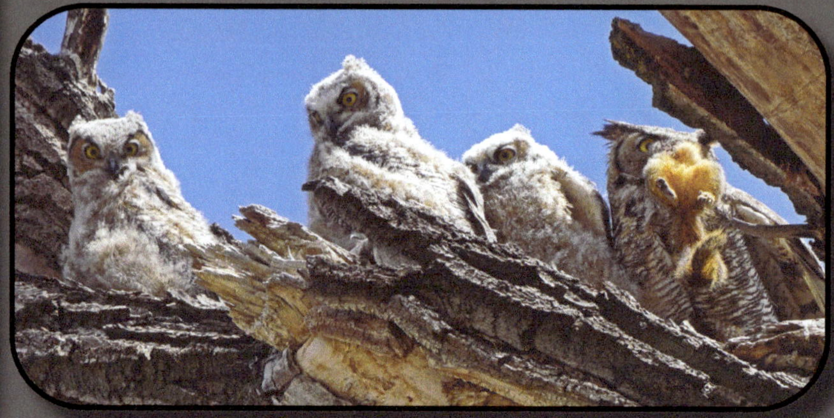

The adult (right) brings food to the owlets

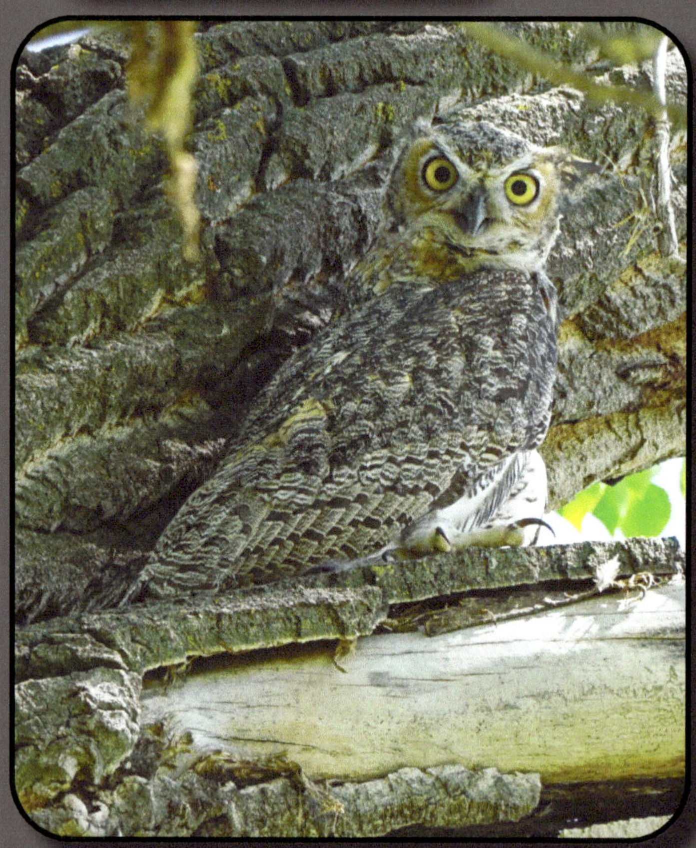

Camouflaged owlet

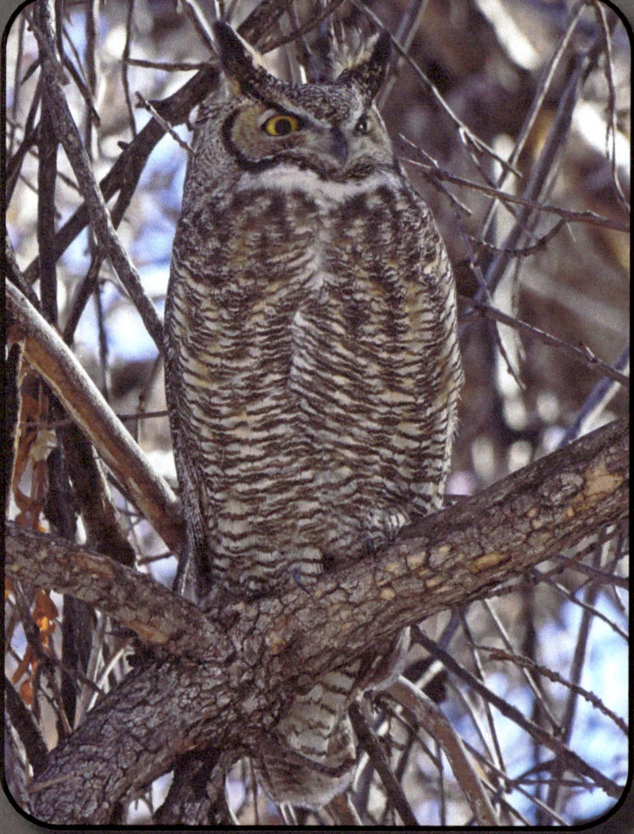

Adult male GHO

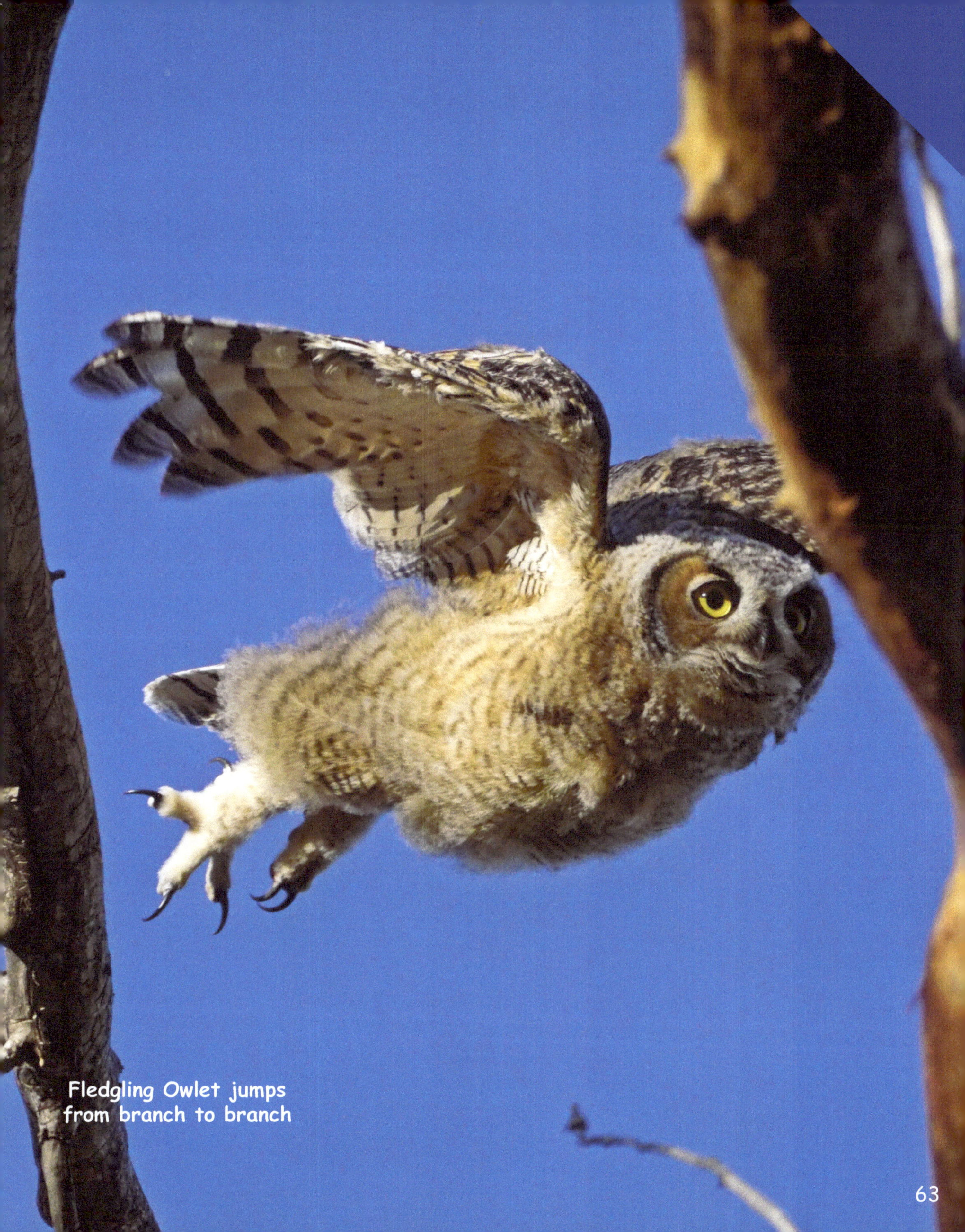

Fledgling Owlet jumps
from branch to branch

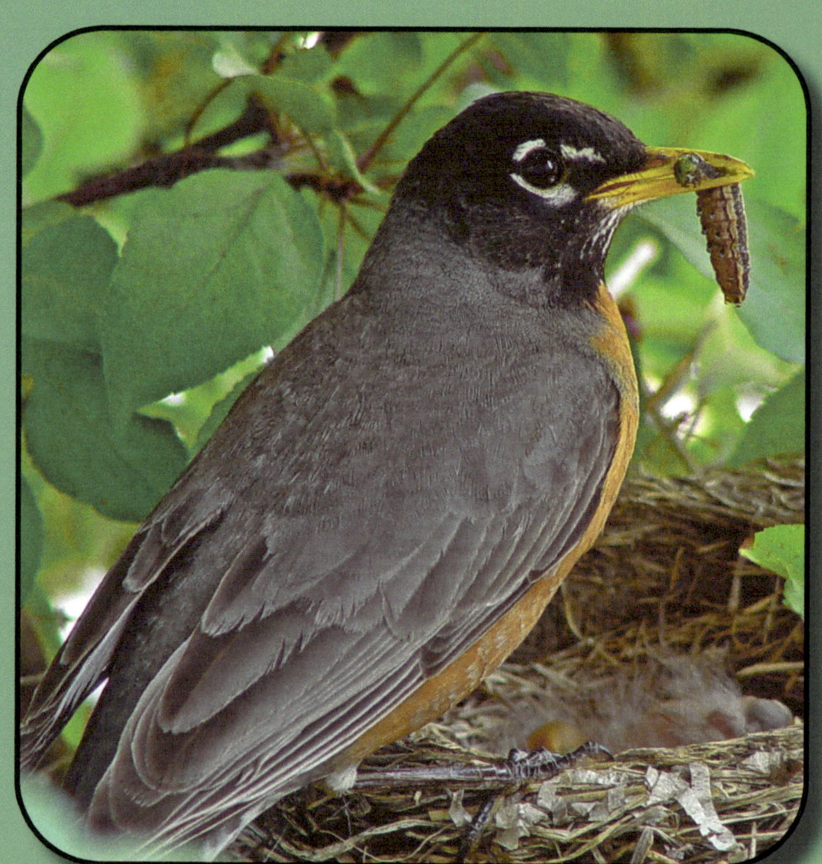

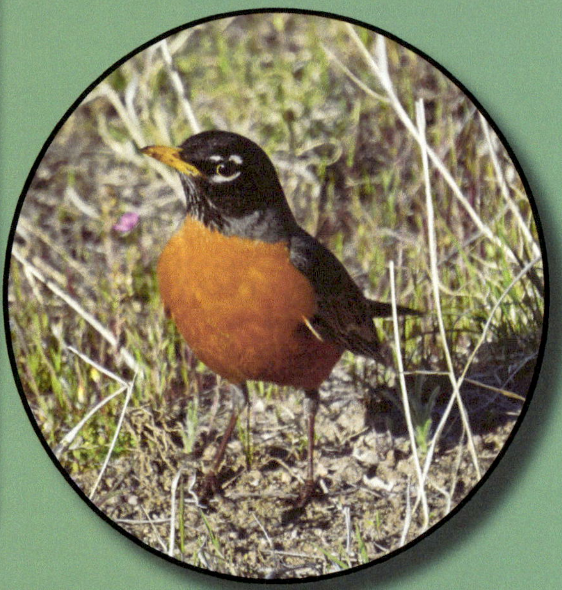

American Robins are common year-round across the country. In summer, they are usually seen on grassy lawns and fields searching for earthworms. Nests in open woodland or edge habitat.

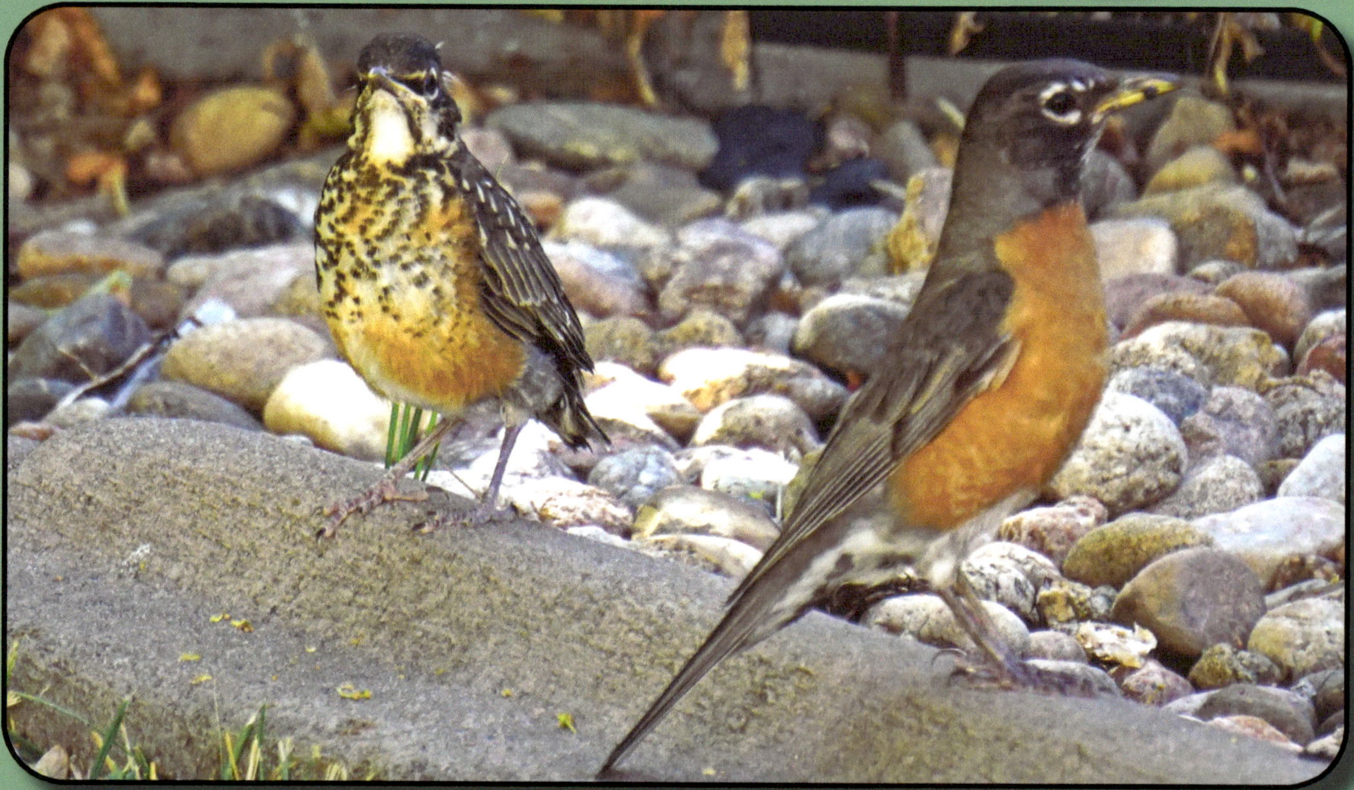

Juvenile (left) and adult Robin

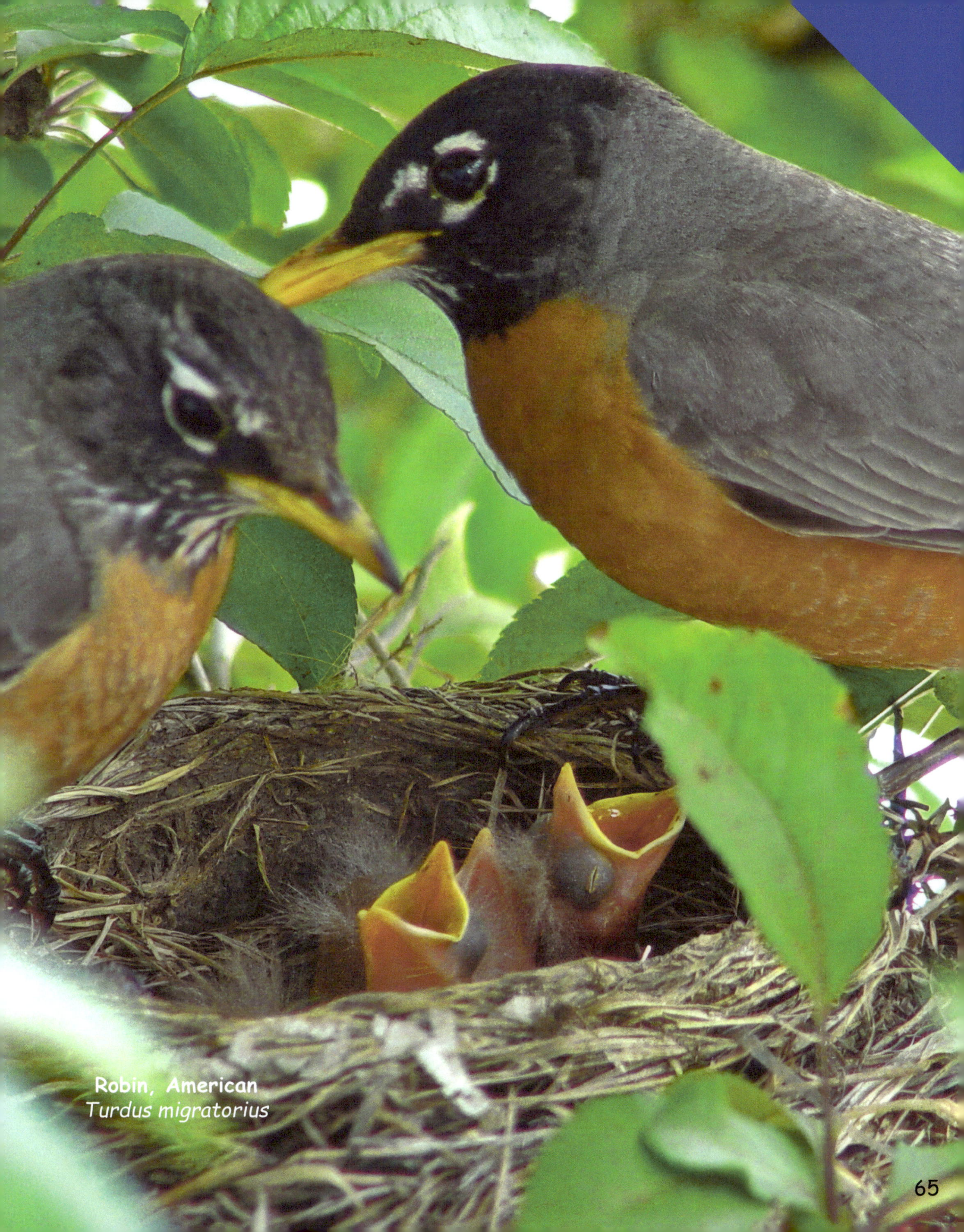
Robin, American
Turdus migratorius

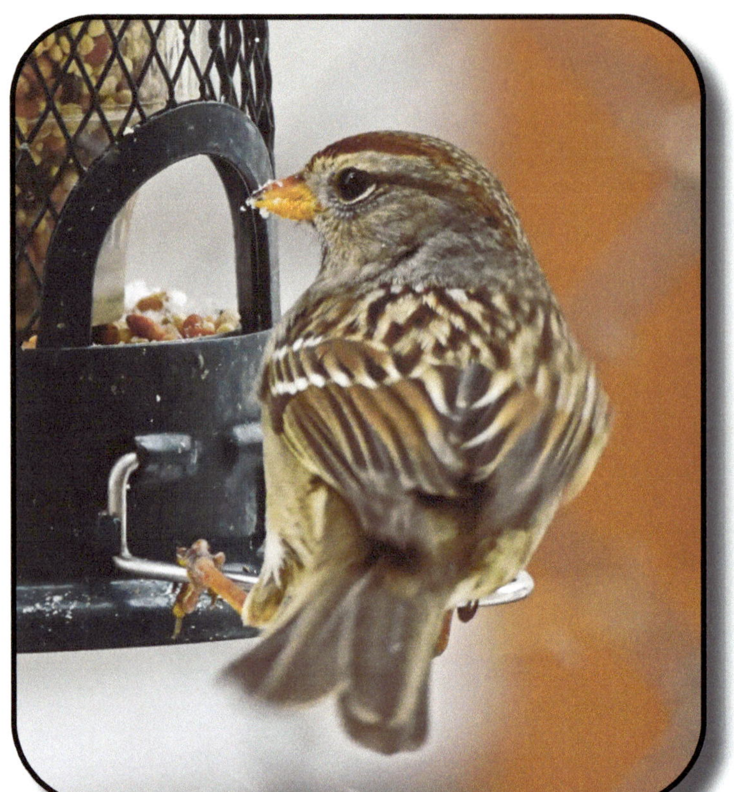

Female House Sparrow

House Sparrows are common and widespread. They nest in any sheltered cavity, from birdhouses to streetlights etc. Often seen in small flocks.

Male has a black breast..

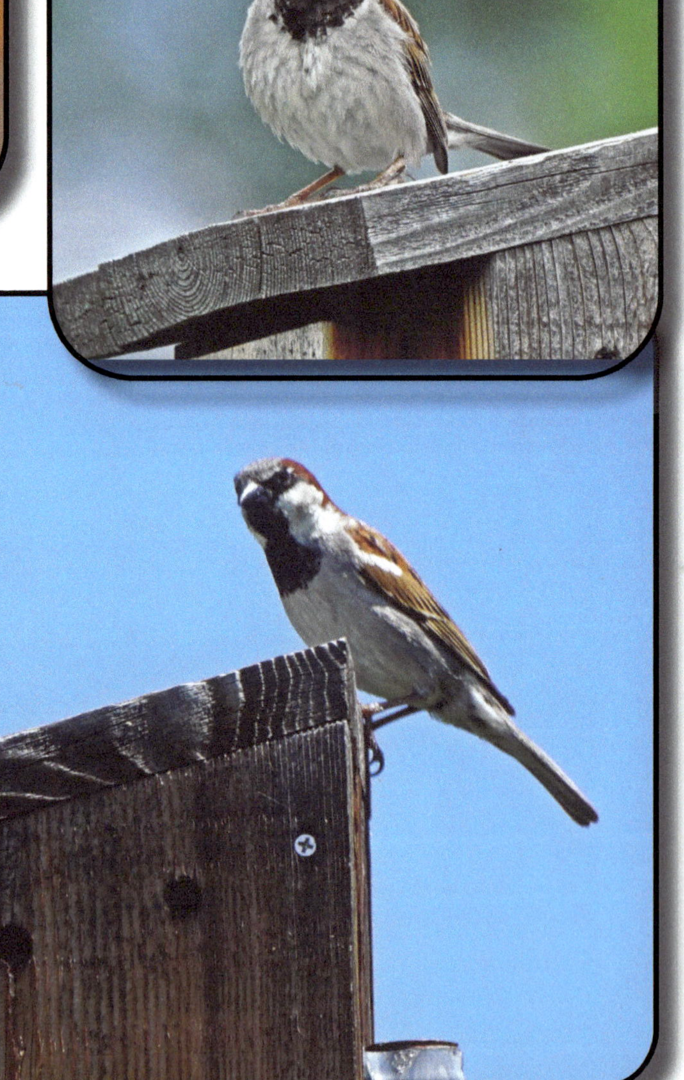

Male House Sparrow (right) and a House Finch

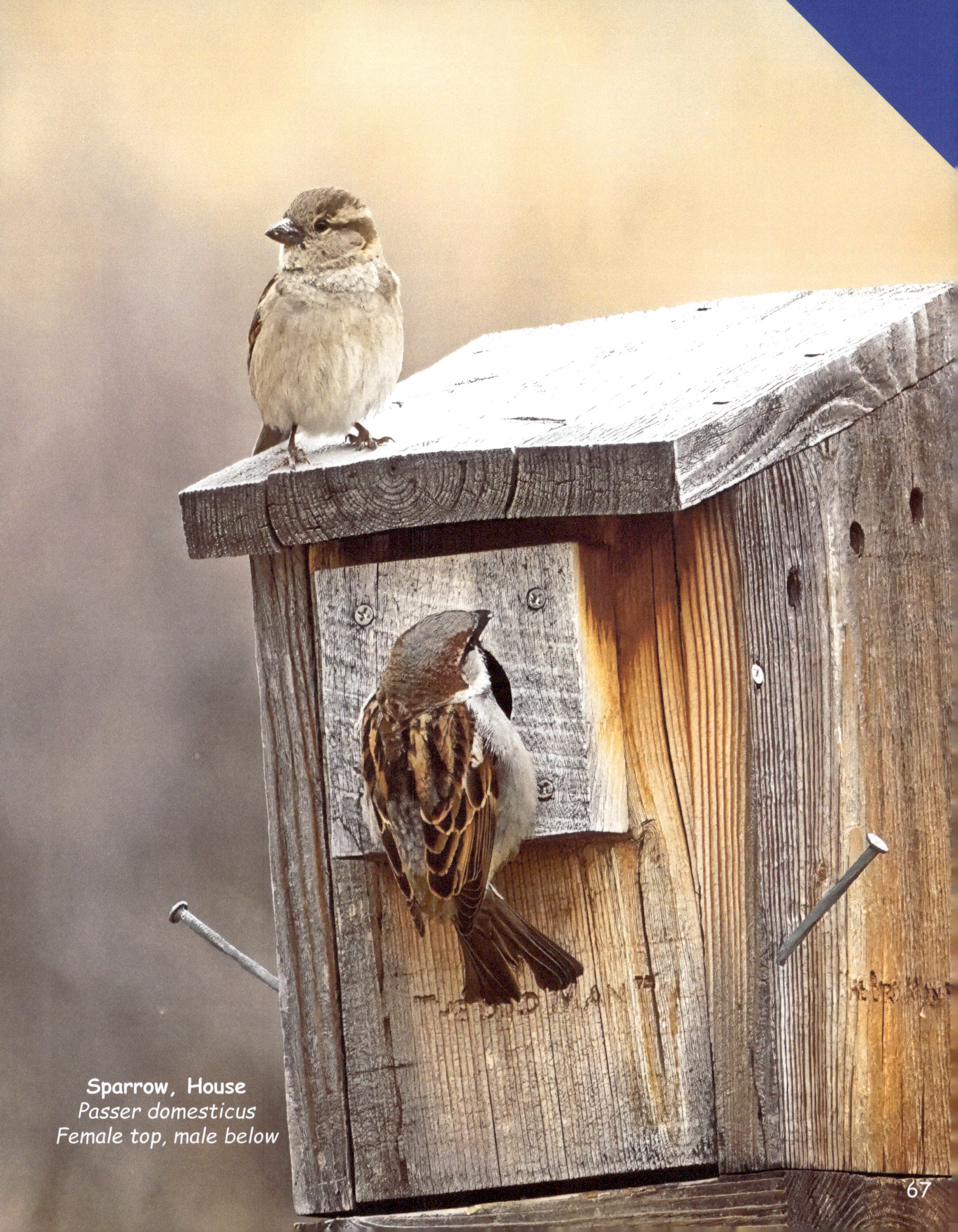

Sparrow, House
Passer domesticus
Female top, male below

67

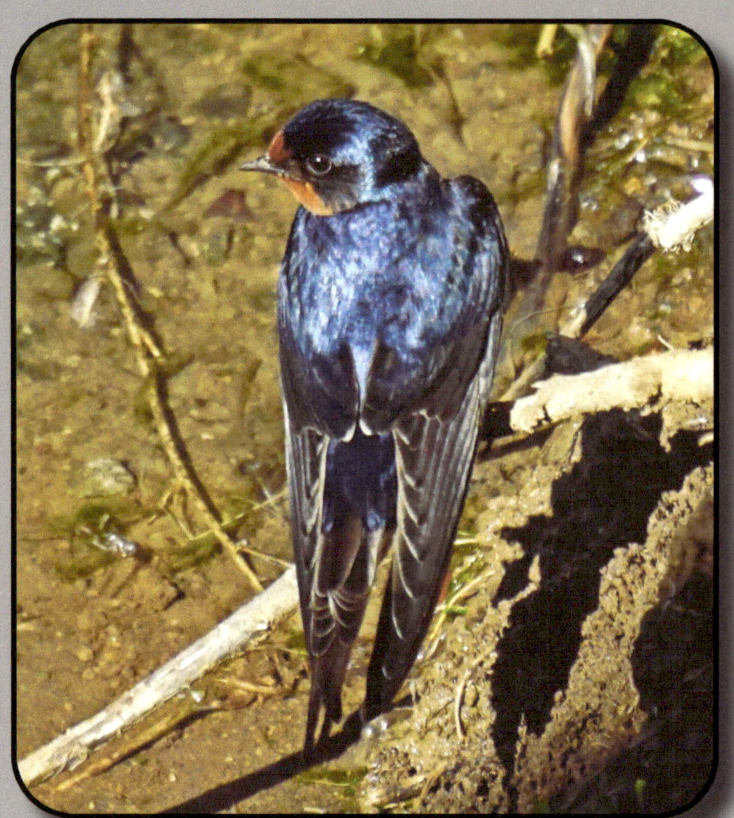

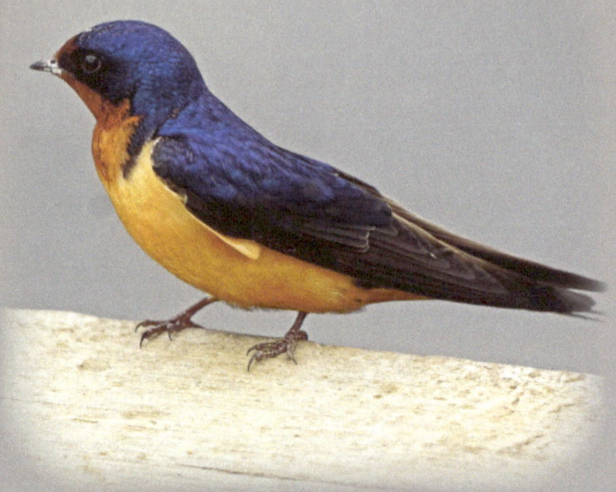

Barn Swallows are common. They nest on structures such as bridges or house eaves where large numbers may congregate. Their nest is a partial bowl of mud.

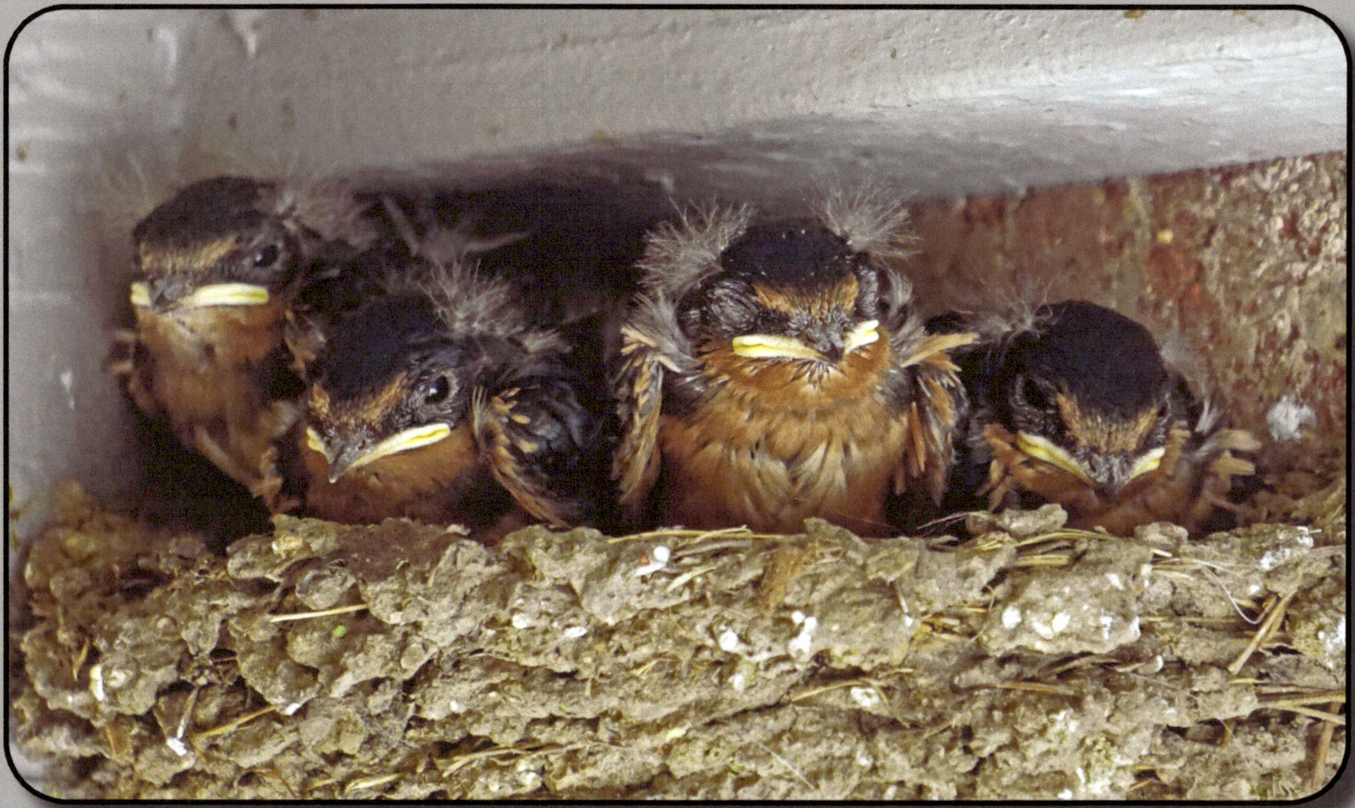

Barn Swallow chicks in their mud nest

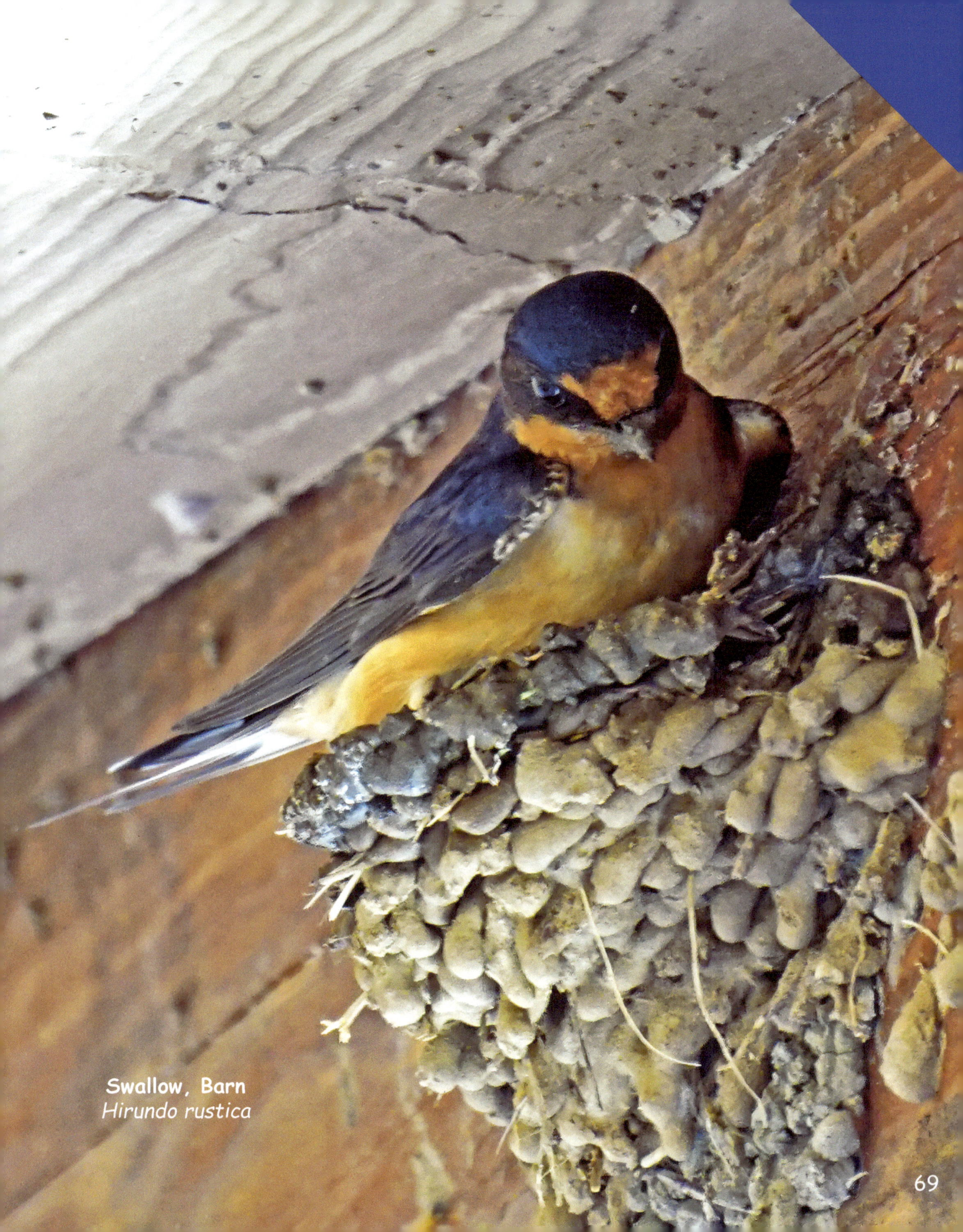

Swallow, Barn
Hirundo rustica

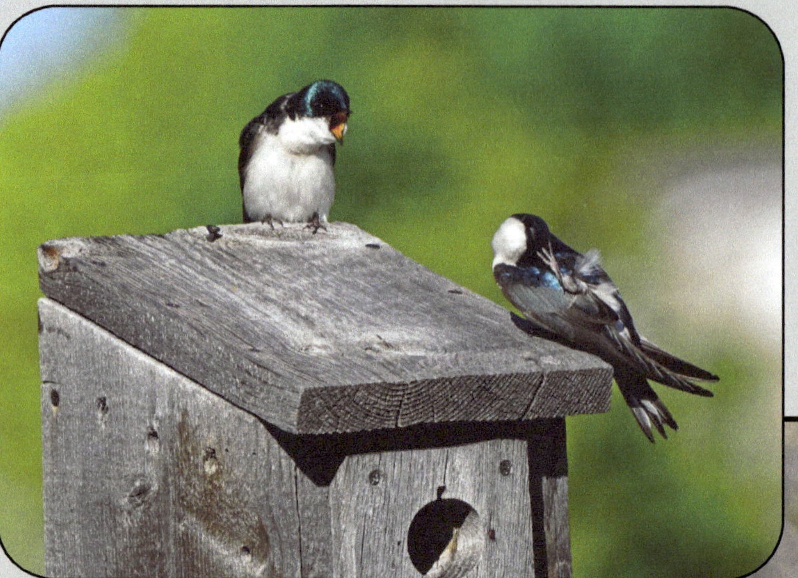

Tree Swallows are common. They nest singly in bird houses along Parker trails. Large numbers may be seen perched on wires or in bushes or reeds.

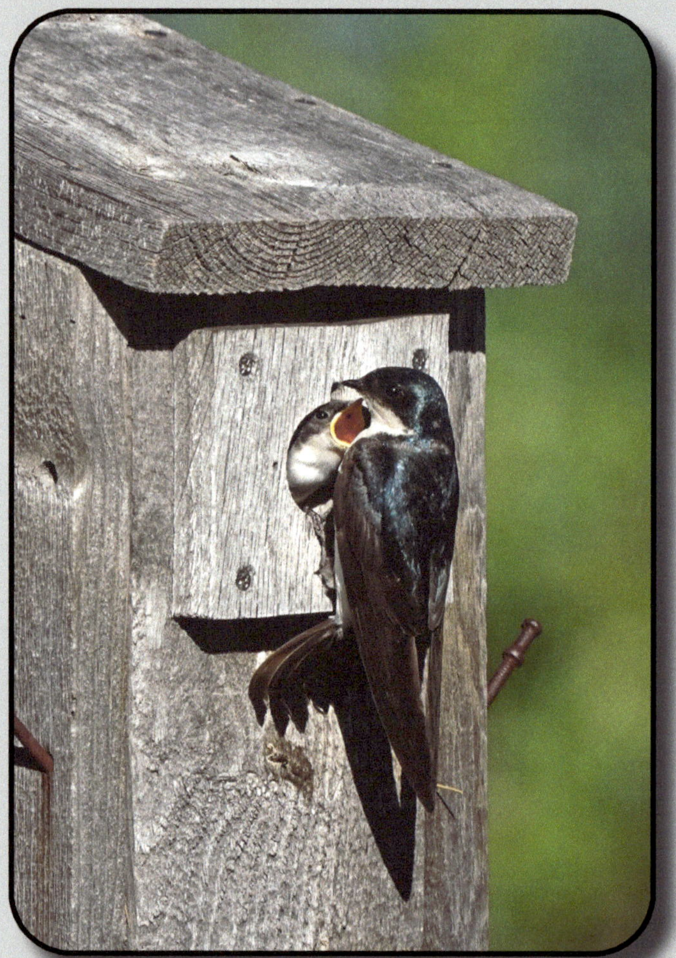

Feeding a chick

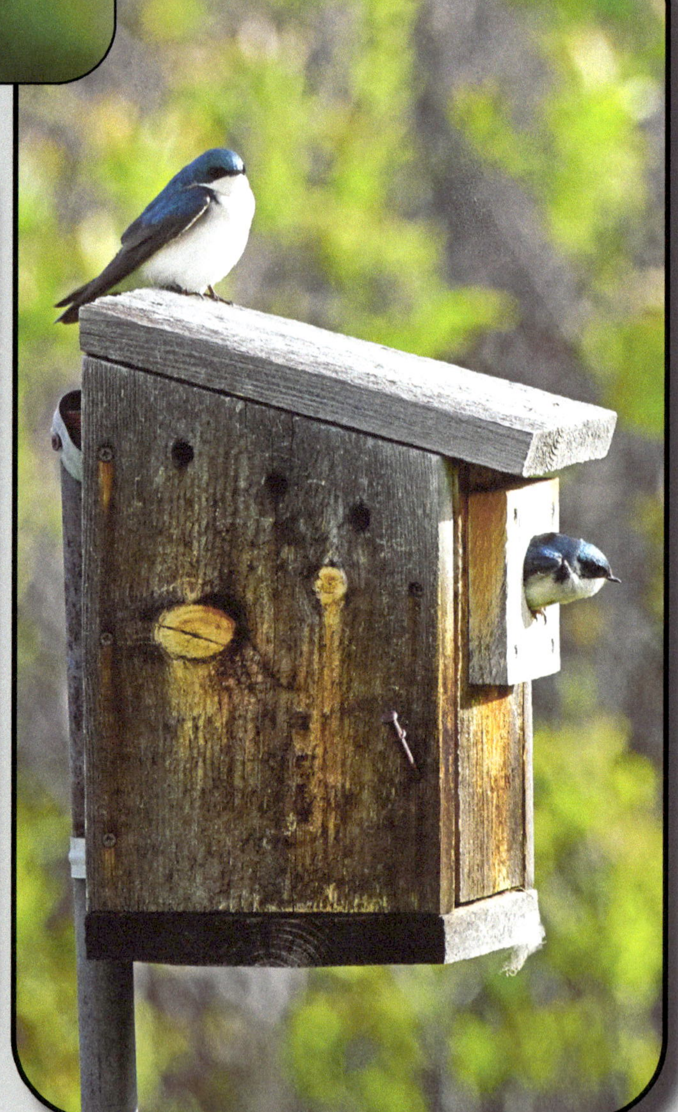

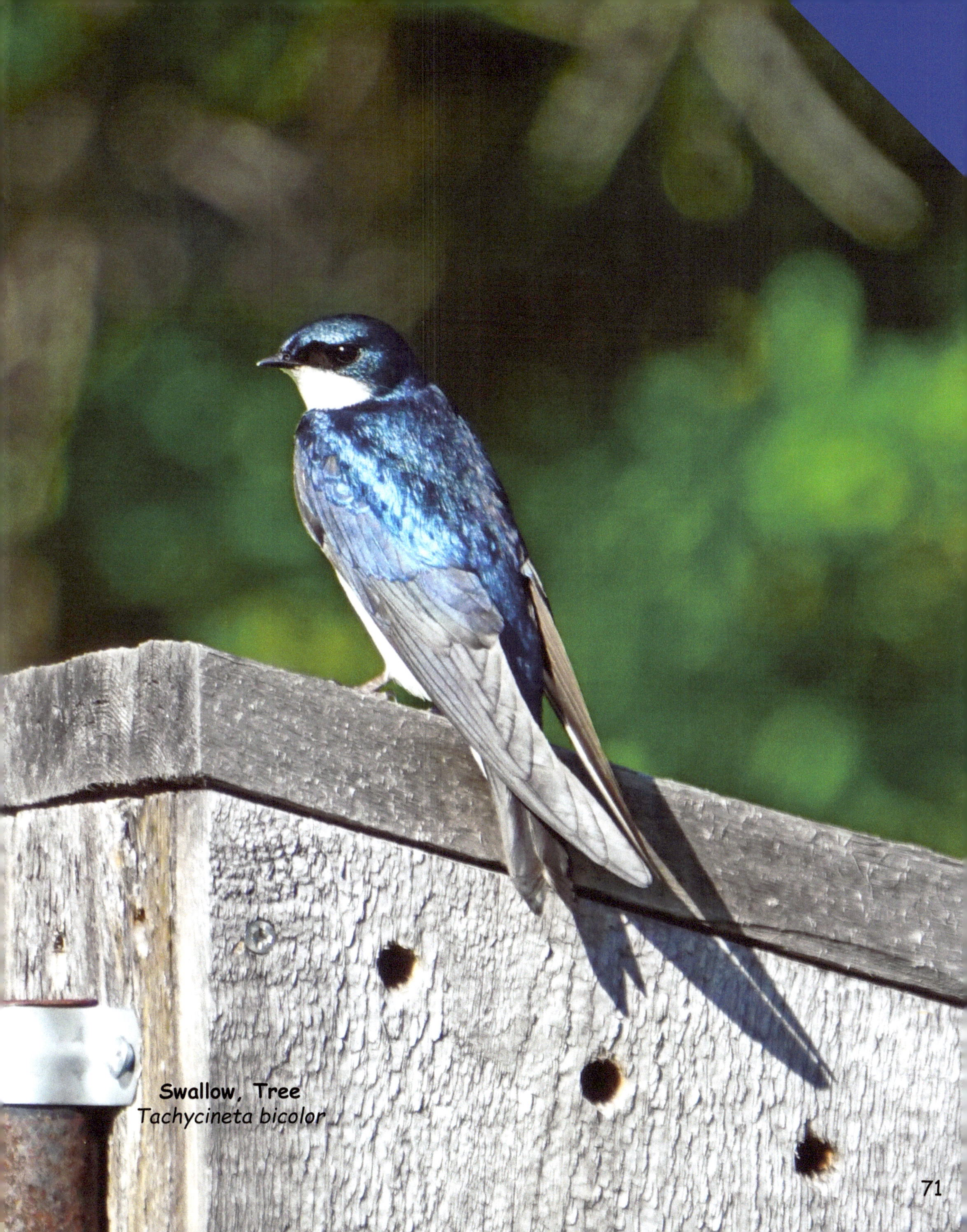

Swallow, Tree
Tachycineta bicolor

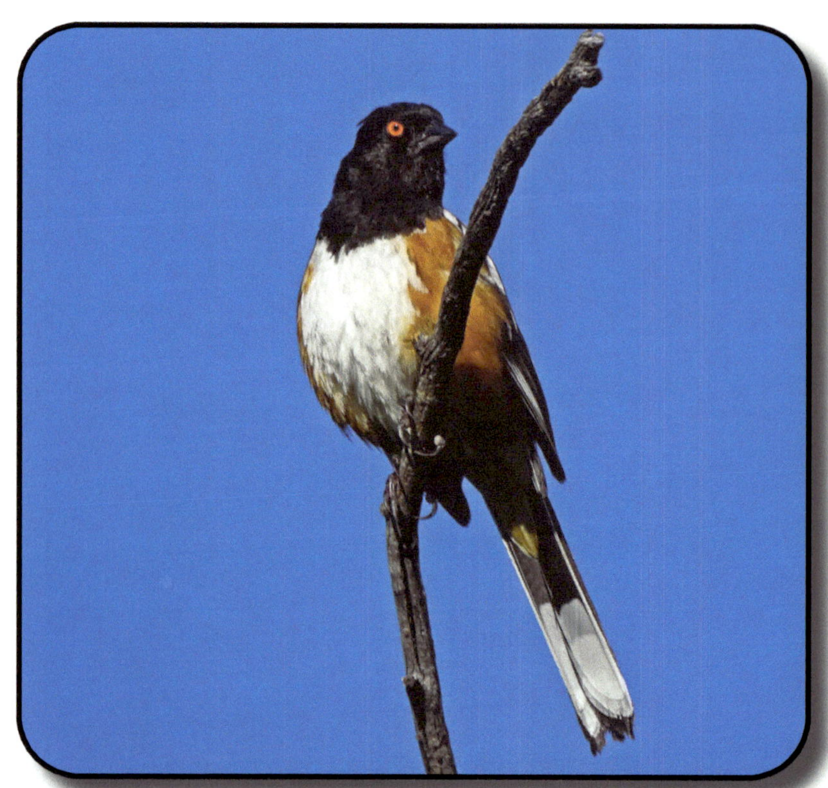

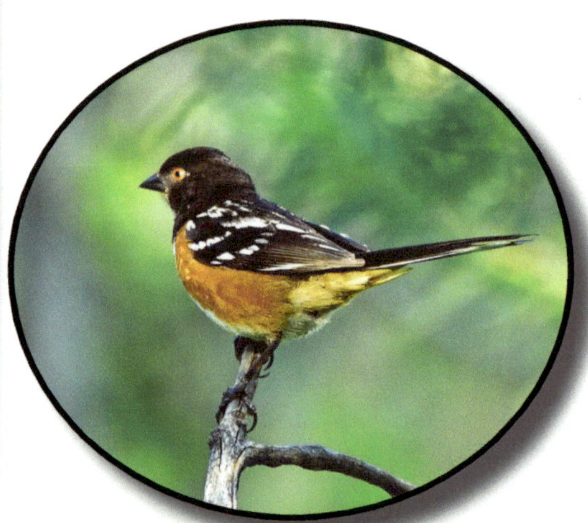

The **Spotted Towhee**, a year-round resident, is common in brushy habitats, usually staying undercover. They forage on the ground in leaf litter for seeds and insects.

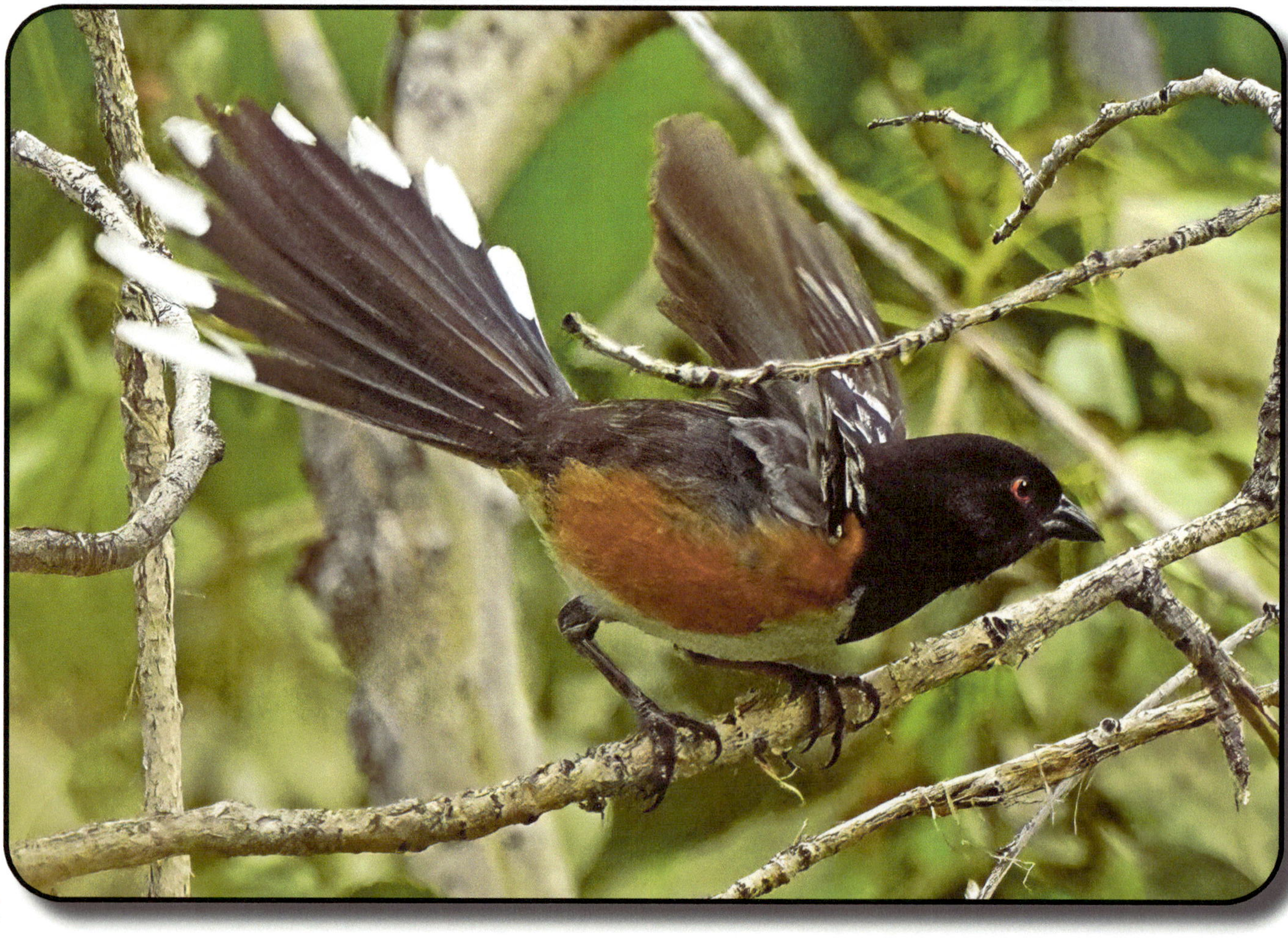

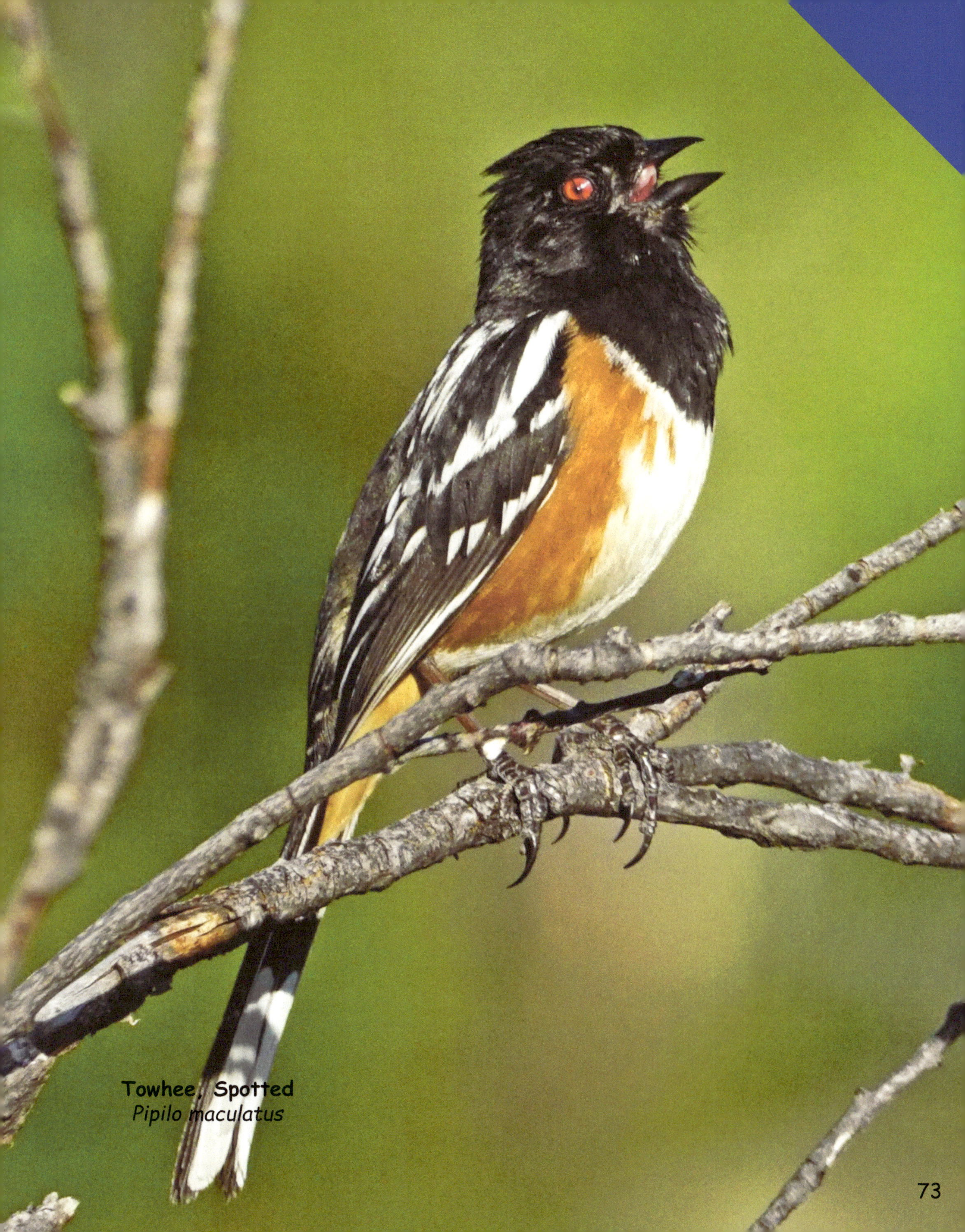

Towhee, Spotted
Pipilo maculatus

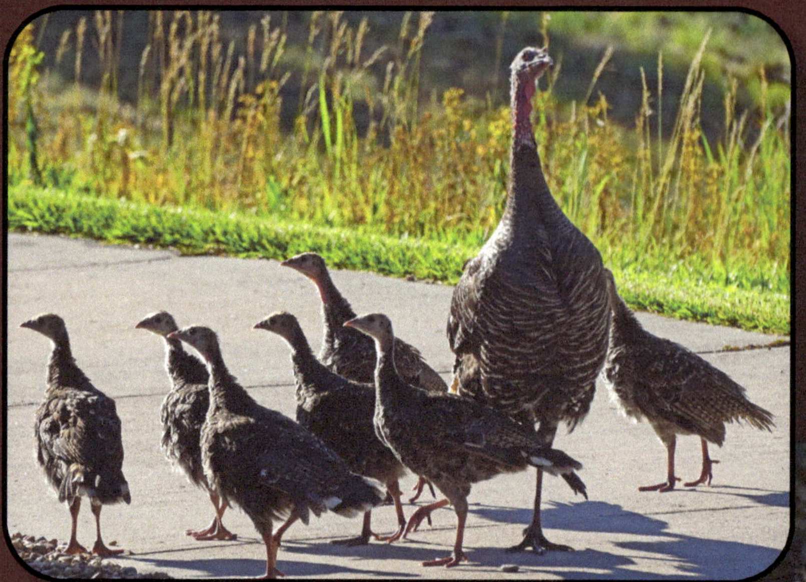

Wild Turkeys are seen from time to time, even on streets in the town center. They are usually found in open woodlands in large flocks. They roost in trees at night.

The chicks can fly short distances when only about a week old.

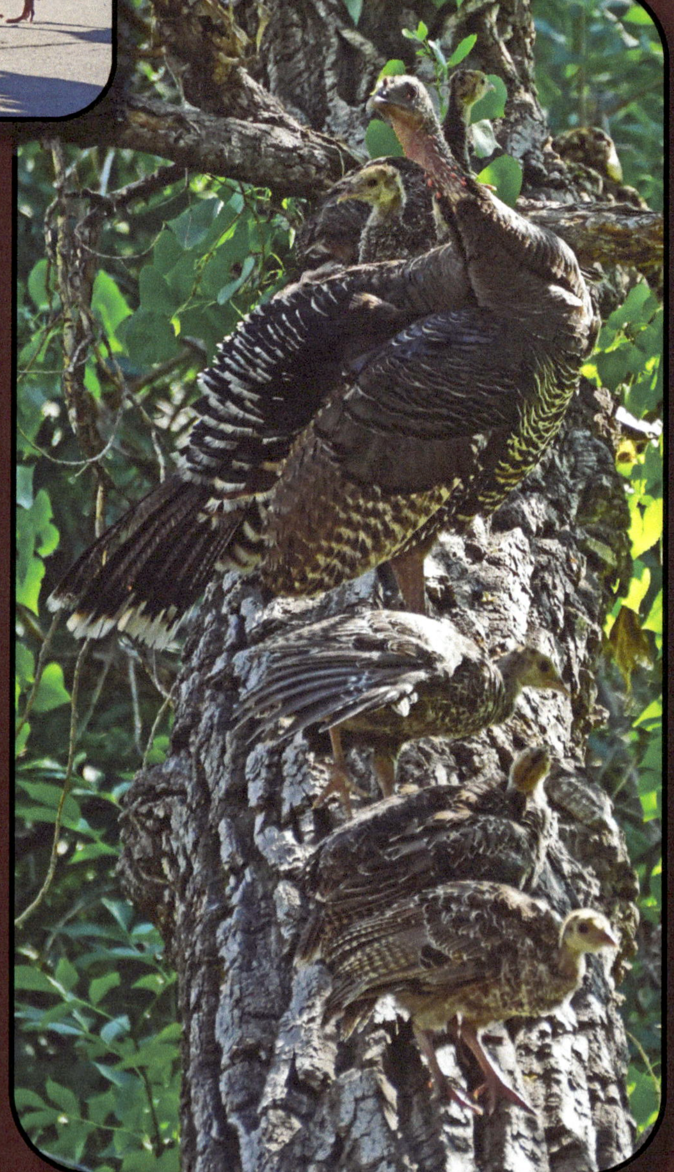

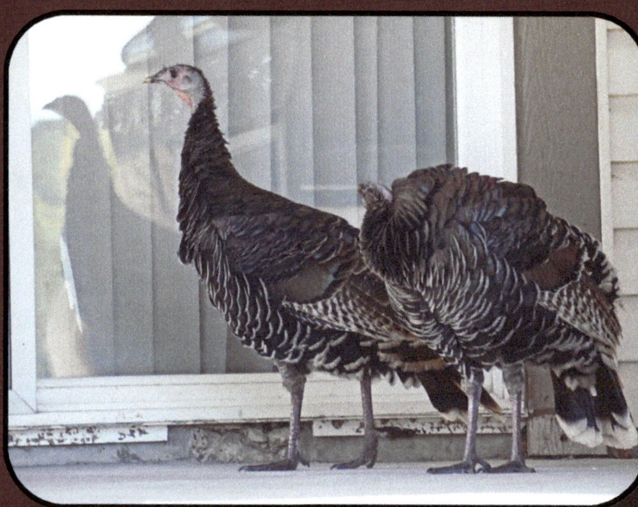

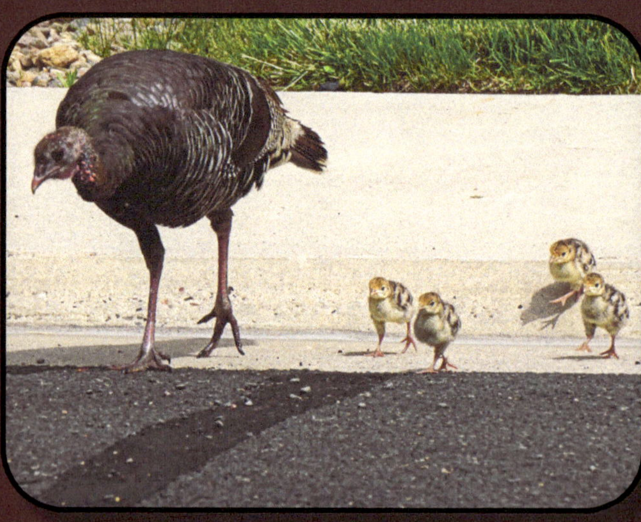

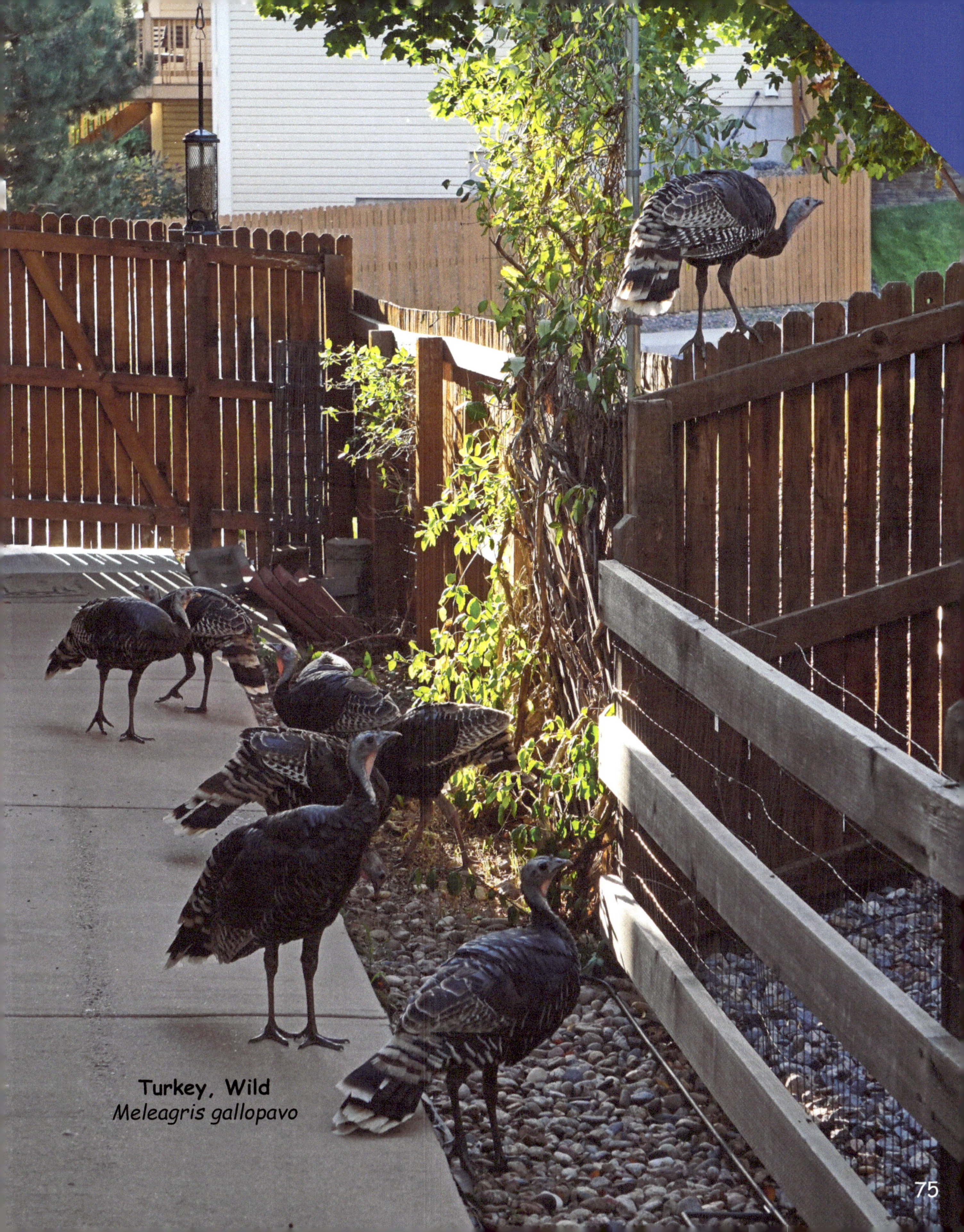

Turkey, Wild
Meleagris gallopavo

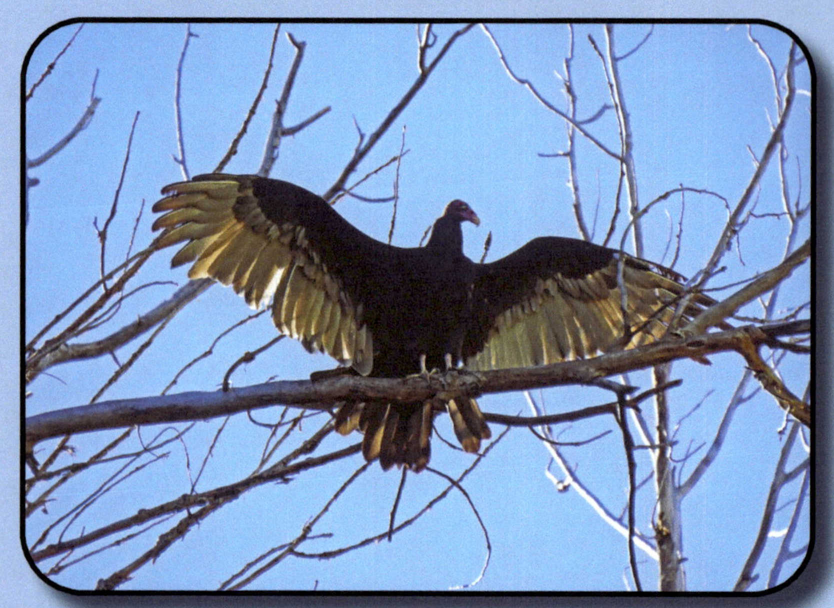

Turkey Vultures are common but most often seen in flight over mixed habitat of woods and open areas. They are not often seen over built-up areas. They feed on carrion found on the ground. Easily identified by their large size and small 'naked' heads.

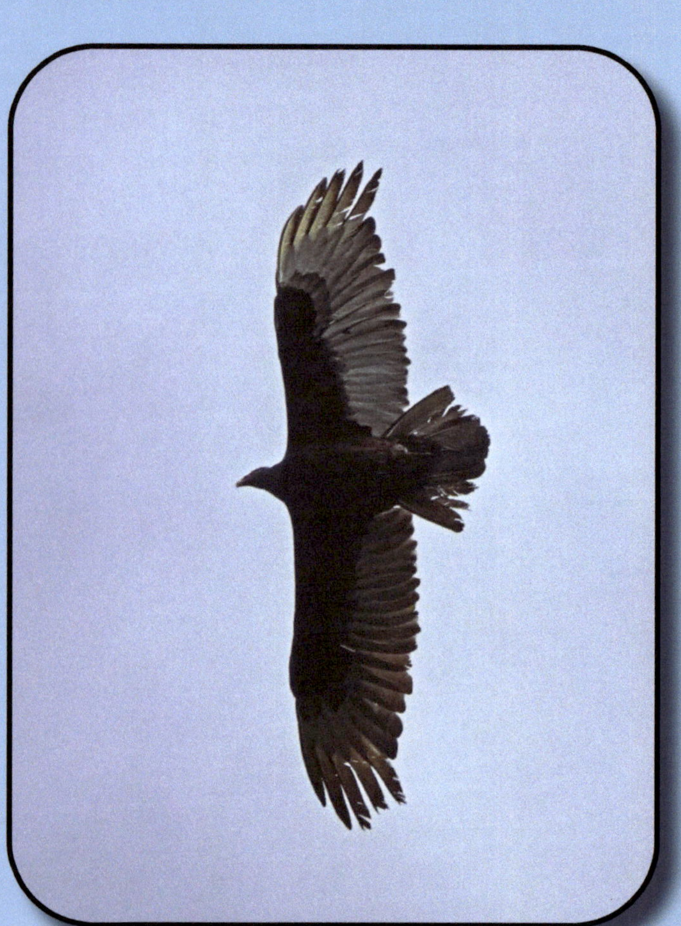

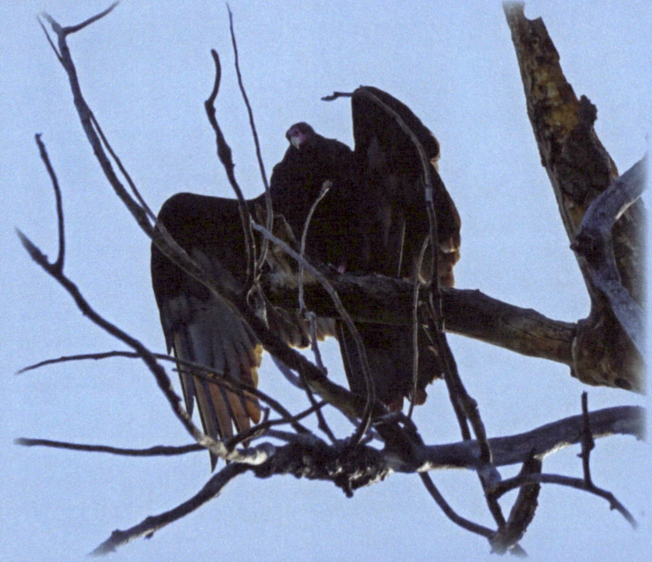

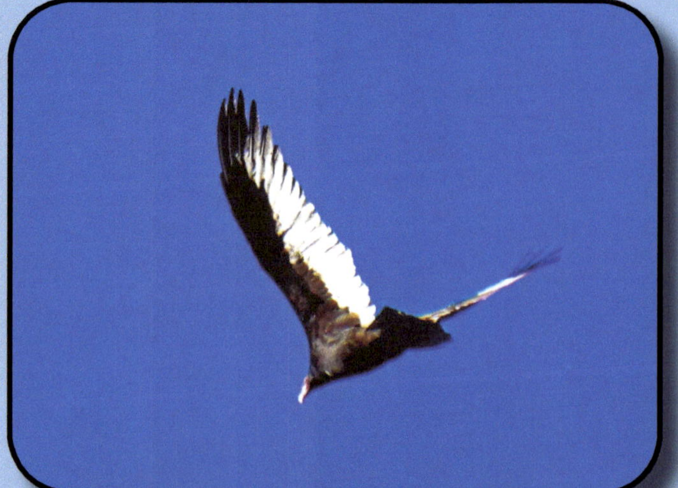

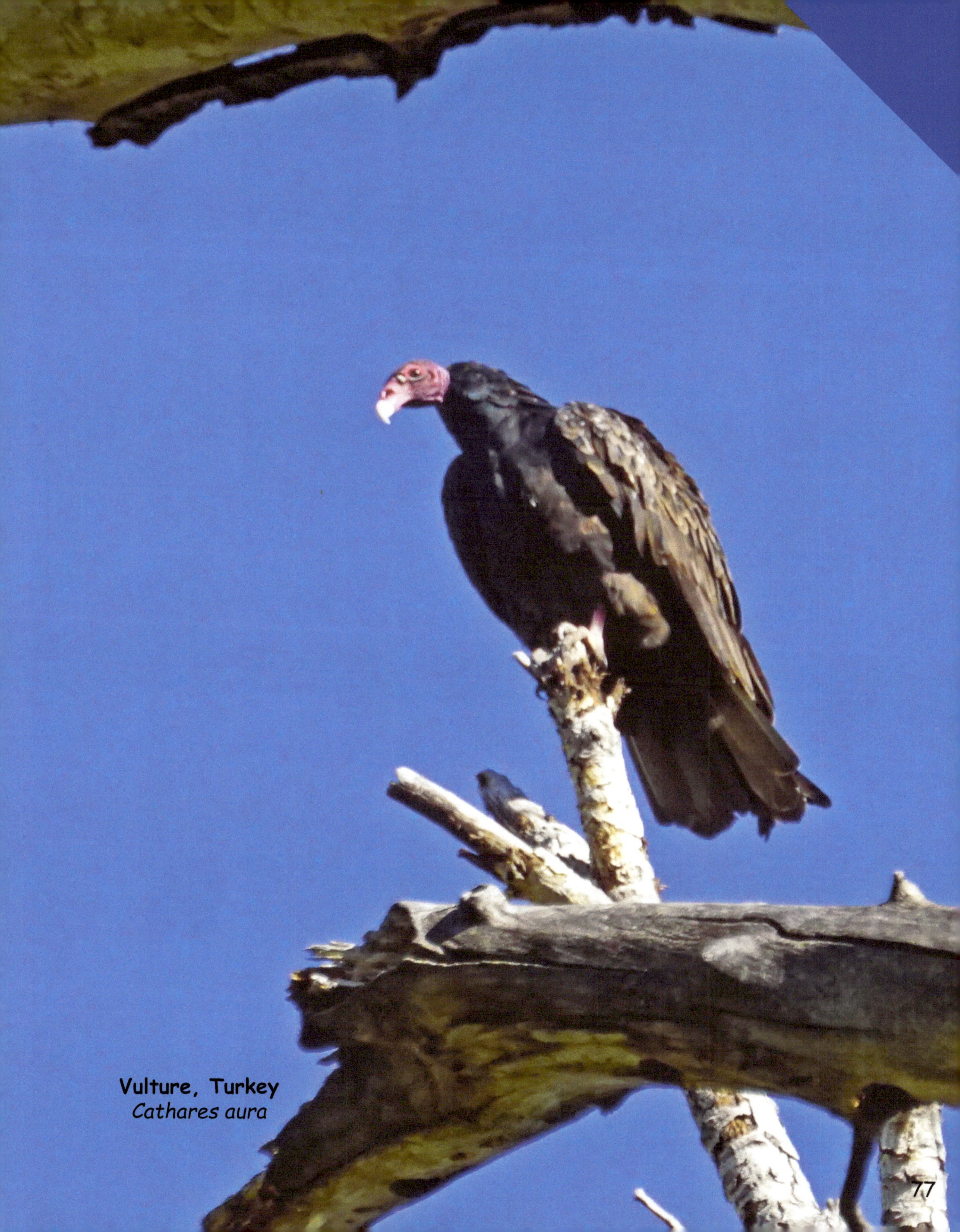

Vulture, Turkey
Cathares aura

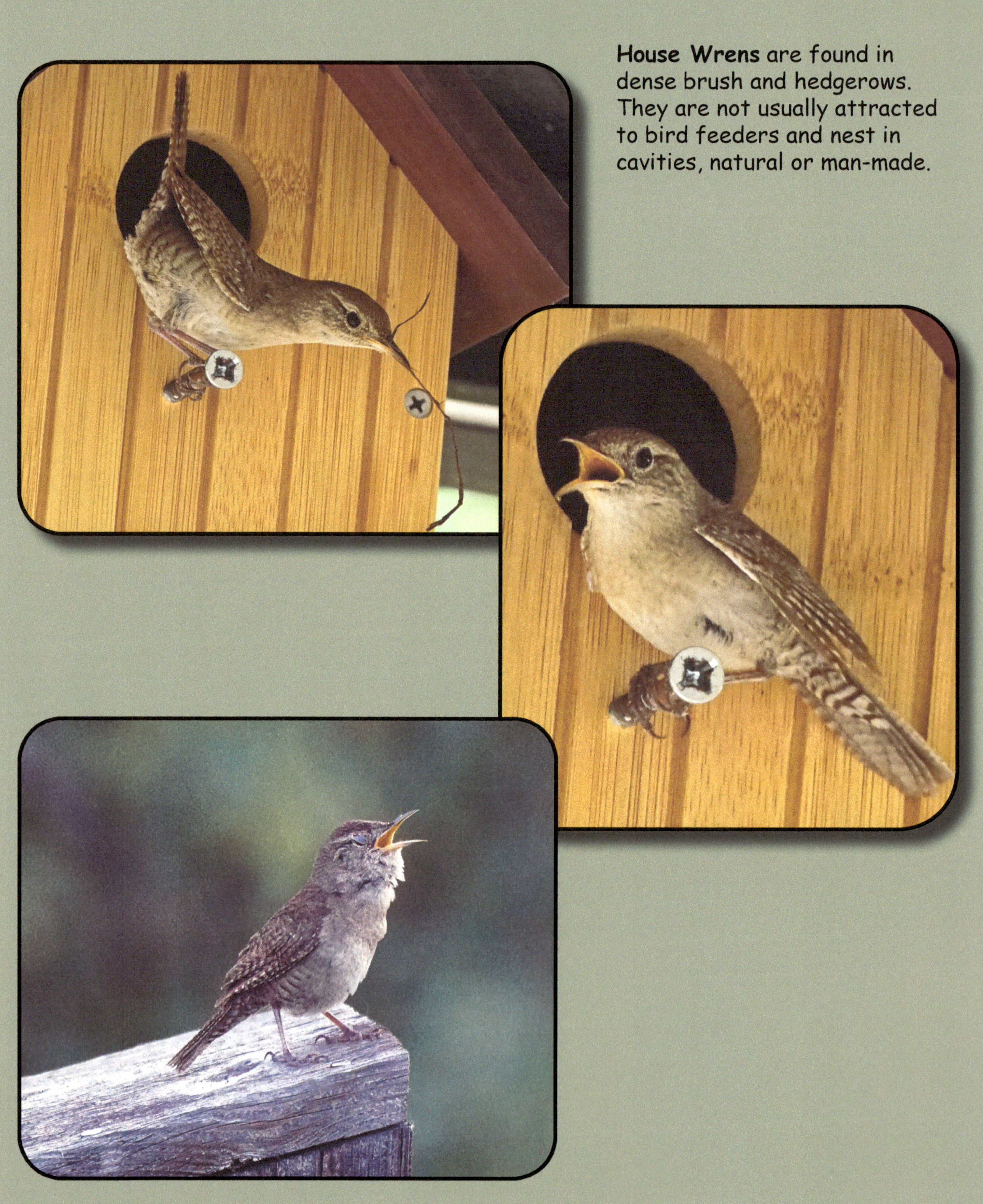

House Wrens are found in dense brush and hedgerows. They are not usually attracted to bird feeders and nest in cavities, natural or man-made.

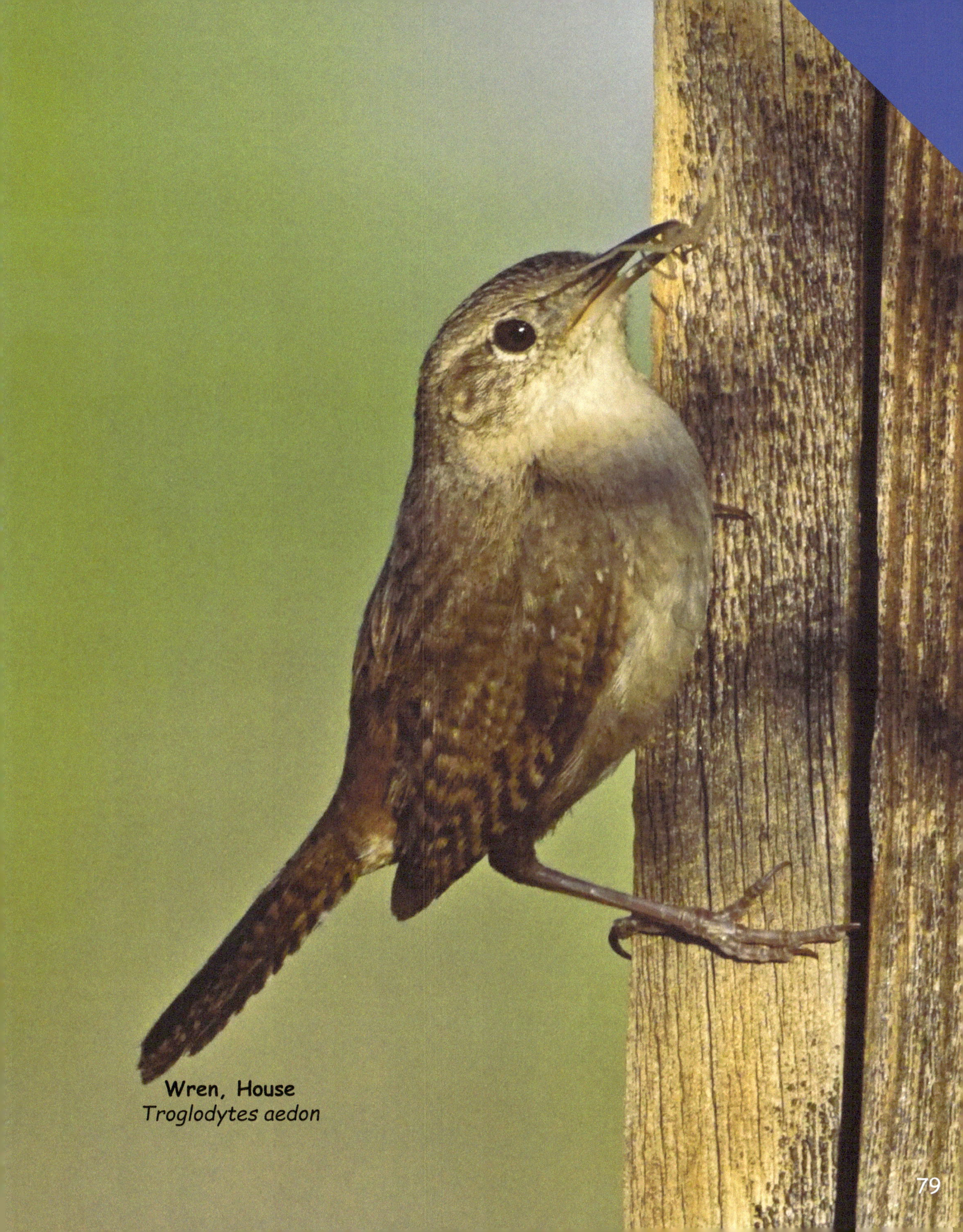

Wren, House
Troglodytes aedon

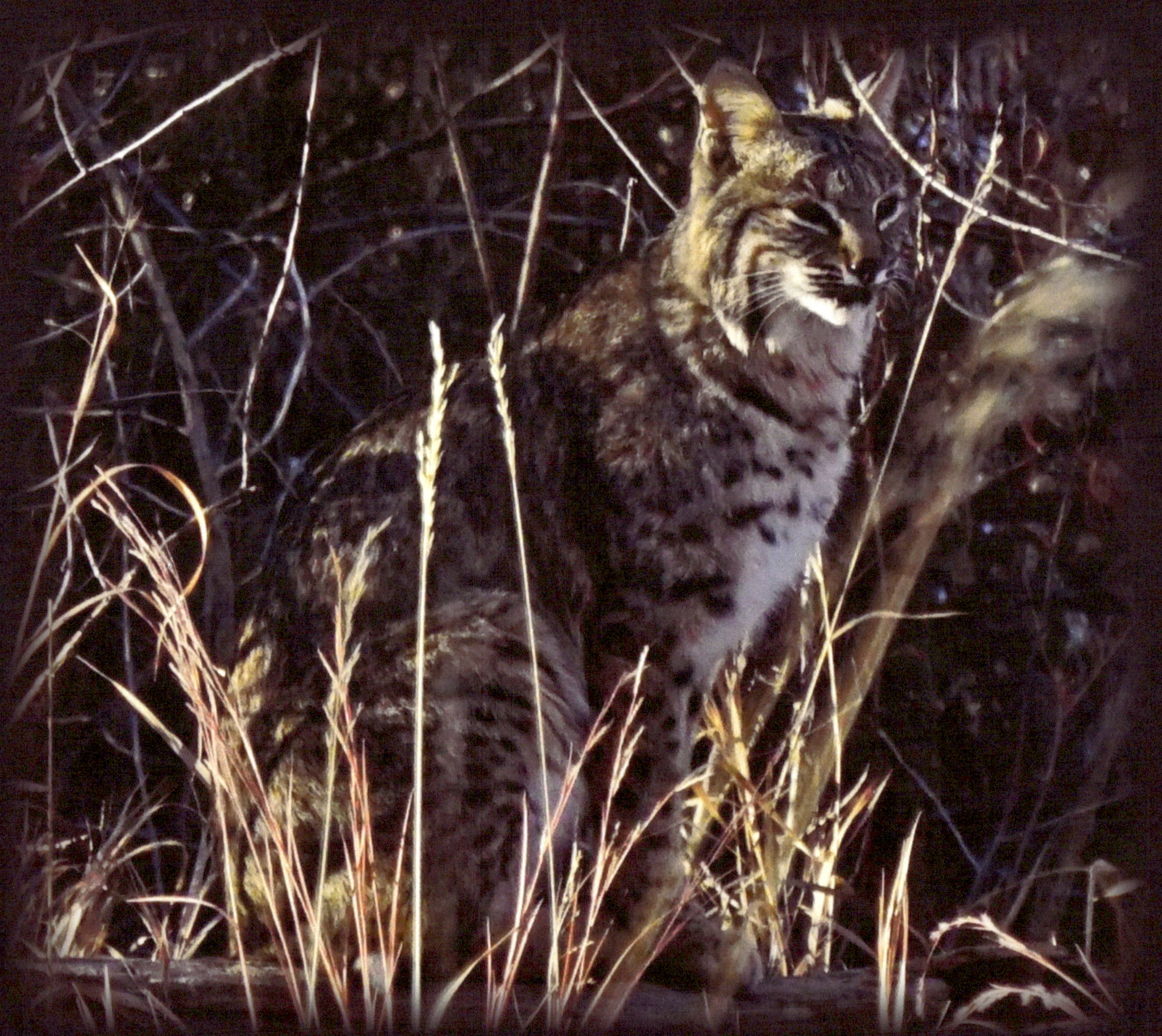

Bobcats are mostly nocturnal and rarely seen during the day. They feed on cottontails, squirrels and other small mammals. The tail is short and back and sides are spotted.

Bobcat photographed at 9:00 a.m. in December

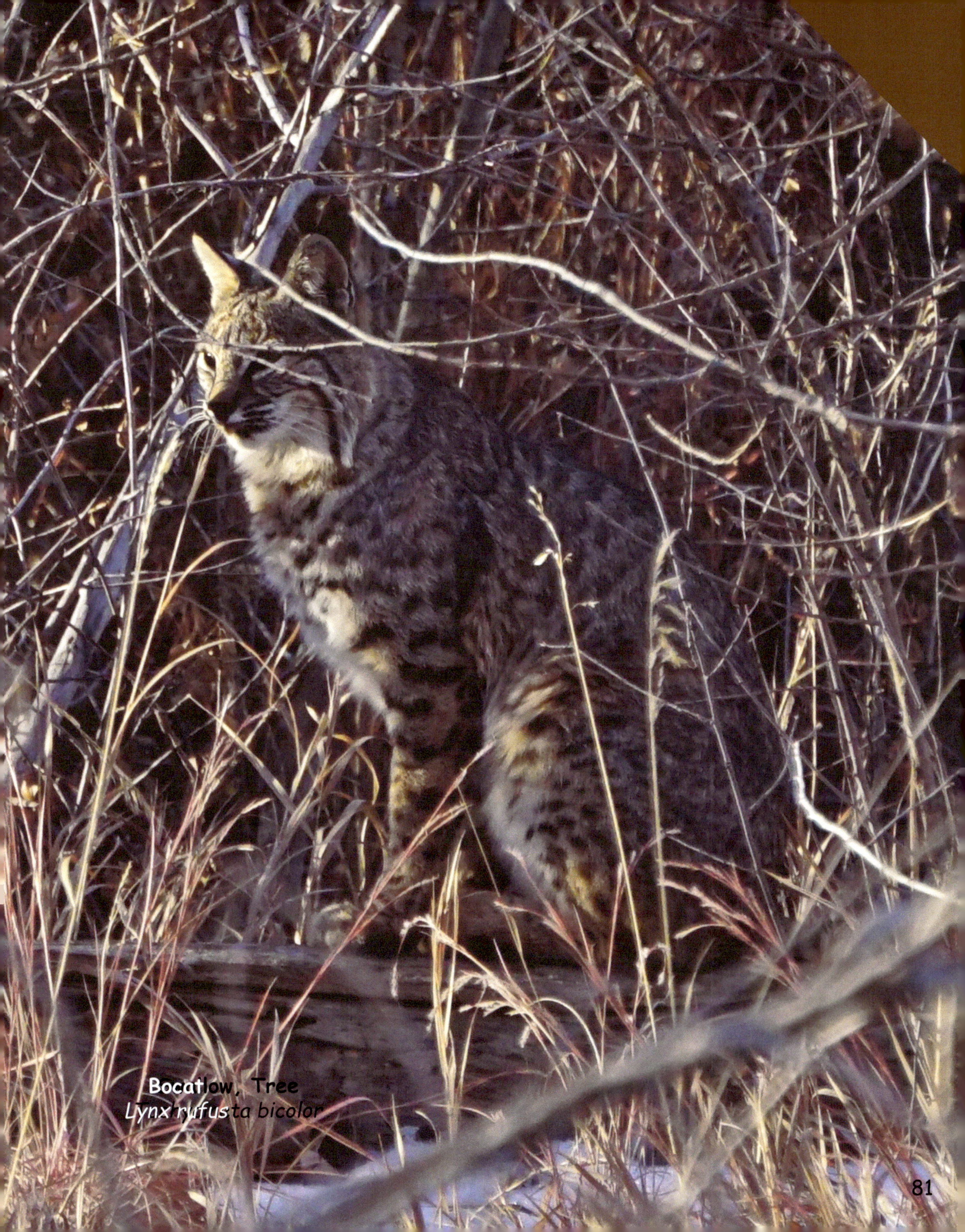
Bocatlow, Tree
Lynx rufusta bicolor

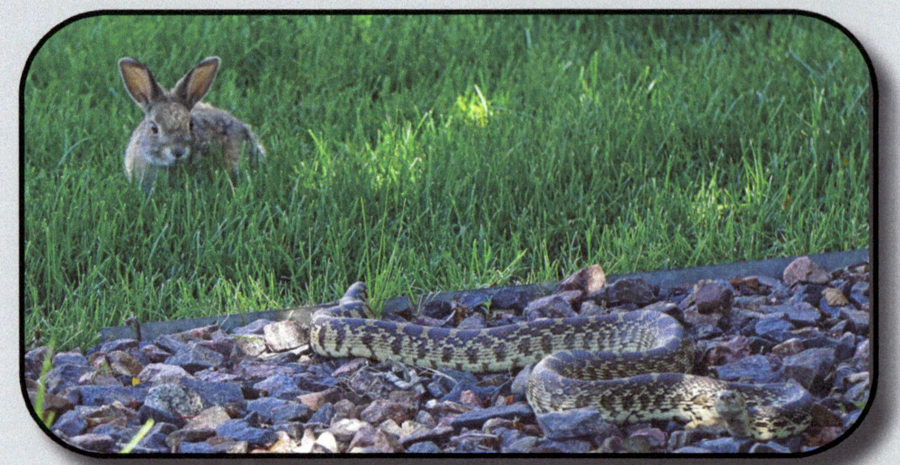

Above: Cottontail and a
Bull Snake

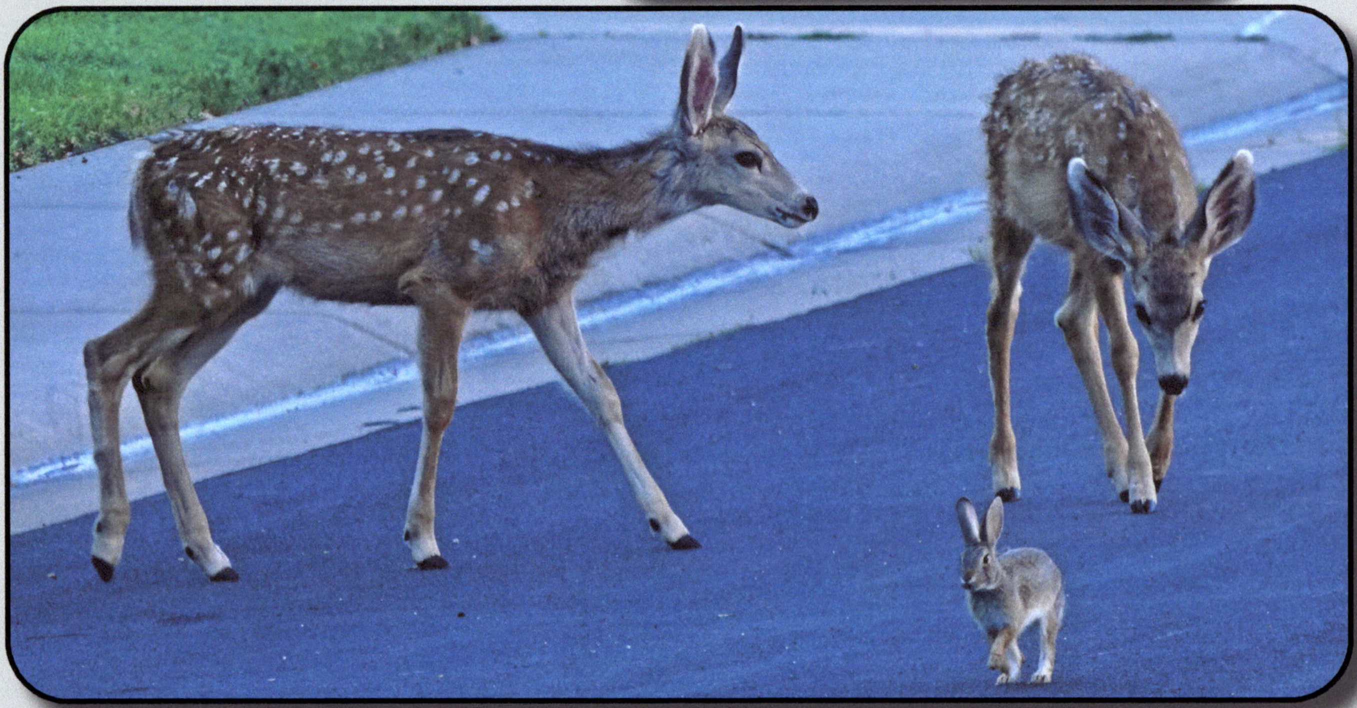

Desert Cottontails are plentiful and "breed like rabbits." Often seen in gardens and along Parker trails where they are at the bottom of the food chain for raptors and predator mammals. Up to six young are born in a fur-lined nest; usually two litters a year.

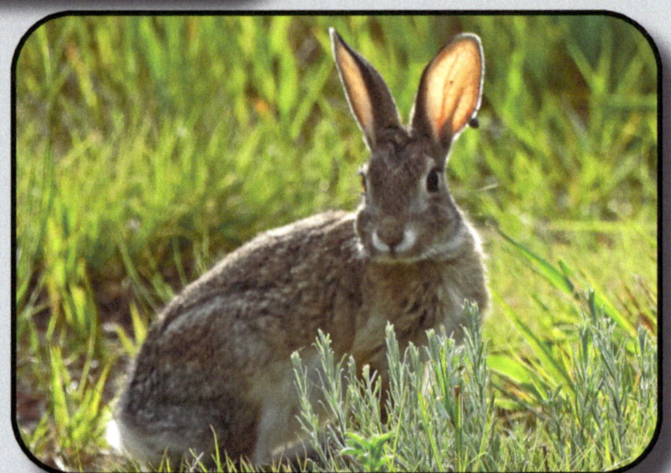

A Cottontail and two Mule Deer fawns on a neighborhood street

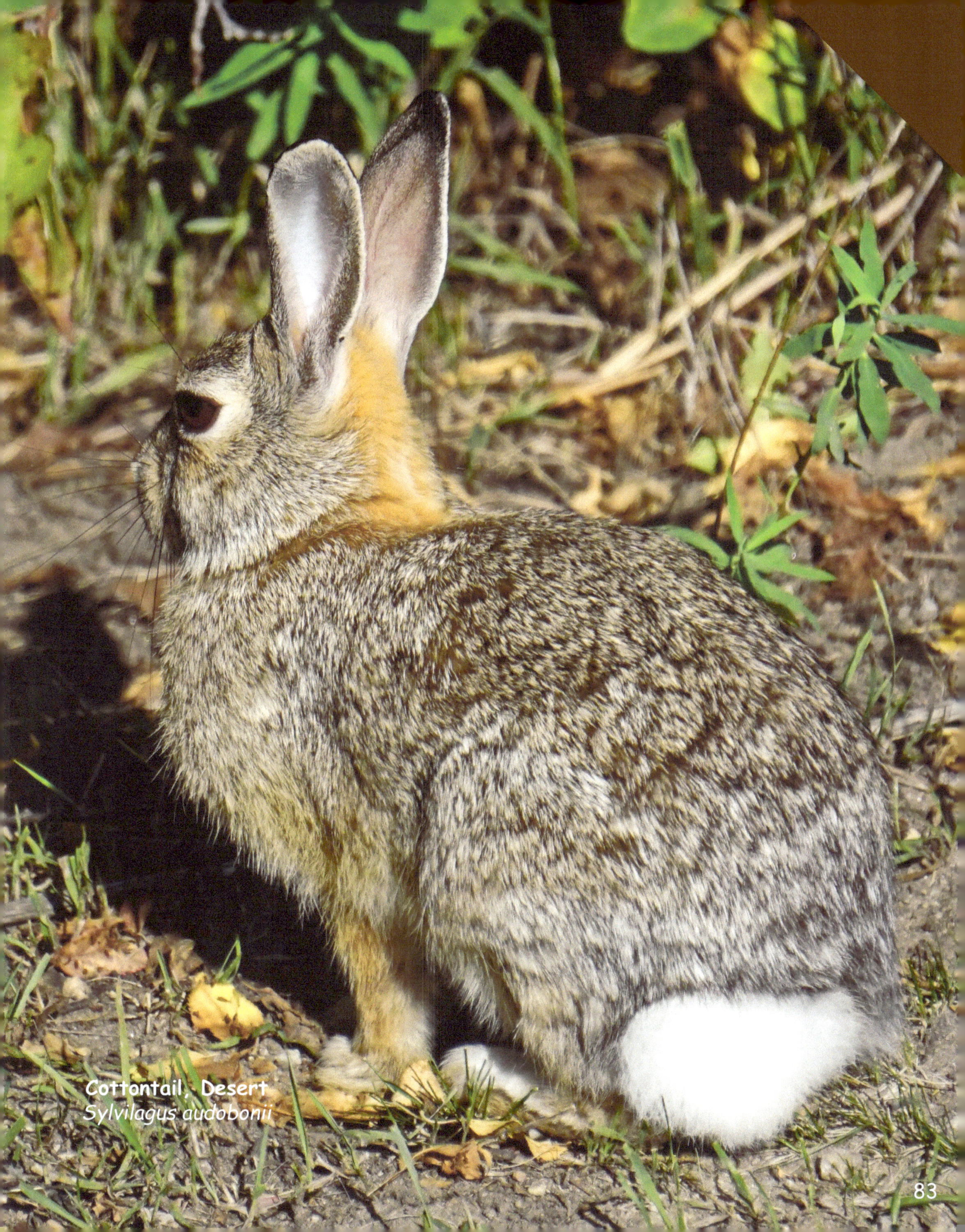

Cottontail, Desert
Sylvilagus audobonii

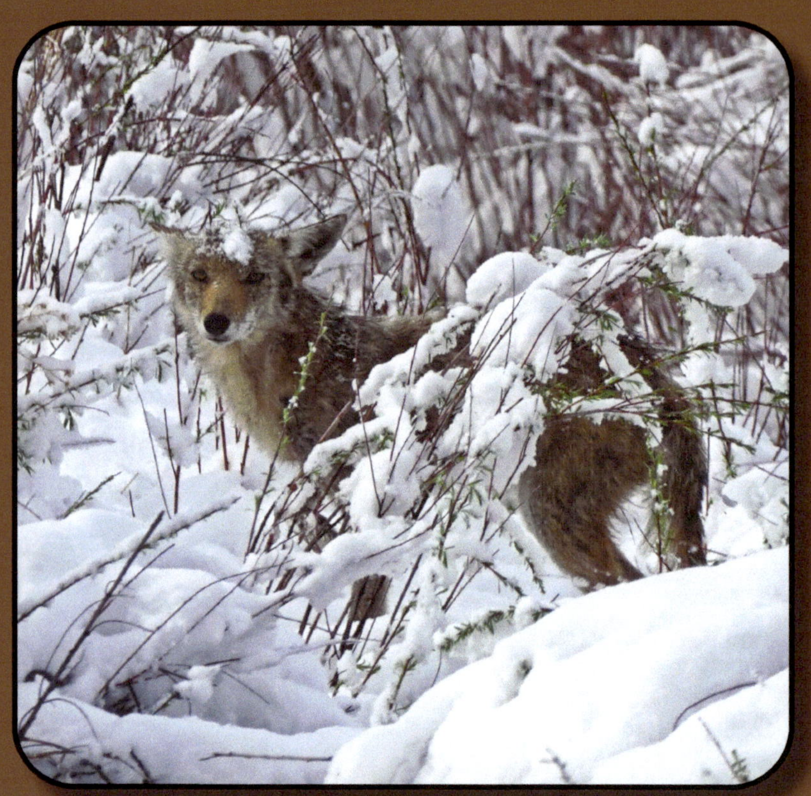

Coyotes are widespread across the country and are occasionally seen scampering through our residential neighborhoods (photo below). They are opportunistic scavengers, preying on rabbits, squirrels and even Mule Deer when hunting in a pack.

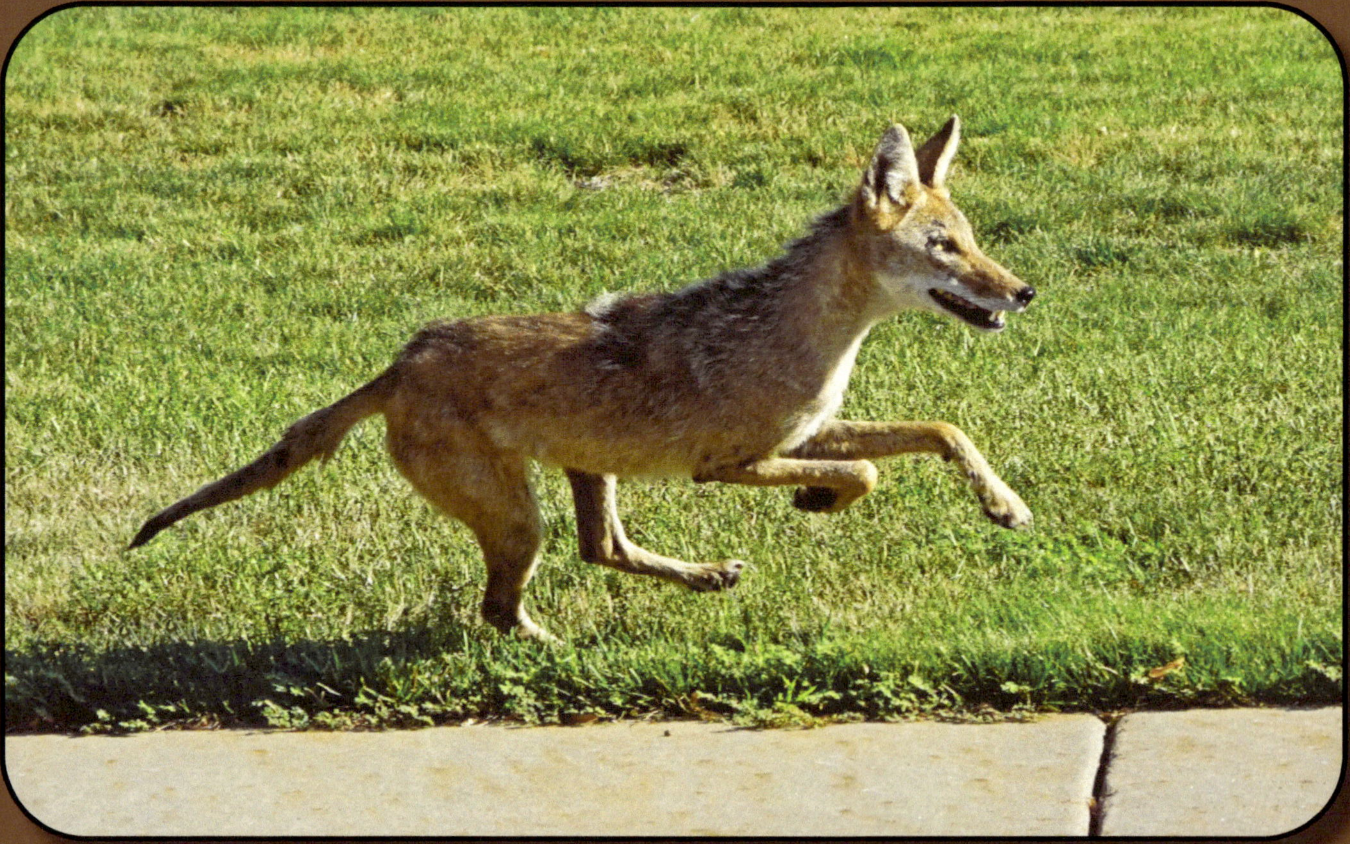

Coyote running through a Parker neighborhood

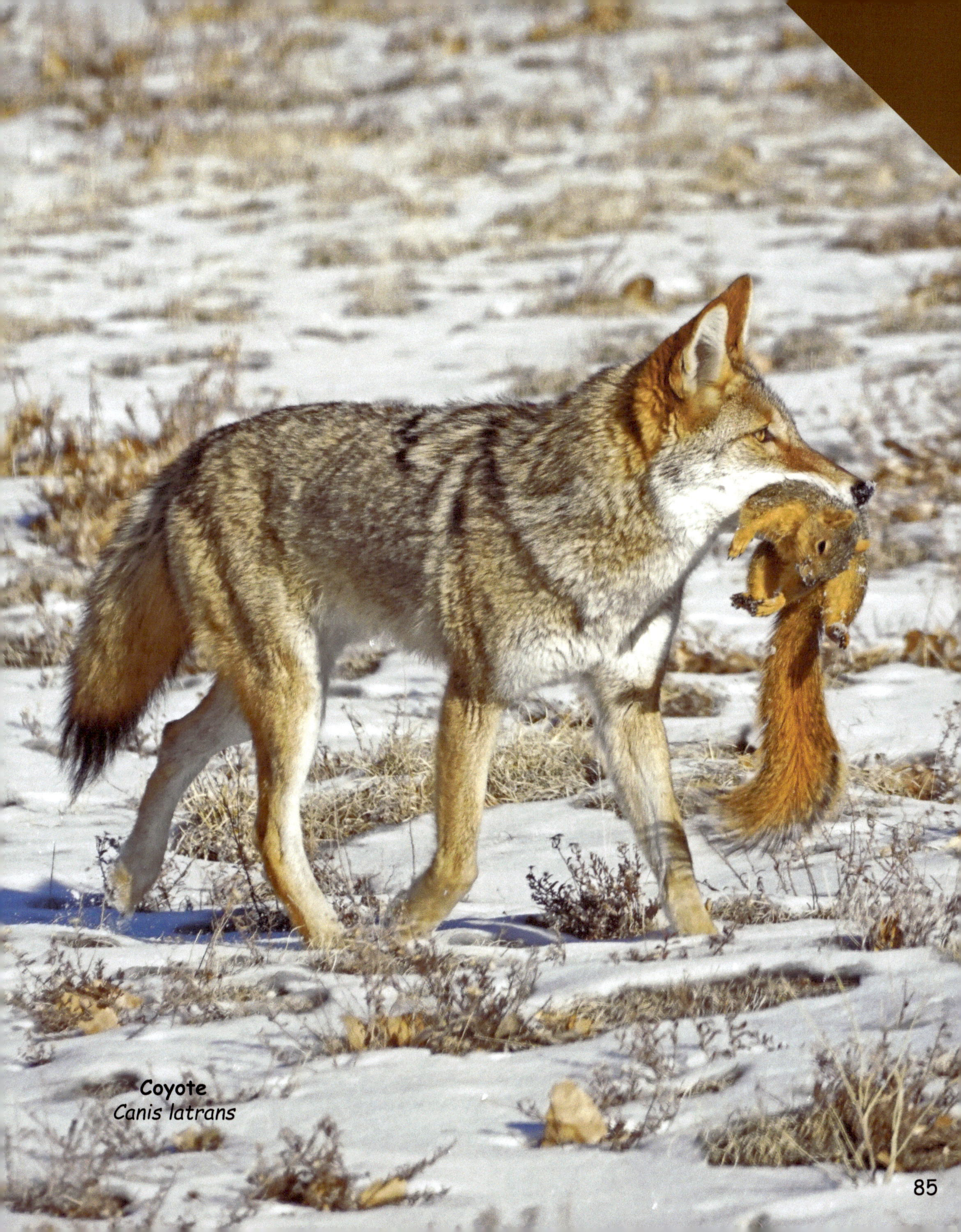

Coyote
Canis latrans

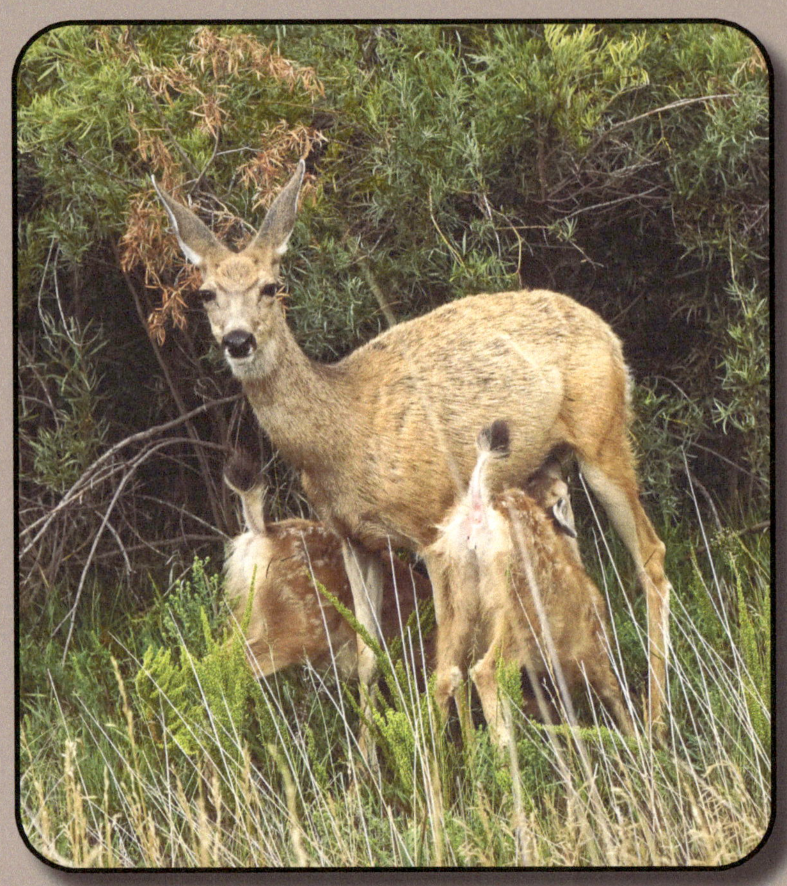

Mule Deer are plentiful in Parker, frequently seen in gardens, open spaces and on the streets. They have a black-tipped tail and large ears. NOTE: **White-tailed Deer** do occur in Parker but are not as numerous and tend to be found on the outskirts of the town along the wooded areas adjacent to Cherry Creek.

Newborn Mule Deer fawns, born in early June, are hidden in dense vegetation for the first few weeks of their life They lose their distinctive spots in 3 - 4 months.

Mule Deer rarely form large herds but small groups of families will often be seen together.

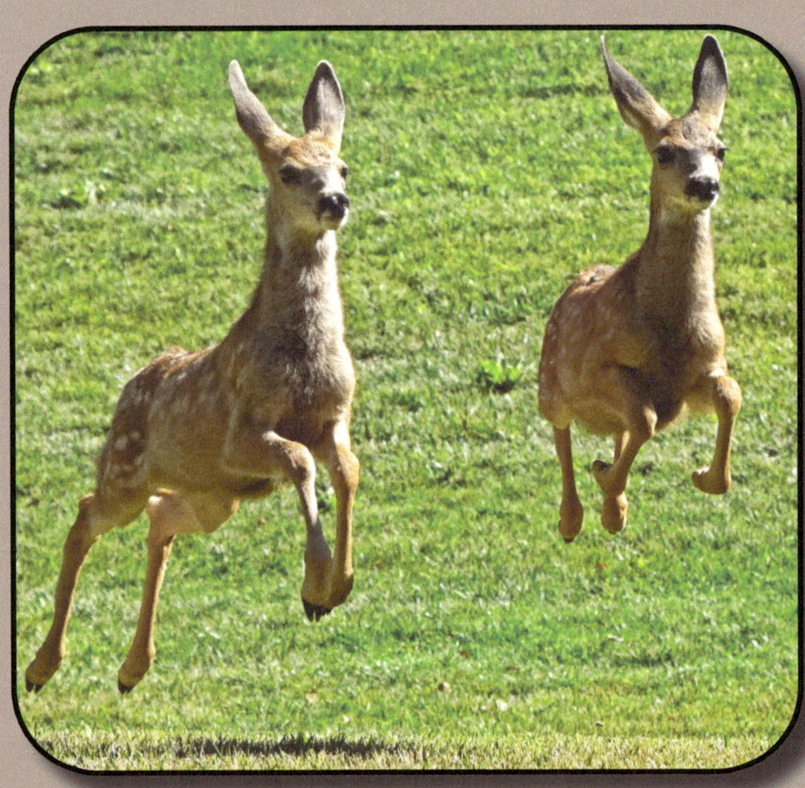

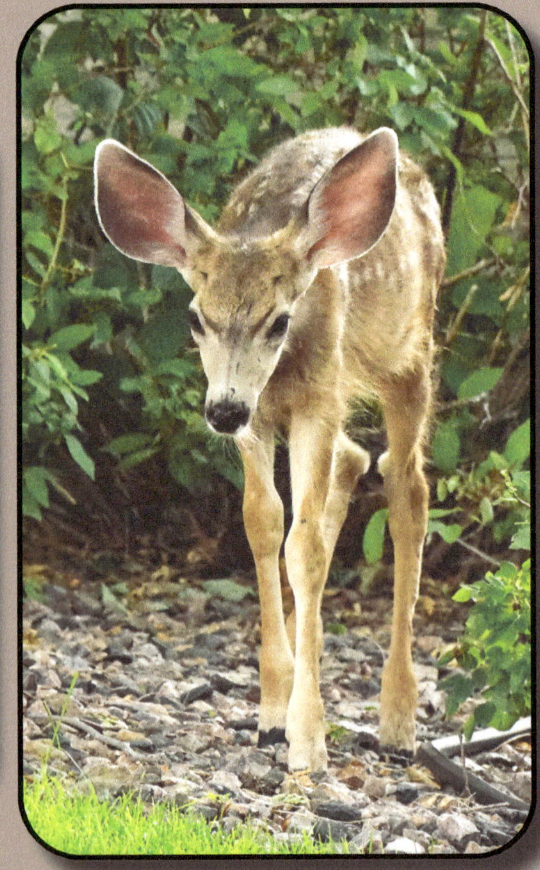

        Fawns "stotting"

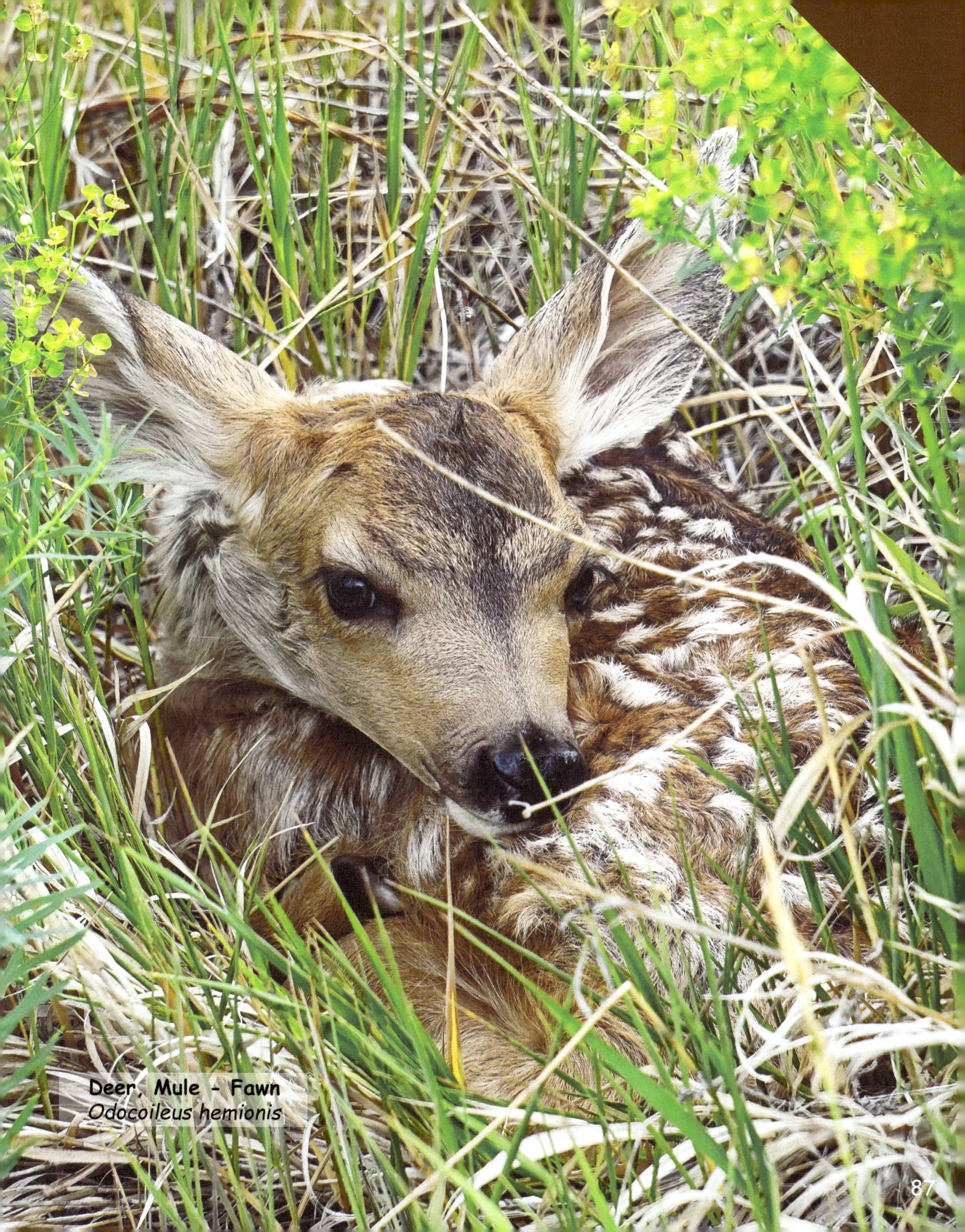
Deer, Mule - Fawn
Odocoileus hemionis

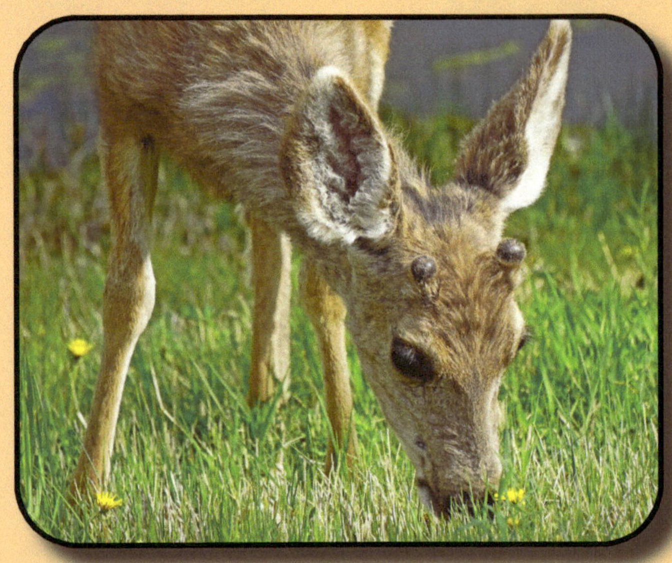

A Mule Deer buck's antlers begin to grow in April/May each year, When fully grown (October) the velvet is shed or rubbed off. Antlers will fall off again in Mar/April.

Left: Antlers appear in the first months of life of a young buck

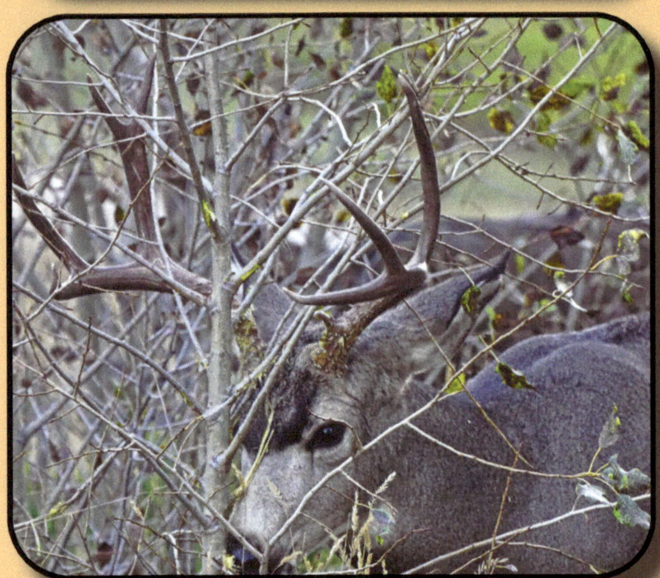

Rubbing the velvet off

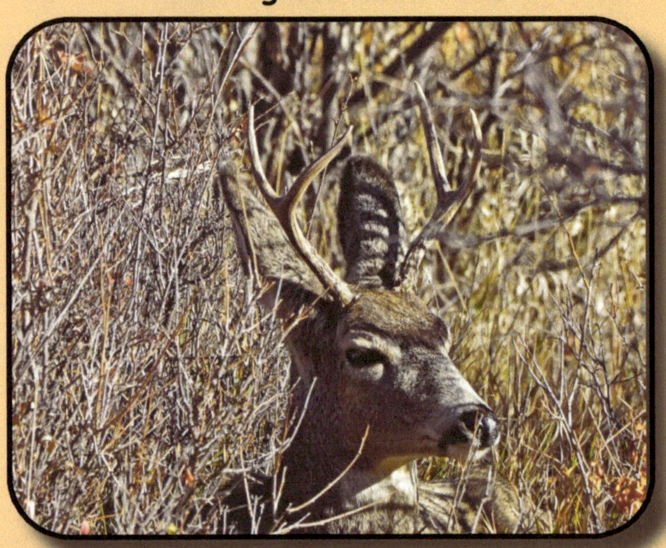

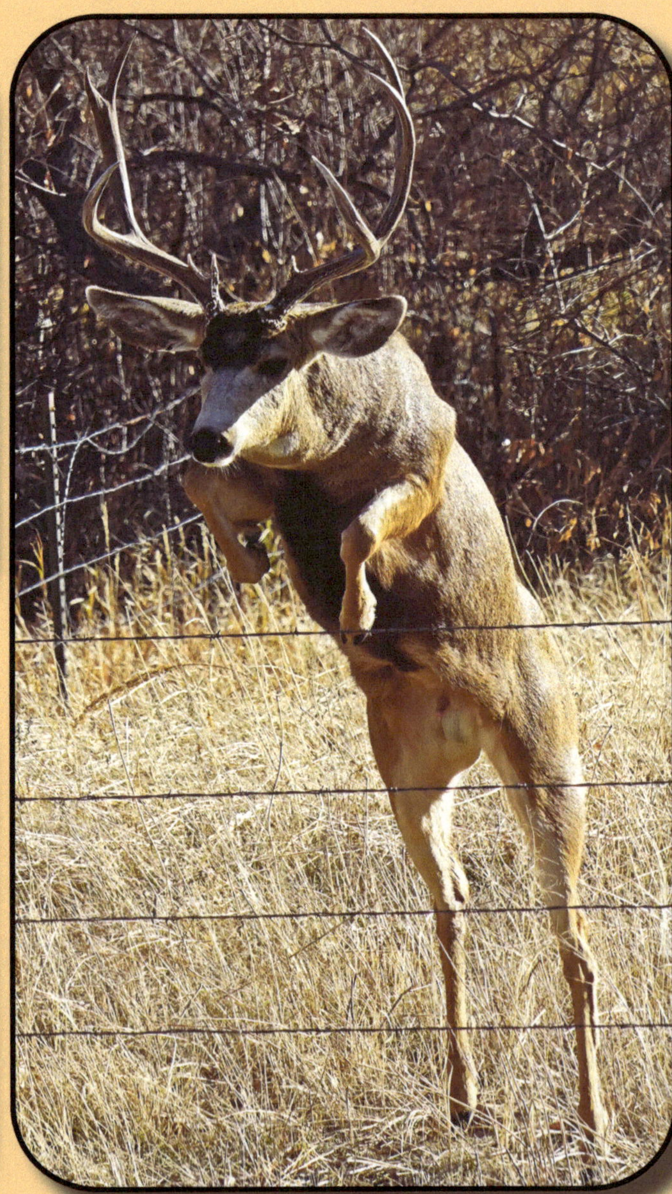

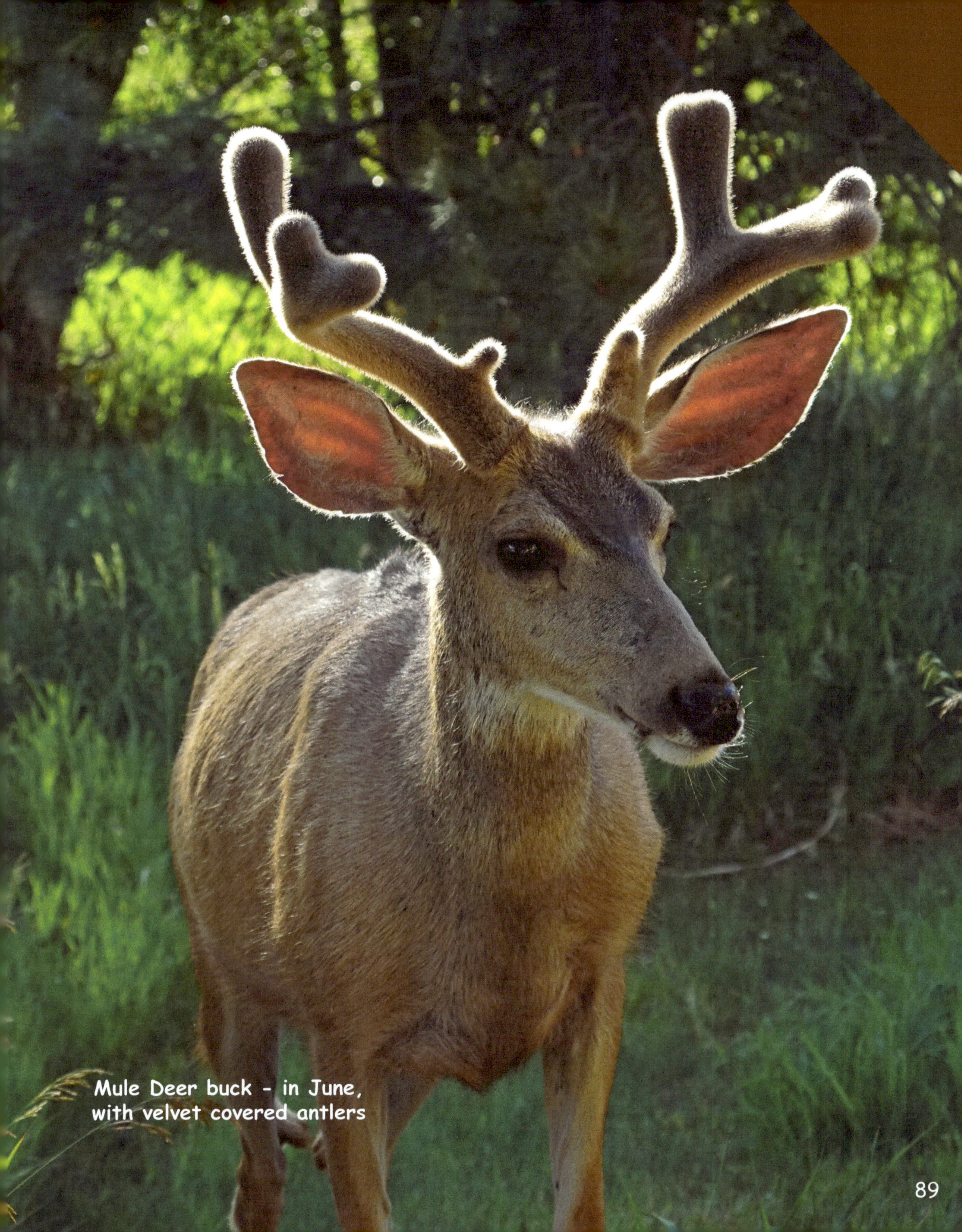
Mule Deer buck - in June,
with velvet covered antlers

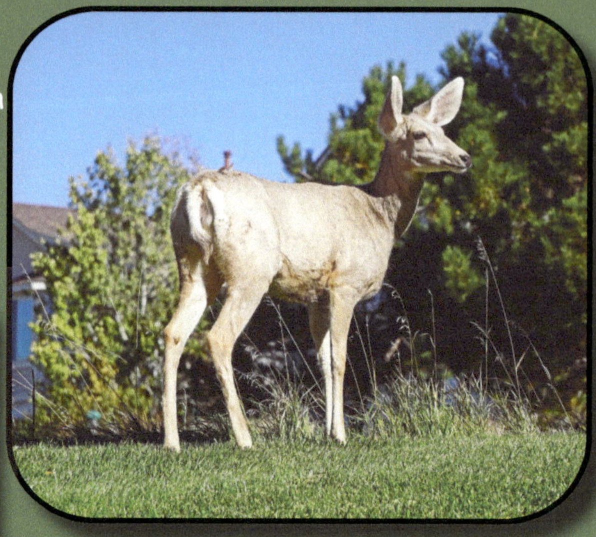

LEUCISTIC Mule Deer have been seen in recent years in the Parker area. *Leucism* is a genetic condition that result in partial loss of pigmentation in an animal, causing white, pale, or patchy coloration of the skin, hair, feathers, scales, or cuticles. The eyes are normal in color.

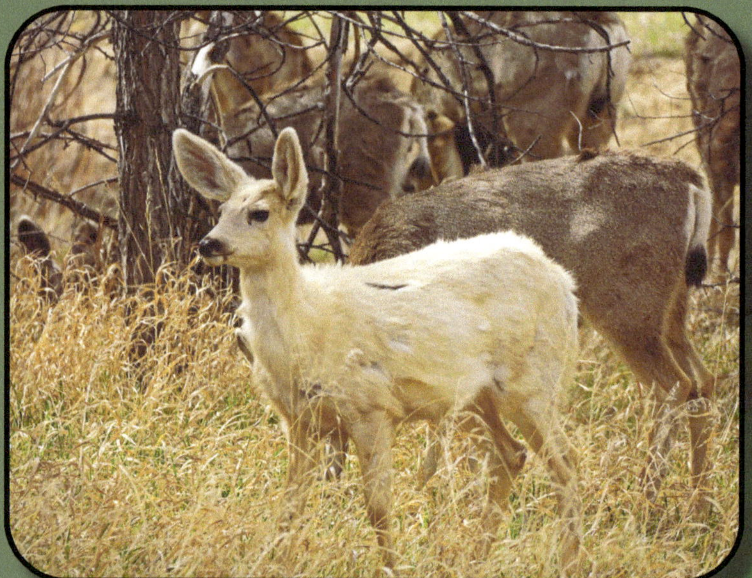

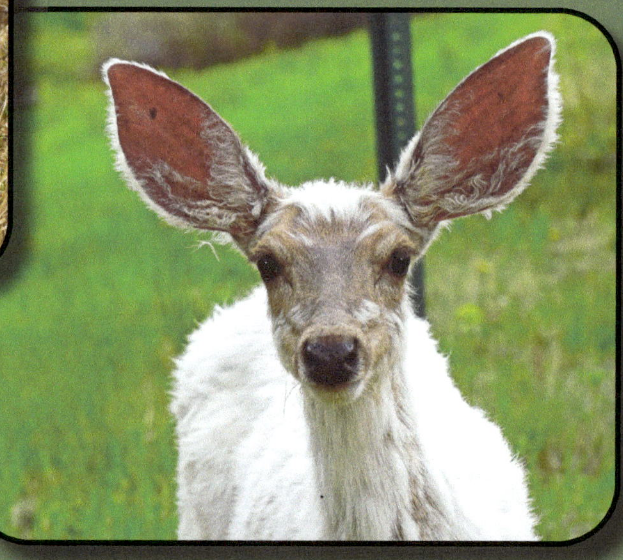

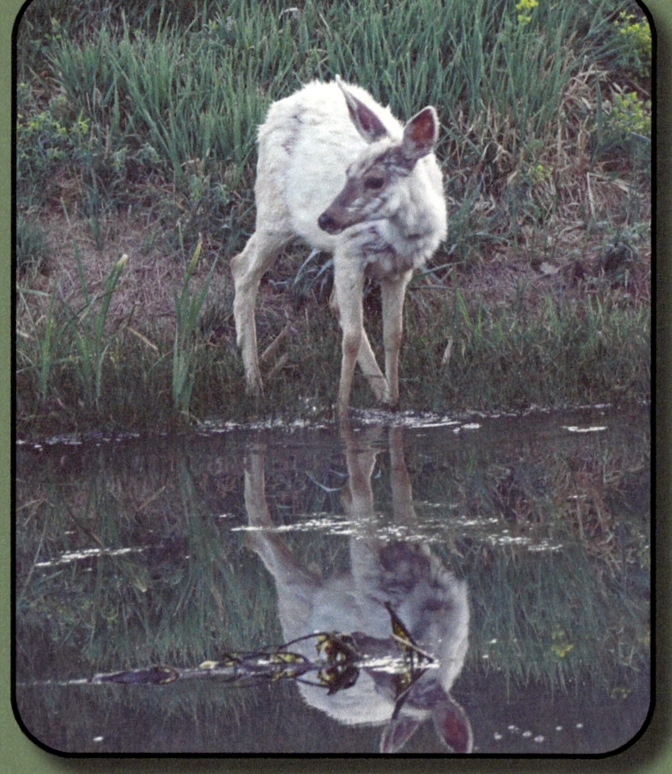

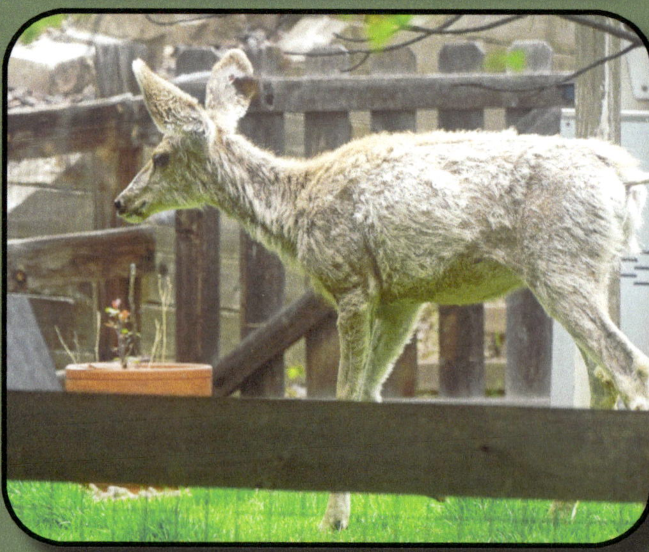

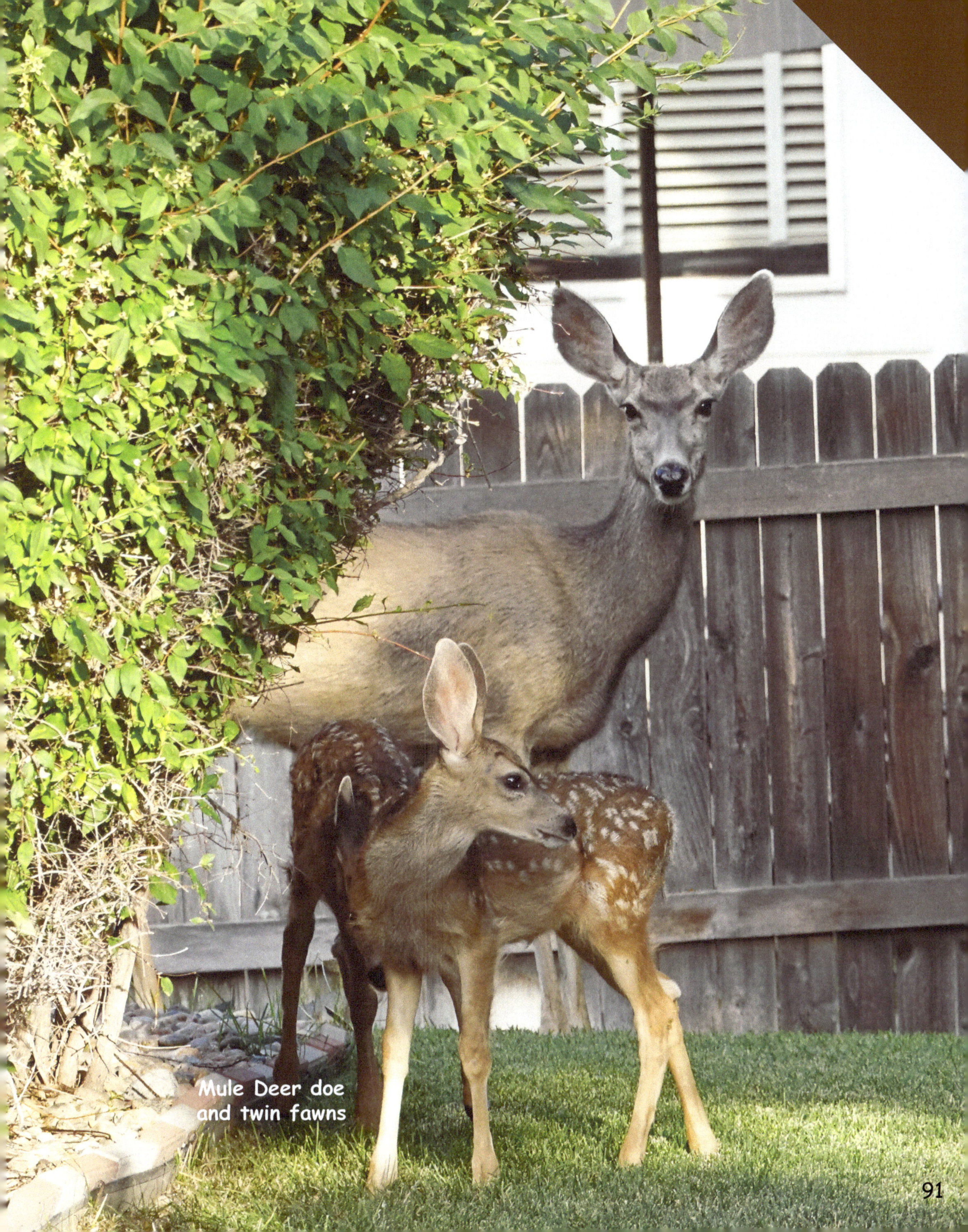

Mule Deer doe
and twin fawns

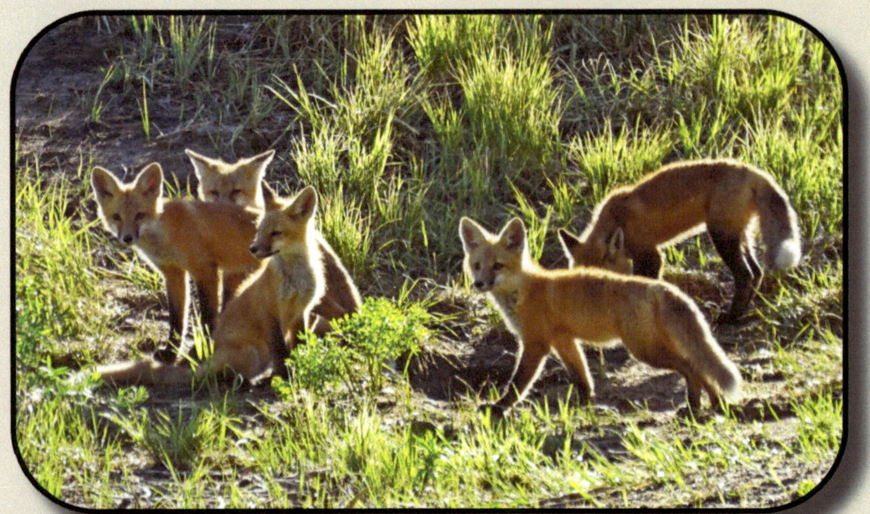

Red Foxes are adaptable to and found in a range of habitats. Dens can be found under decks or in hollowed out Prairie Dog holes. Each litter may have up to five kits. Male and female mate for life.

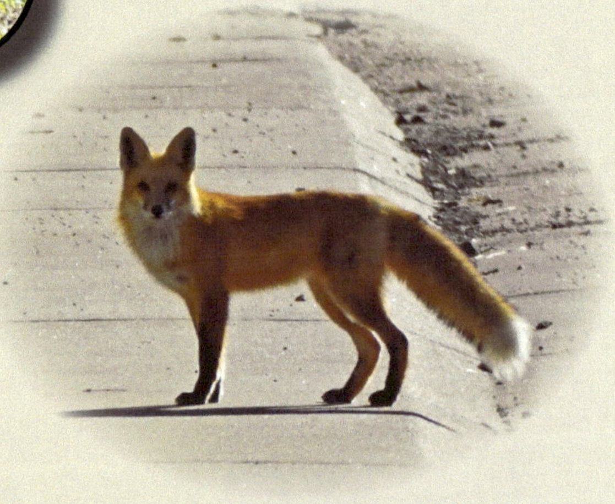

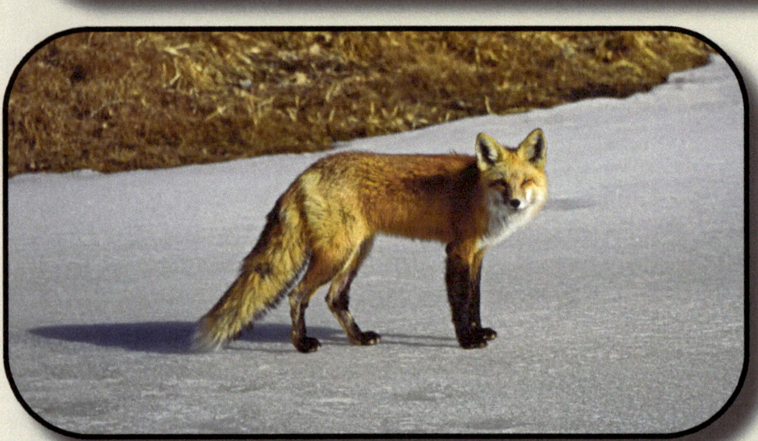

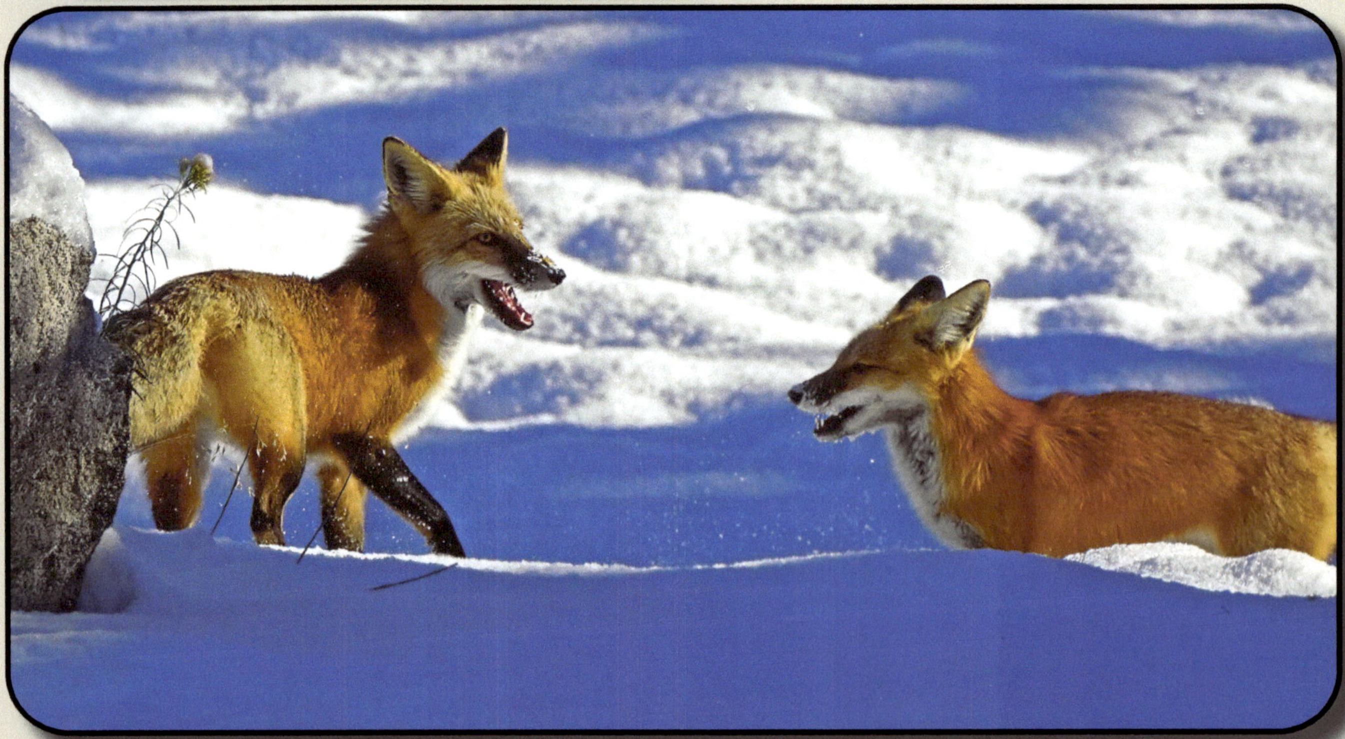

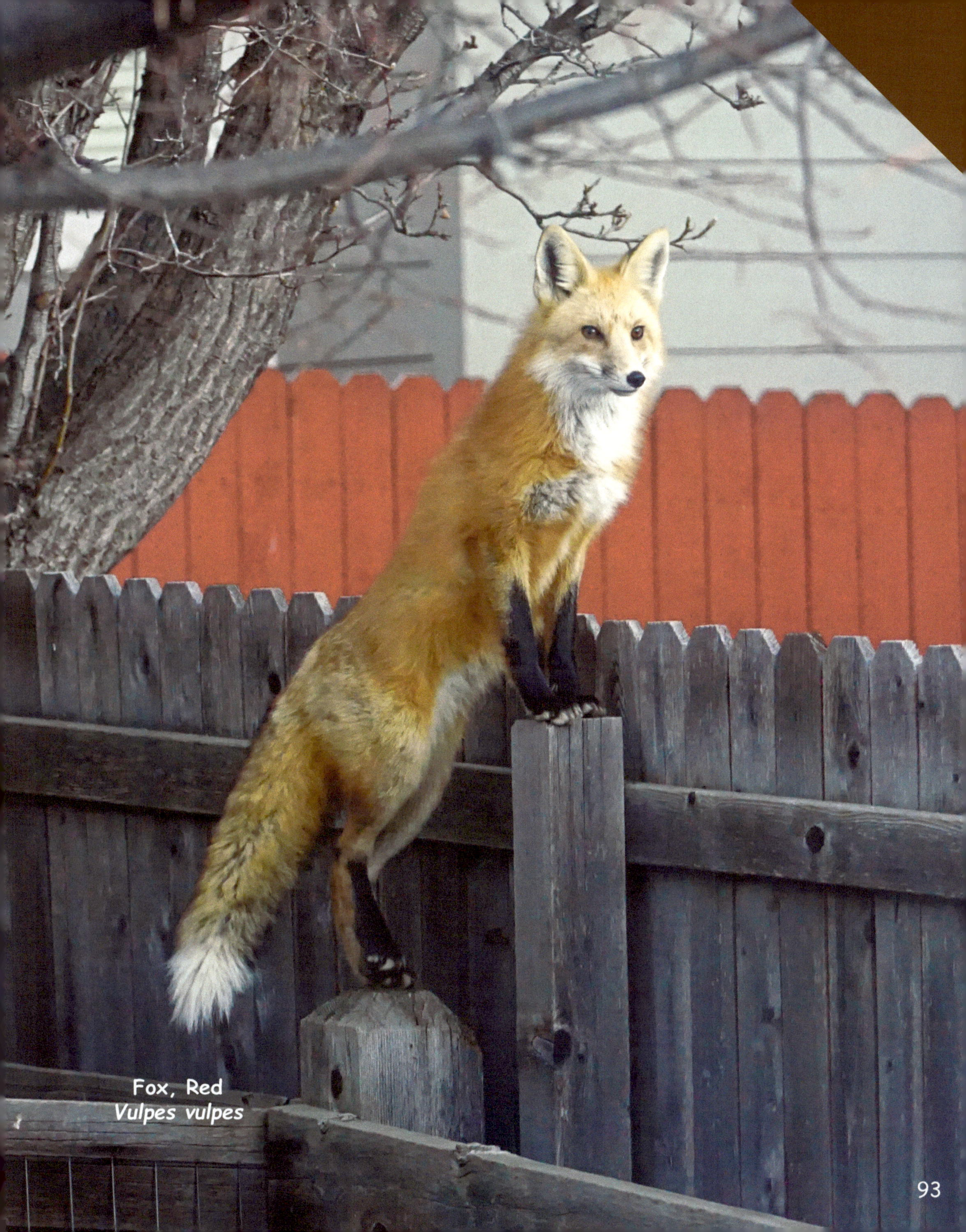
Fox, Red
Vulpes vulpes

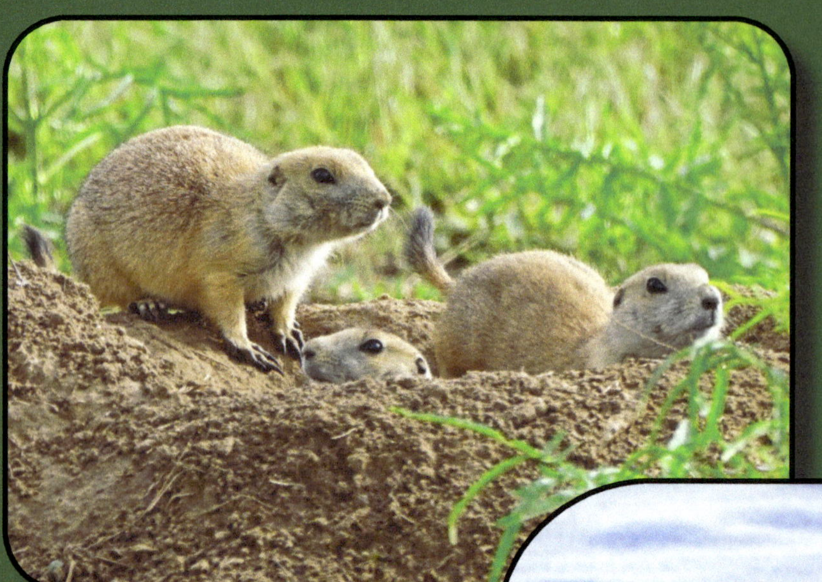

Look for **Black-tailed Prairie Dog** burrows in <u>undeveloped</u> open spaces in and around the Town of Parker. Single litters of 4-5 young are born underground in Apr/May. Burrows ("towns") are guarded by a sentry which stands on a heap of dirt and 'barks' at the sign of danger. Prairie Dogs are a type of ground squirrel.

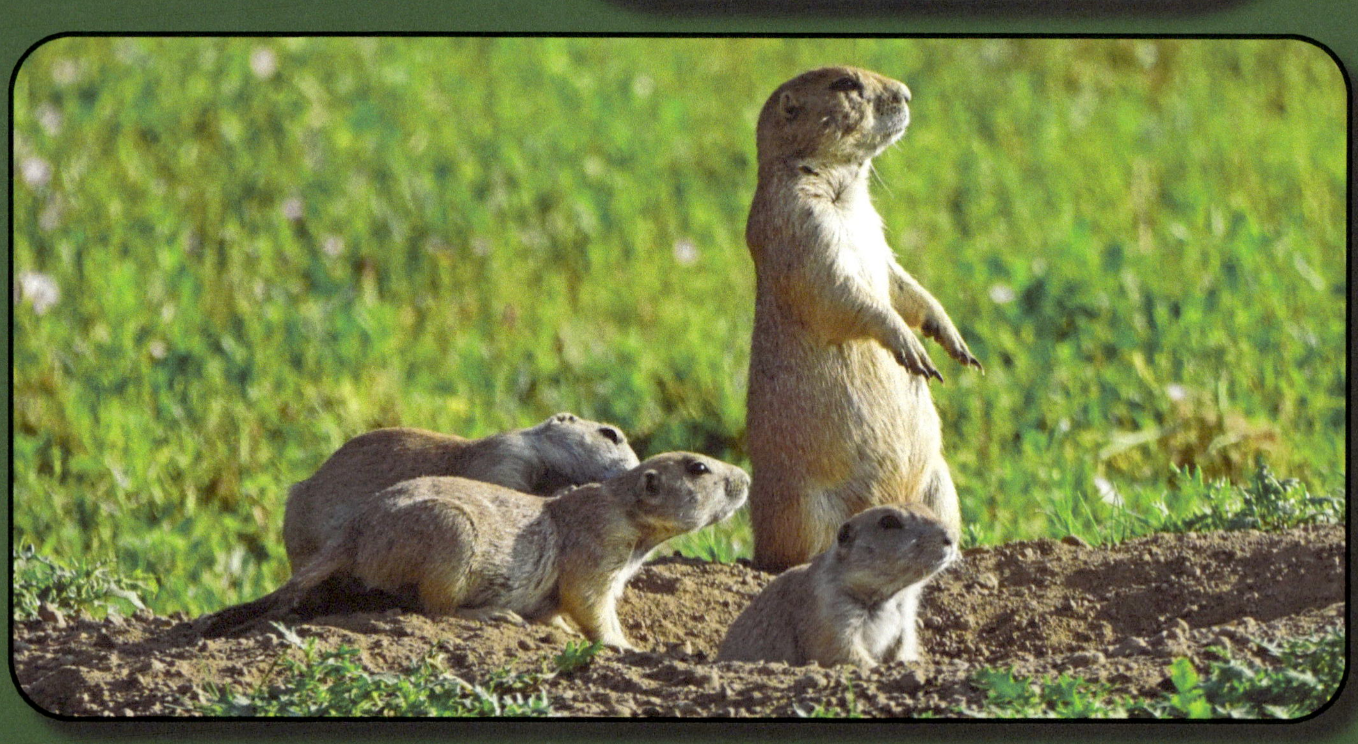

A female may birth a litter of 4-5 young each year

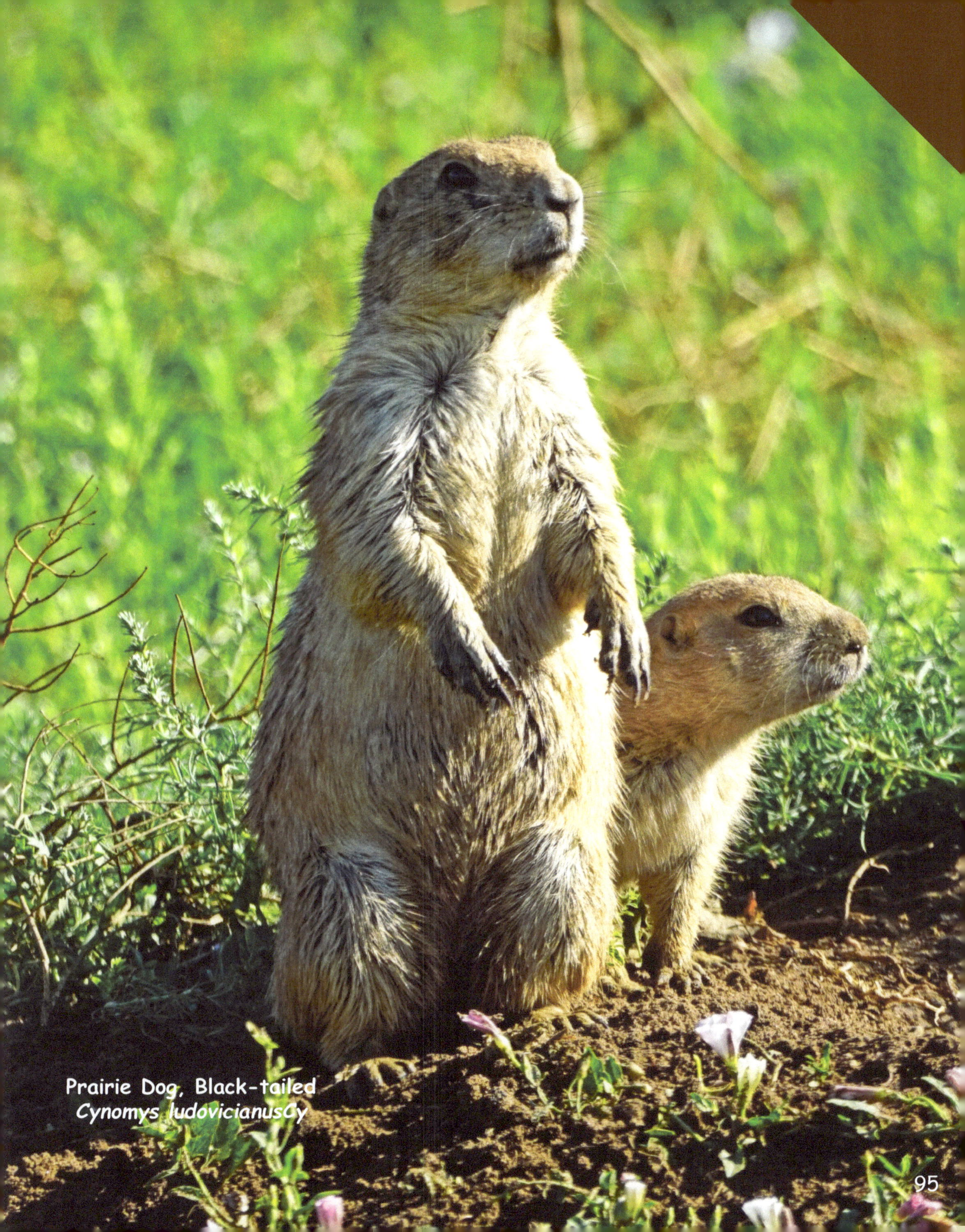
Prairie Dog, Black-tailed
Cynomys ludovicianusCy

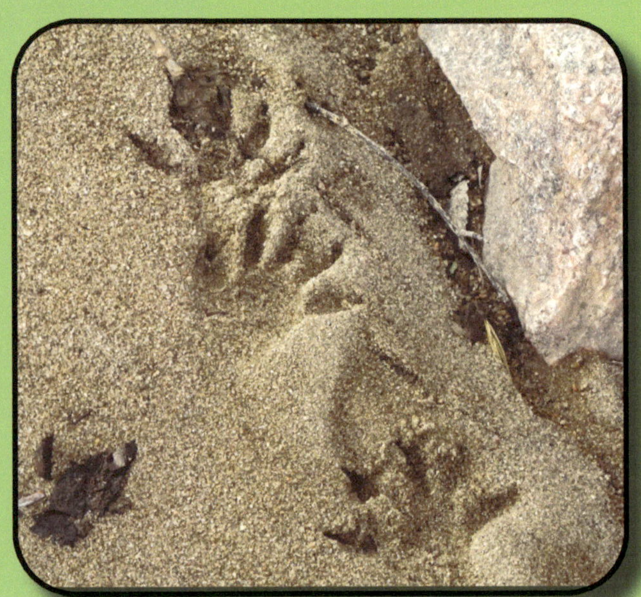
Raccoon's paw prints

Raccoons, with their "bandit's mask" face pattern occur in almost all habitats, and Parker residents are familiar with them. A true omnivore, it often raids garbage and will eat almost anything. A single litter of 2-5 kits is born in late spring. They are nocturnal foragers, resting in trees during the day. Raccoons are highly intelligent and resourceful with extremely dexterous front paws.

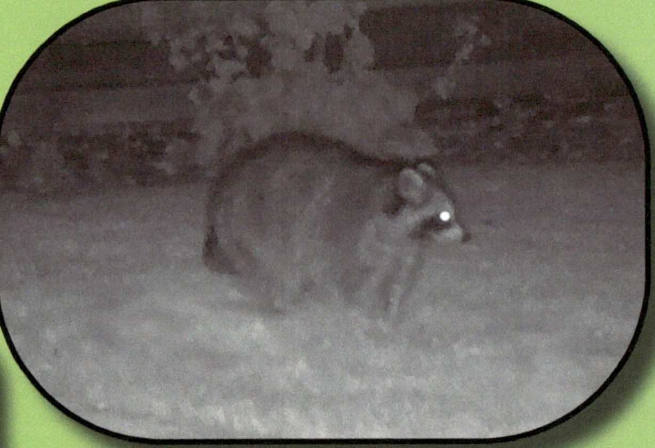
Night time visitor

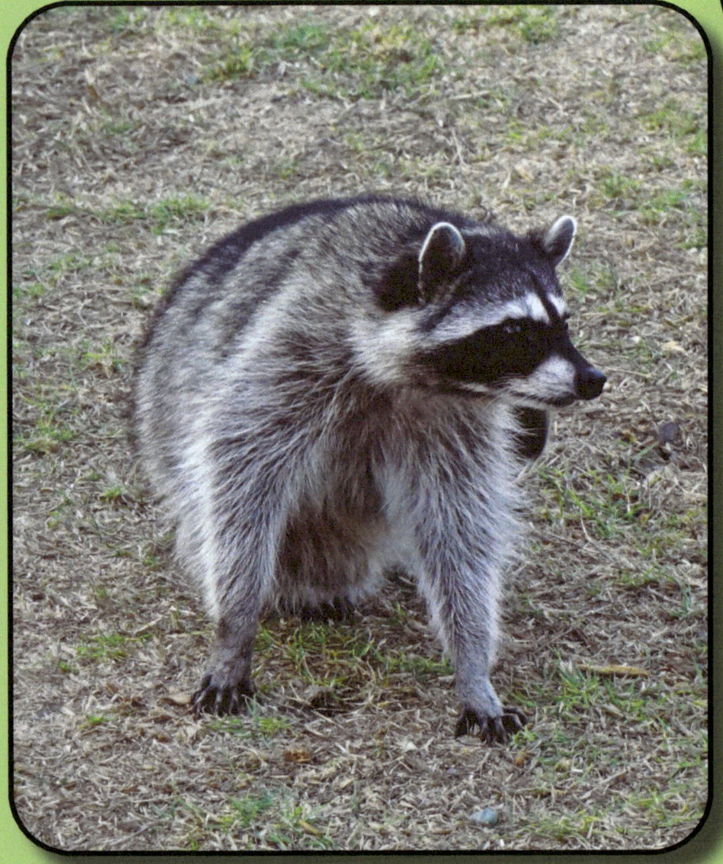
Northern or "Common" Raccoon

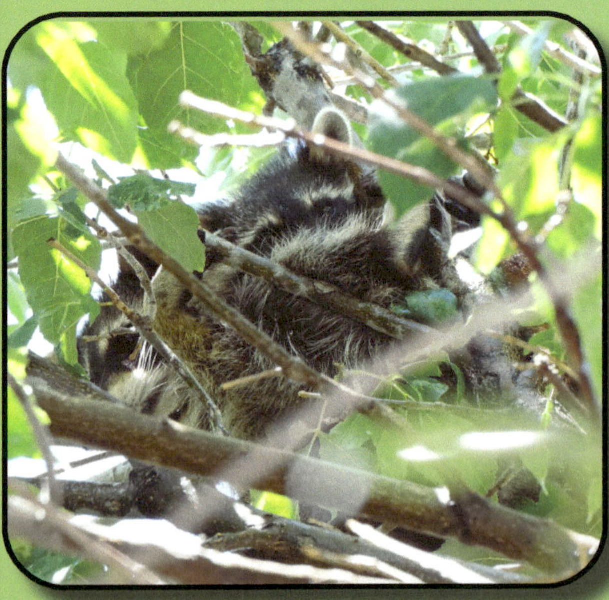
Raccoon adult with her kit

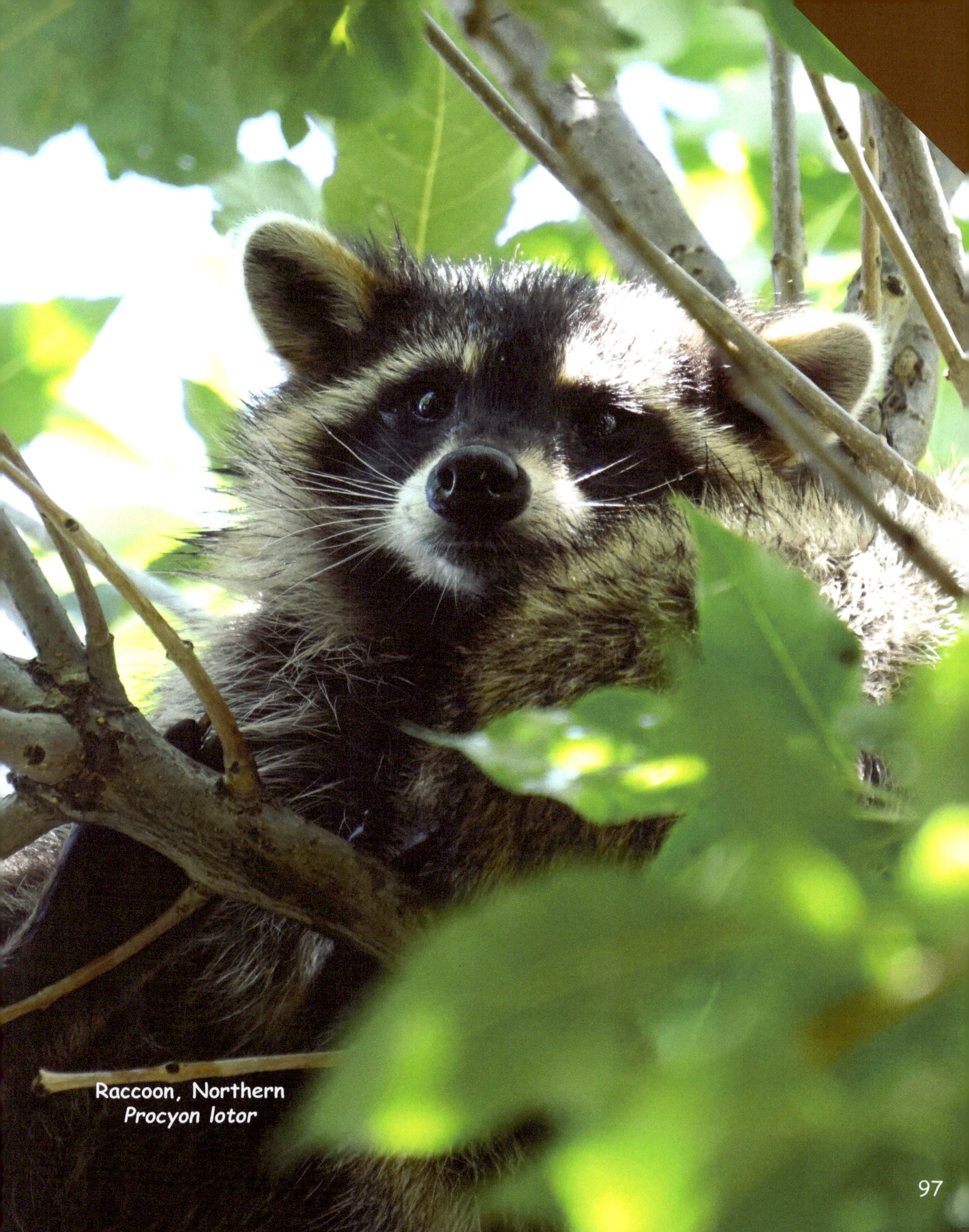

Raccoon, Northern
Procyon lotor

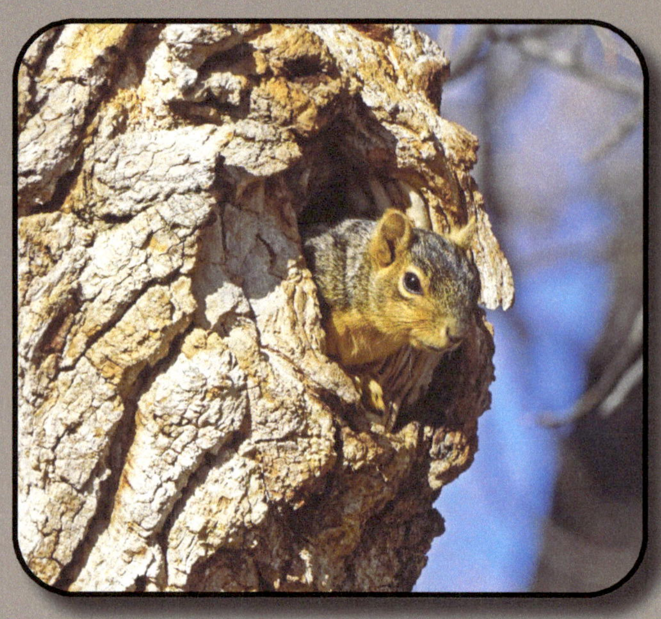

Tree cavity squirrel's den

There is a large population of **Fox Squirrels** in the Parker area. It is the largest North American tree squirrel. They produce two litters each year (late January and July) with an average of three per litter.

Tree cavities, usually those formed by woodpeckers, are remodeled into winter dens and often serve as nurseries for late winter litters. If existing trees lack cavities, leaf nests known as **'dreys'** are built by cutting twigs with leaves and weaving them into warm, waterproof shelters.

Squirrels are diurnal and spend most of their time on the ground.

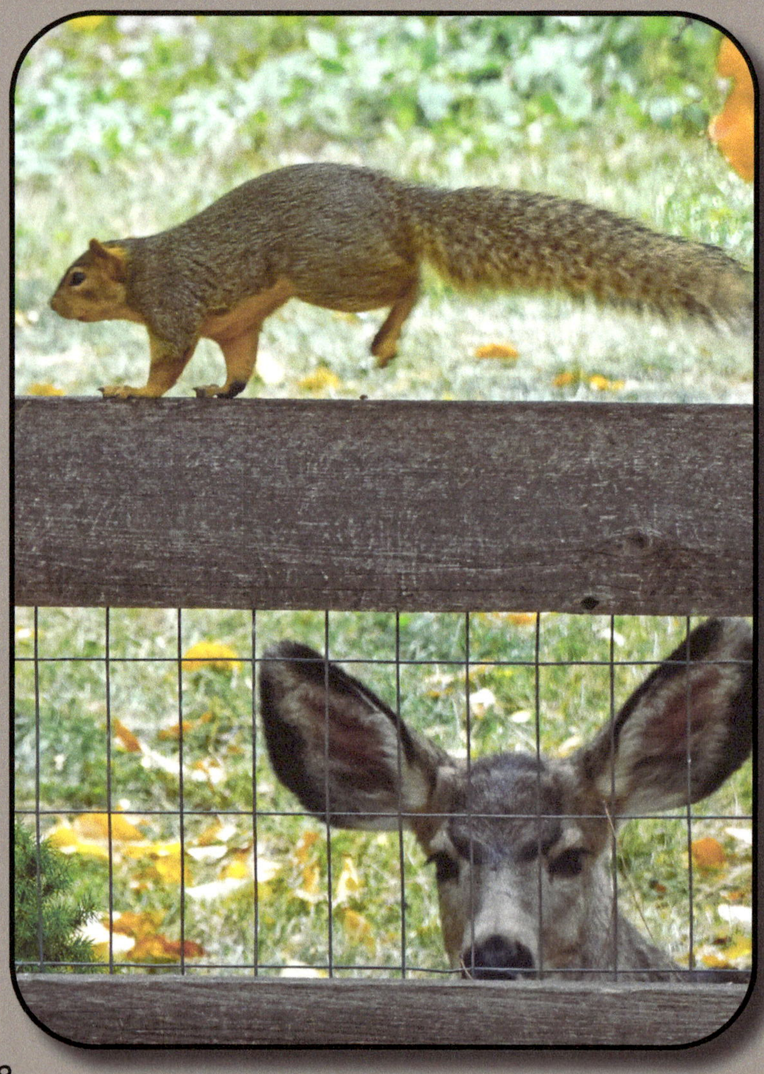

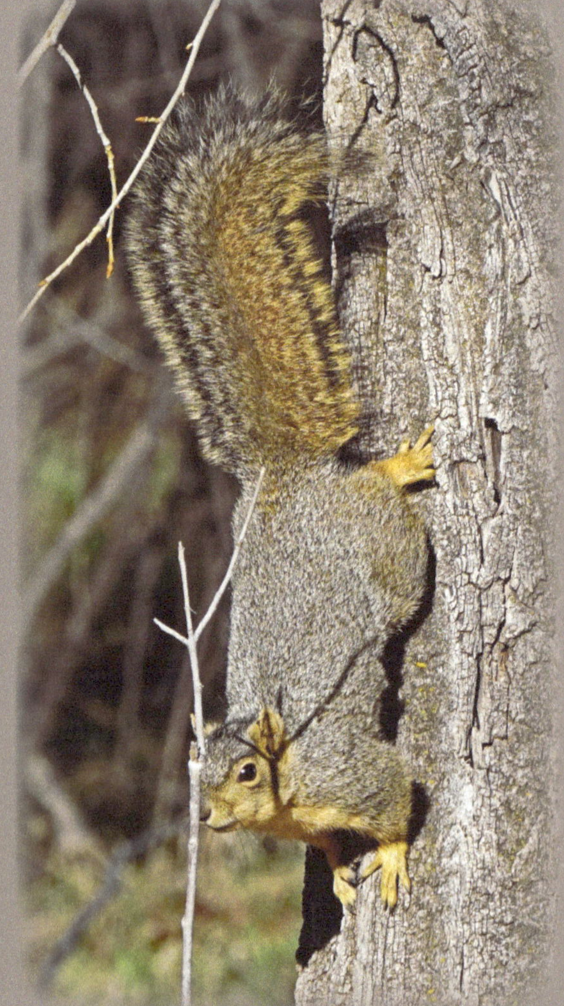

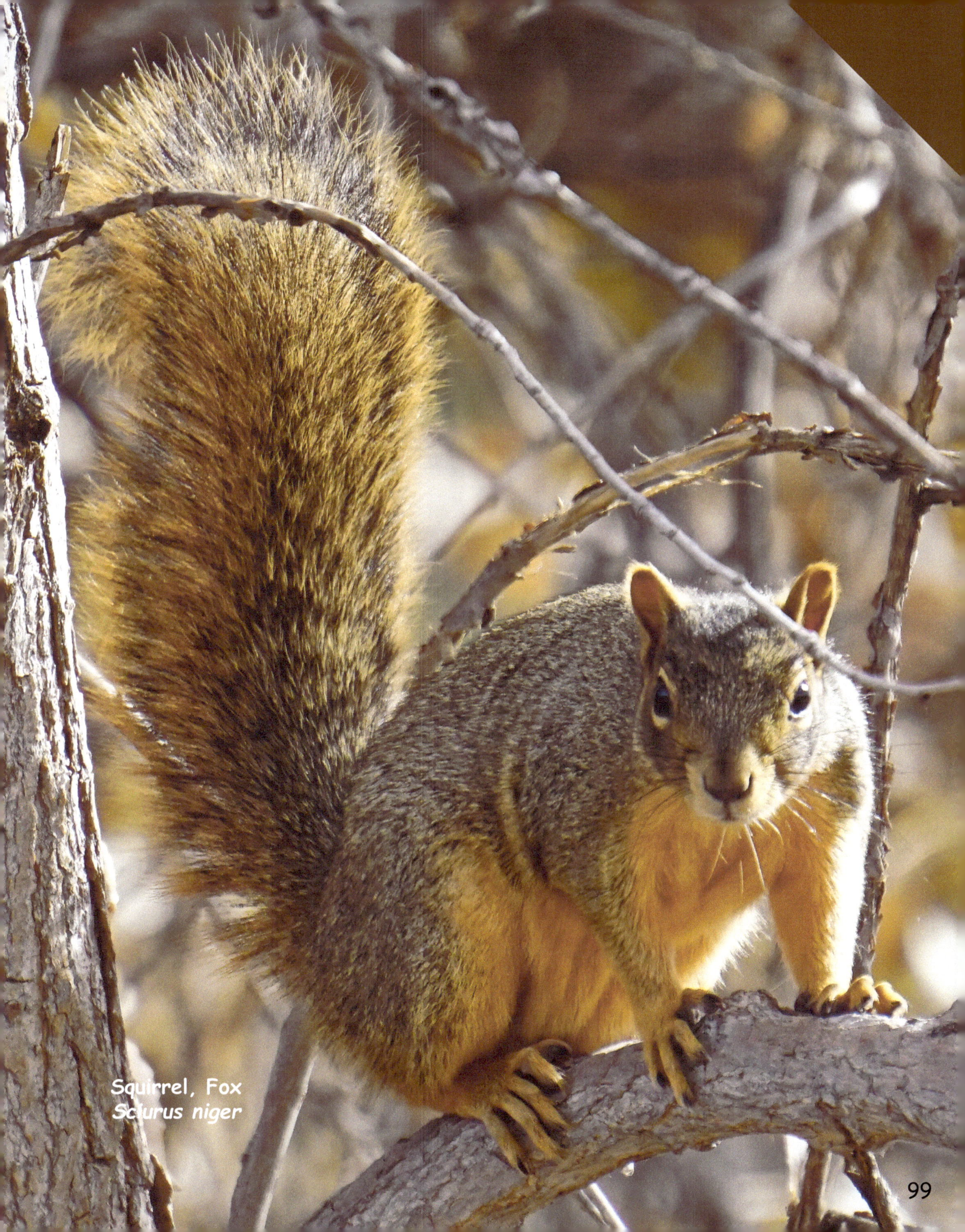

Squirrel, Fox
Sciurus niger

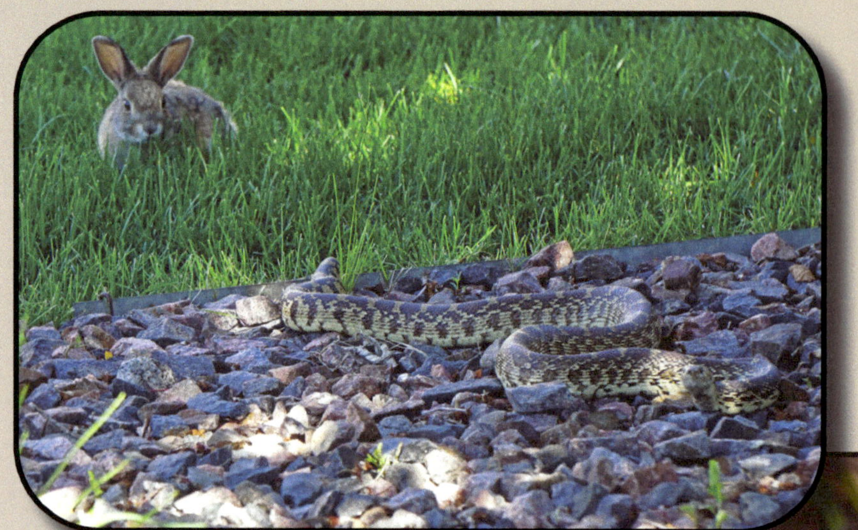

Above: Bullsnake and a Cottontail

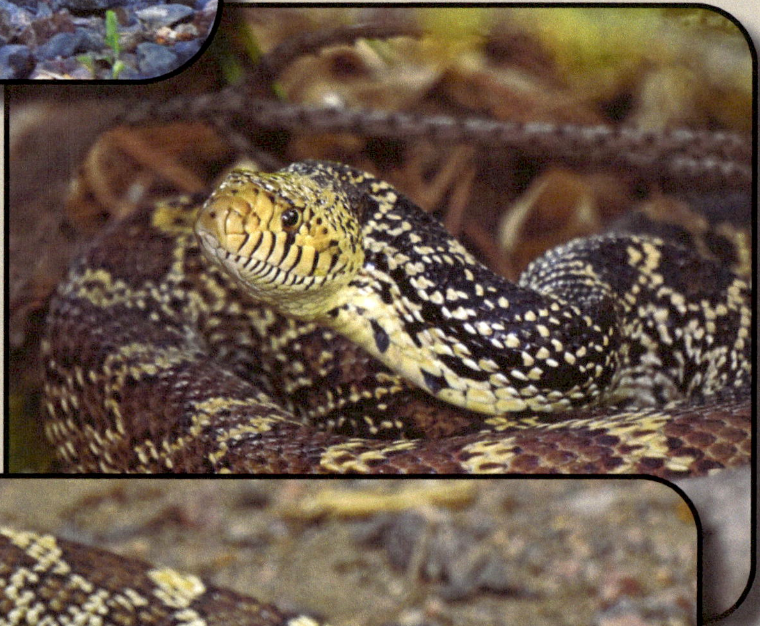

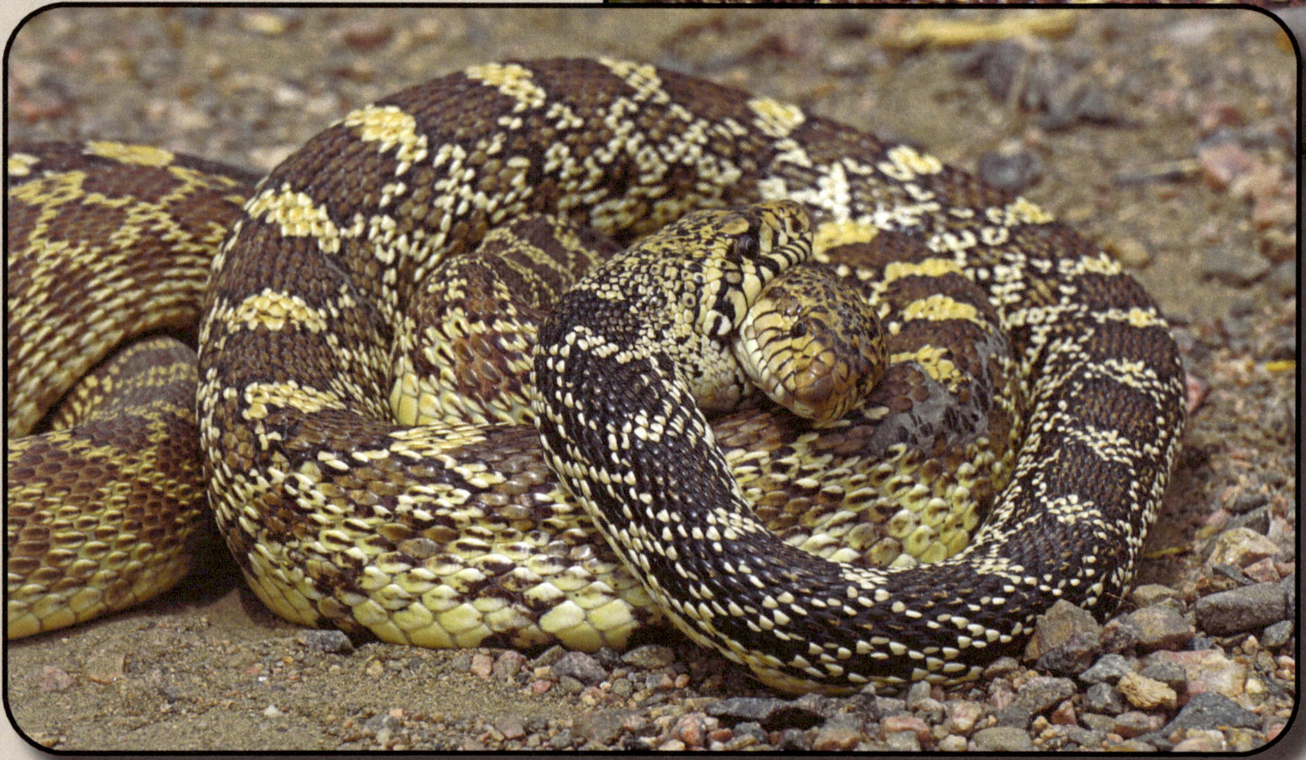

Bullsnakes are heavily built and feed mostly on rodents. Normally active by day but nocturnal in warmer months. They are non-venomous and harmless, but will mimic rattlers when disturbed. They may reach up to 8ft in length.

Bullsnakes mating

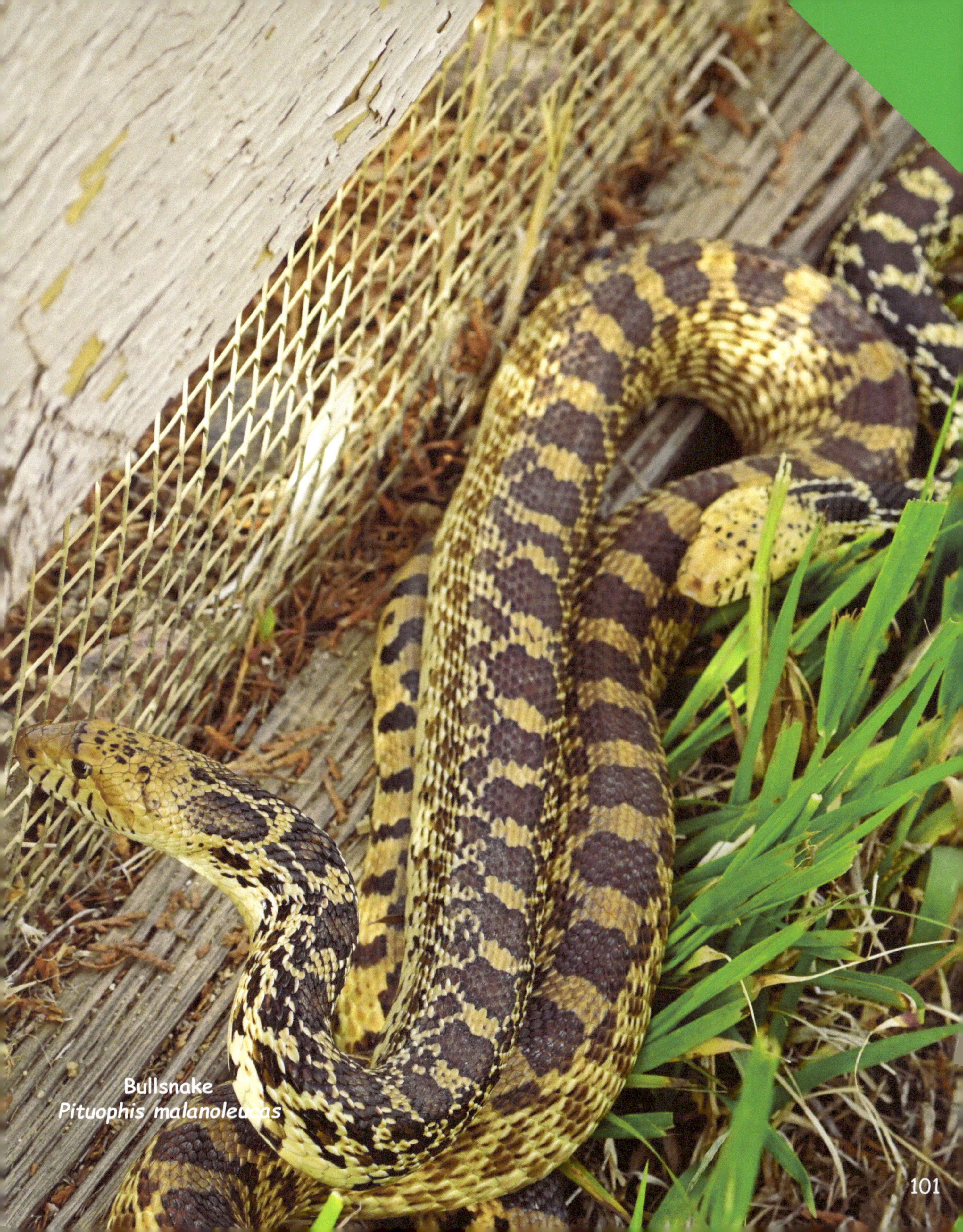

Bullsnake
Pituophis malanoleucas

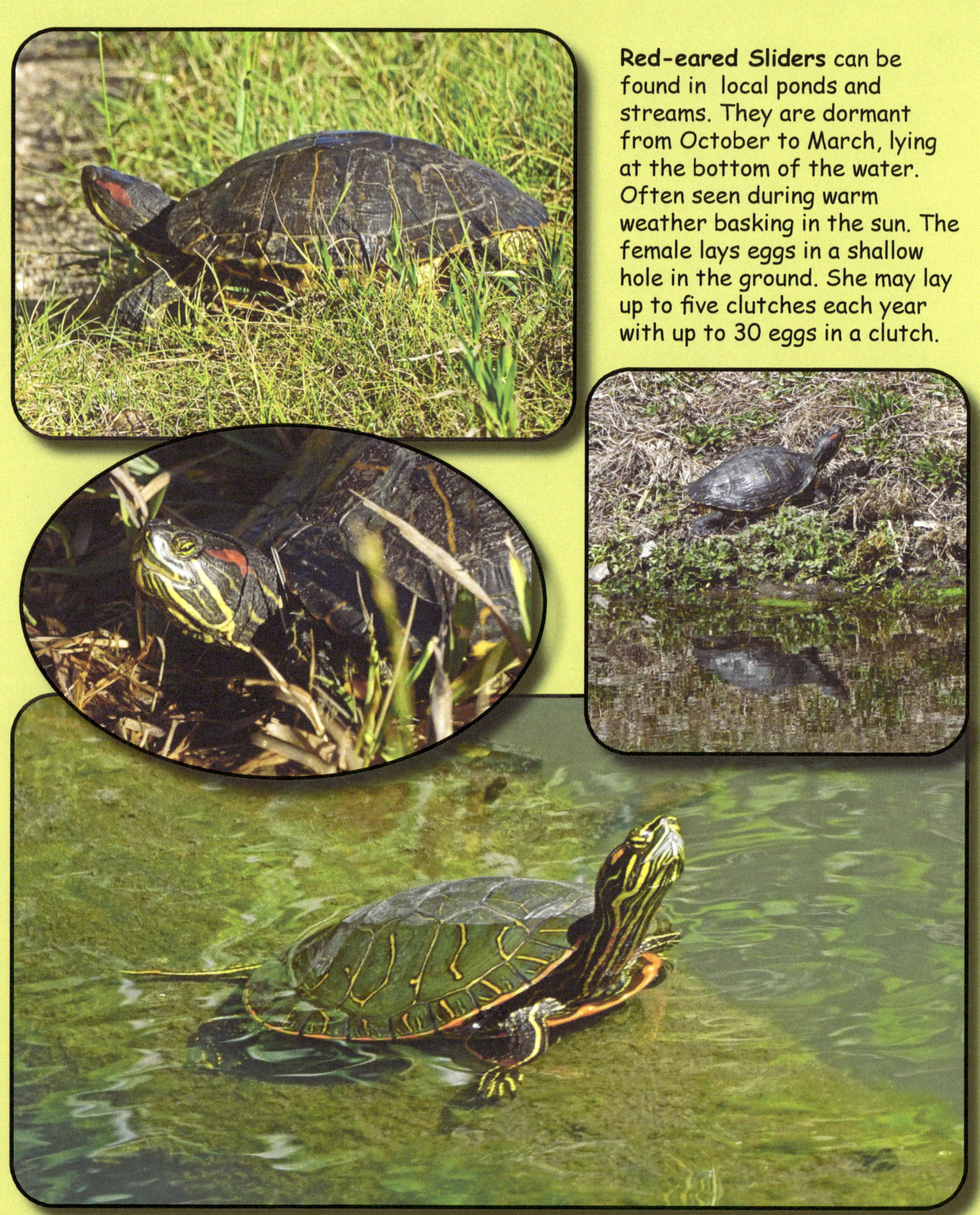

Red-eared Sliders can be found in local ponds and streams. They are dormant from October to March, lying at the bottom of the water. Often seen during warm weather basking in the sun. The female lays eggs in a shallow hole in the ground. She may lay up to five clutches each year with up to 30 eggs in a clutch.

Sliders are popular as pets

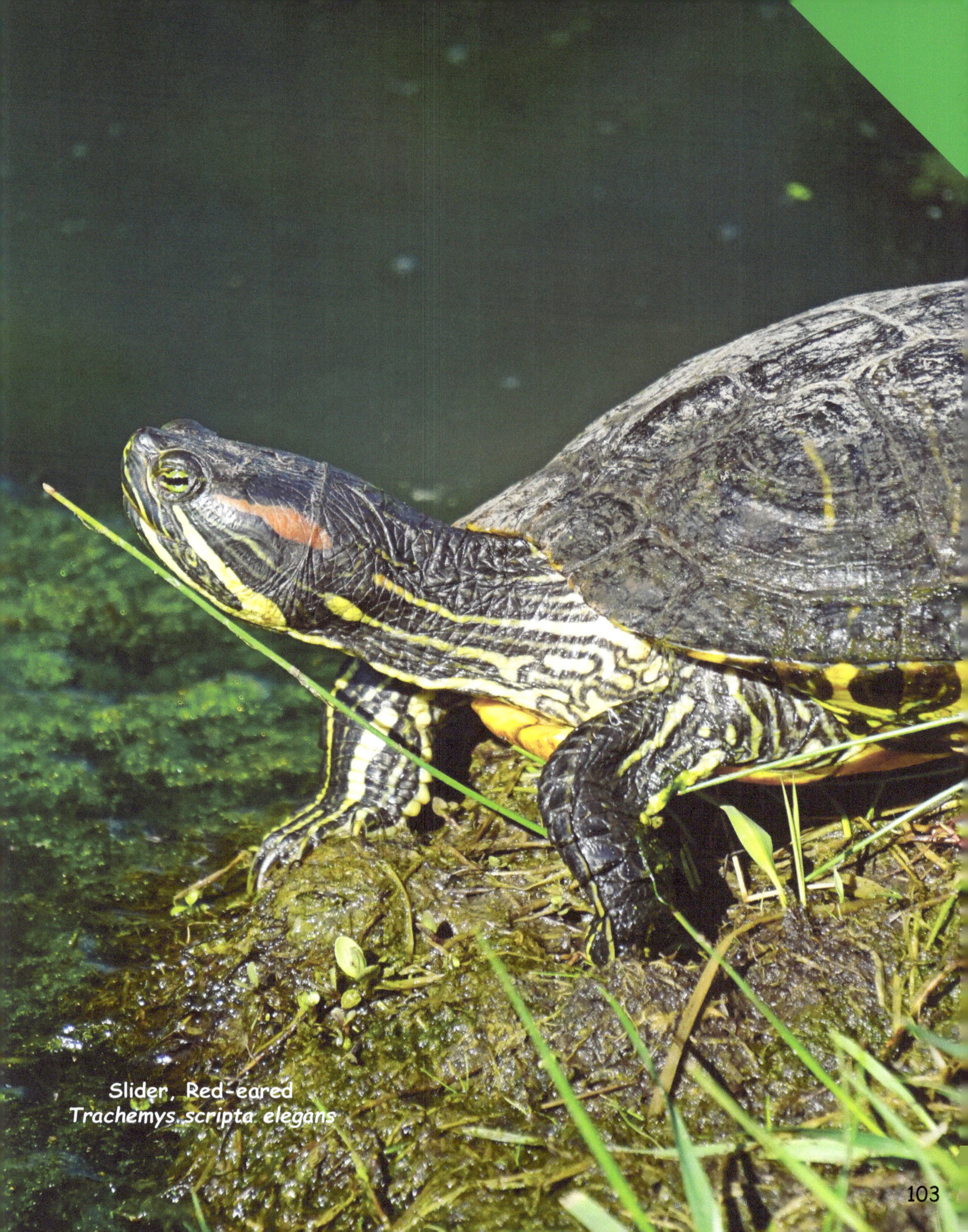

Slider, Red-eared
Trachemys scripta elegans

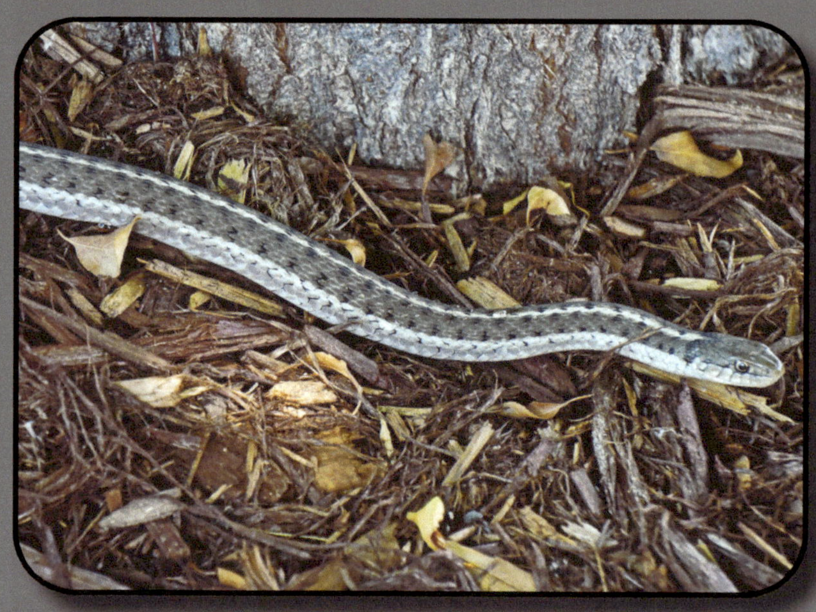

Garter Snakes are common but rarely seen. They are the most widely distributed snake in North America, feeding mainly on amphibians and earthworms. Gives birth to up to 85 live young. Has well-defined back and side stripes.

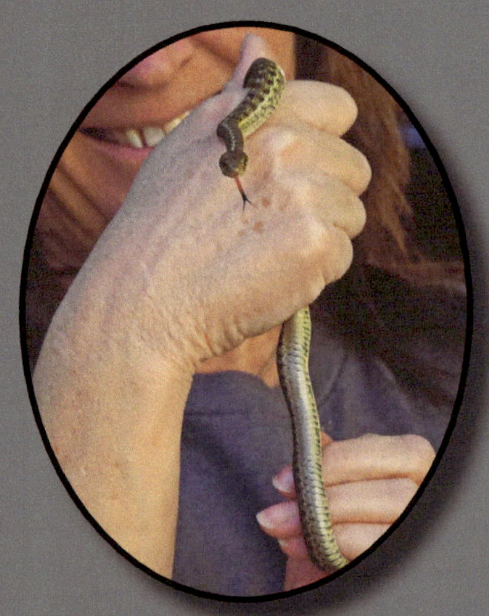

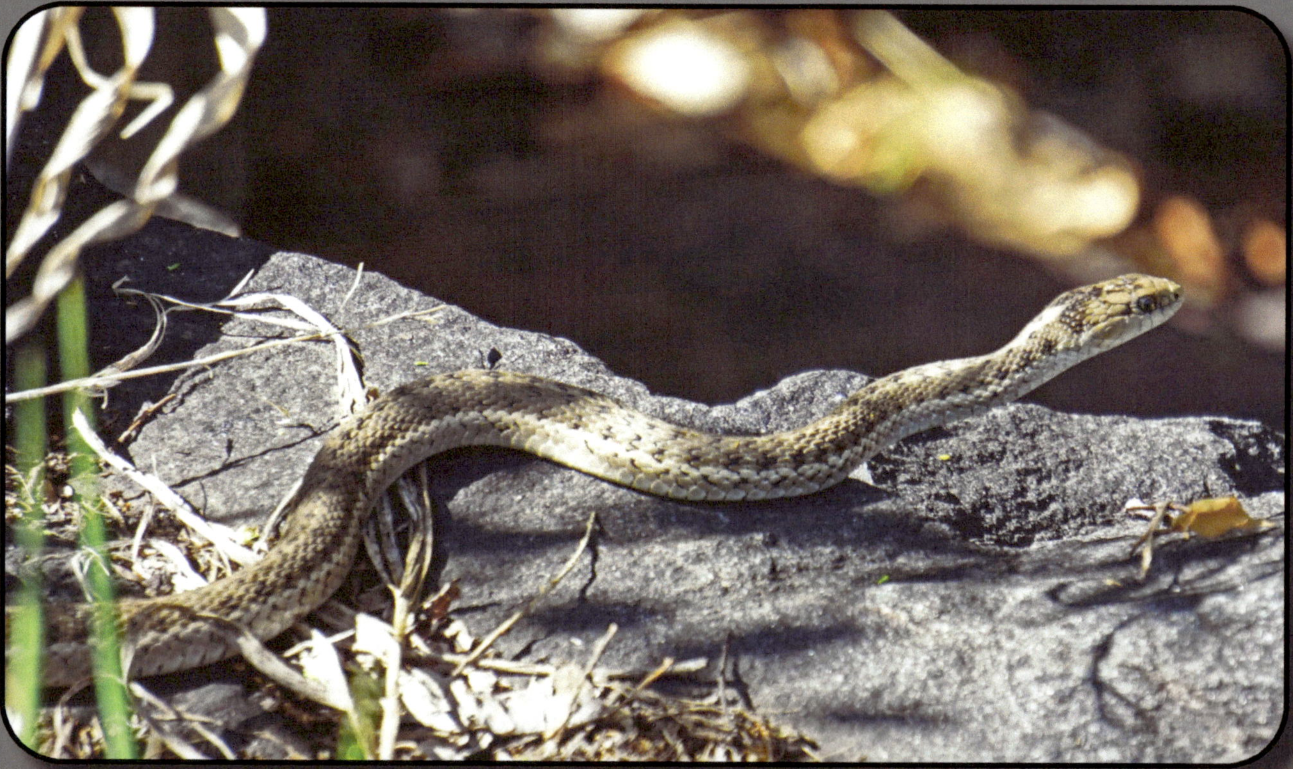

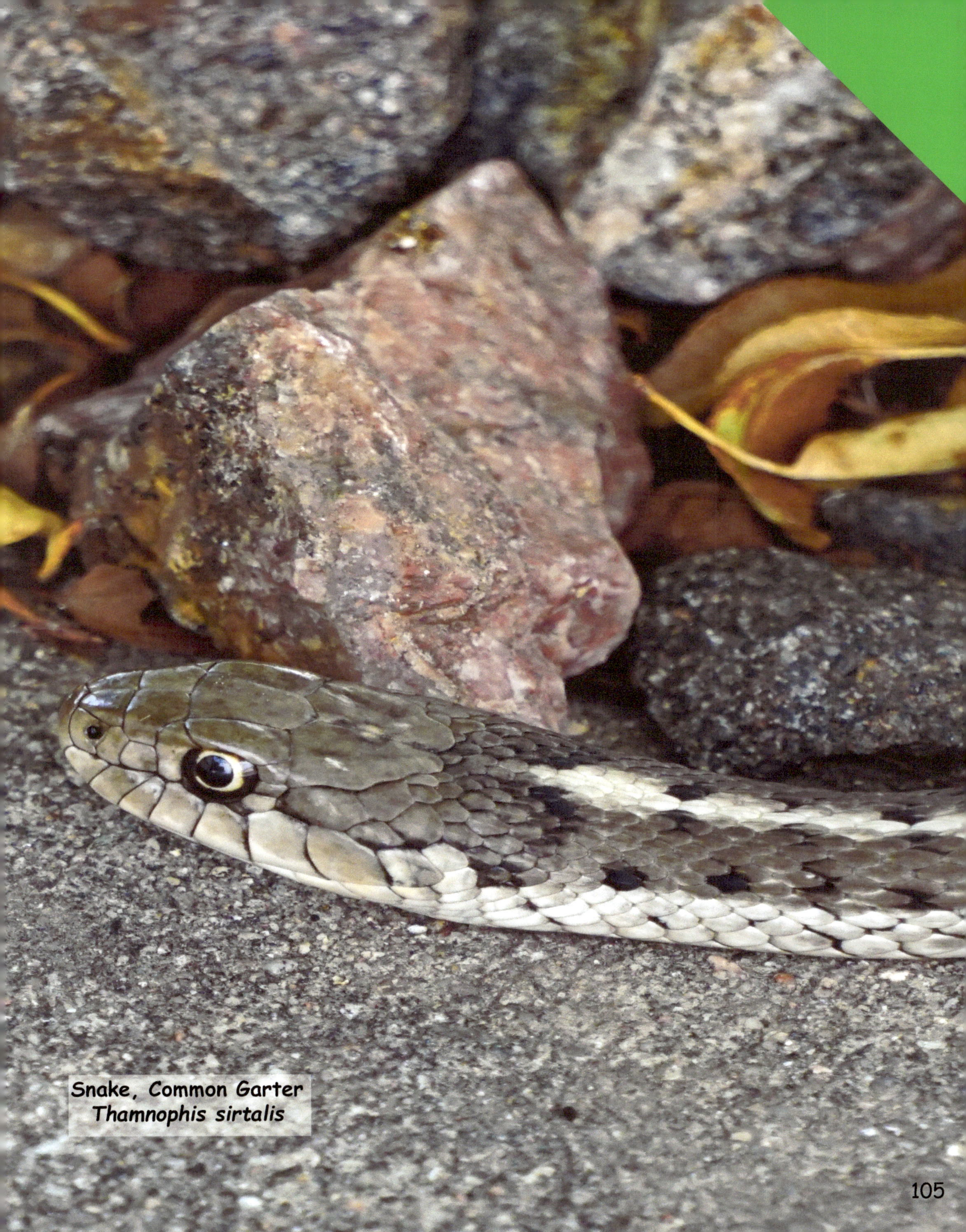

Snake, Common Garter
Thamnophis sirtalis

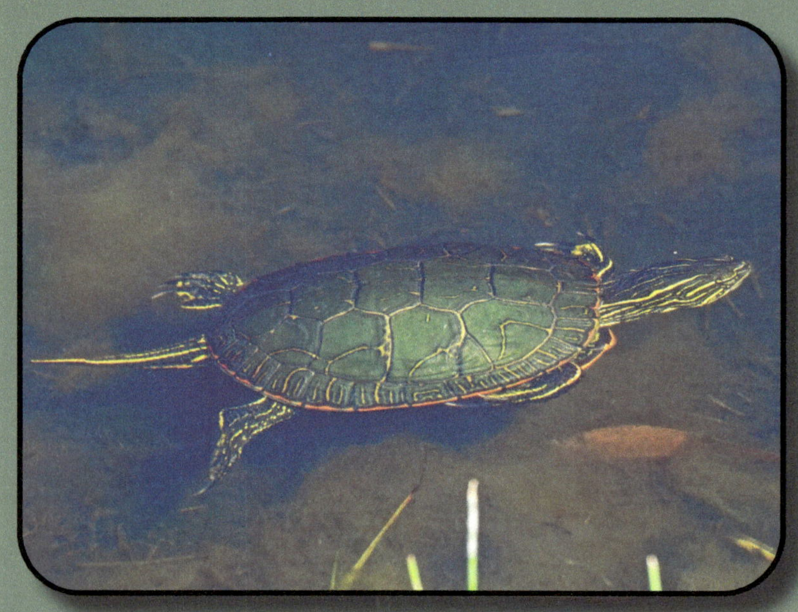

Painted Turtles, the official reptile of Colorado, are seen in most ponds and streams in Parker, often with **Sliders.**

The most widespread turtle in North America, it is specially adapted to tolerate freezing temperatures for extended periods of time. This turtle eats aquatic vegetation, algae, and small water creatures including insects, crustaceans, and fish.

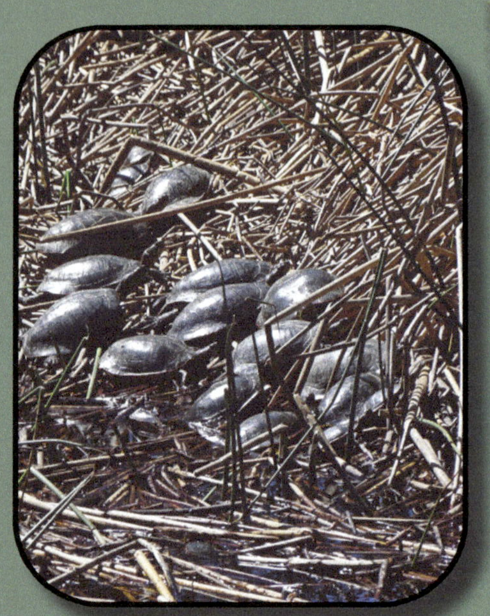

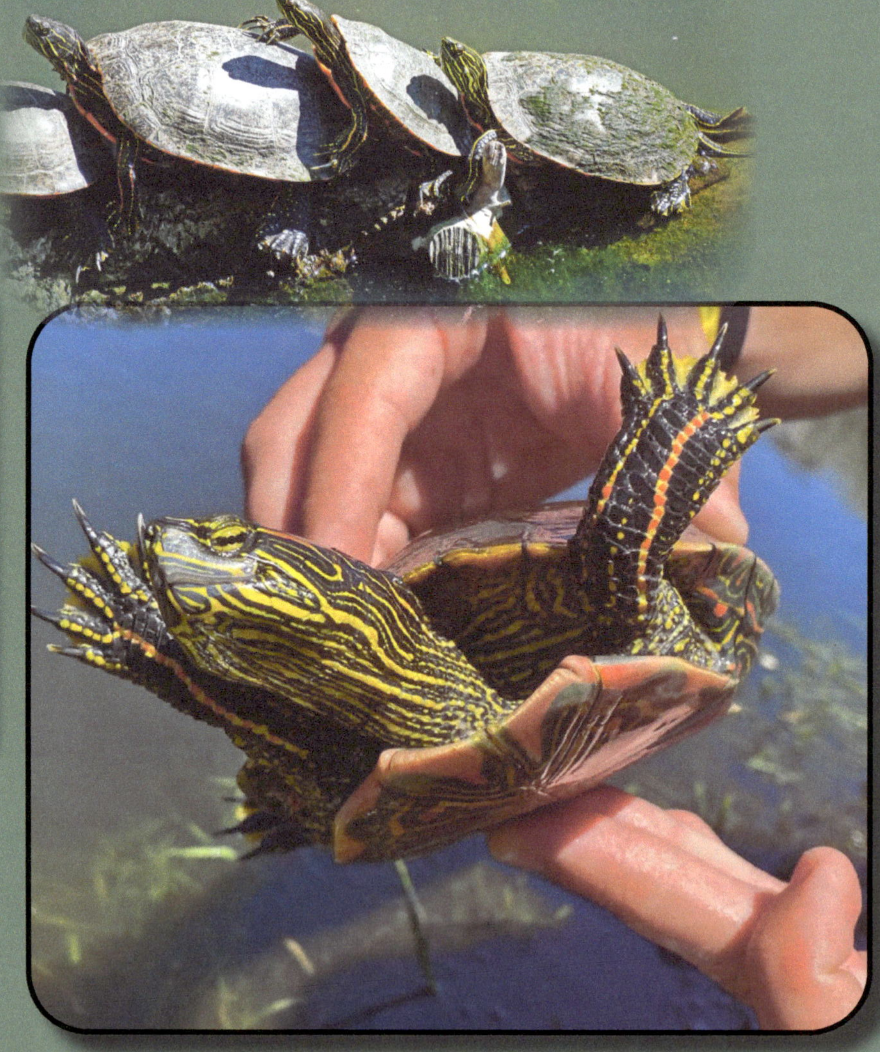

The distinctive markings of the Painted Turtle

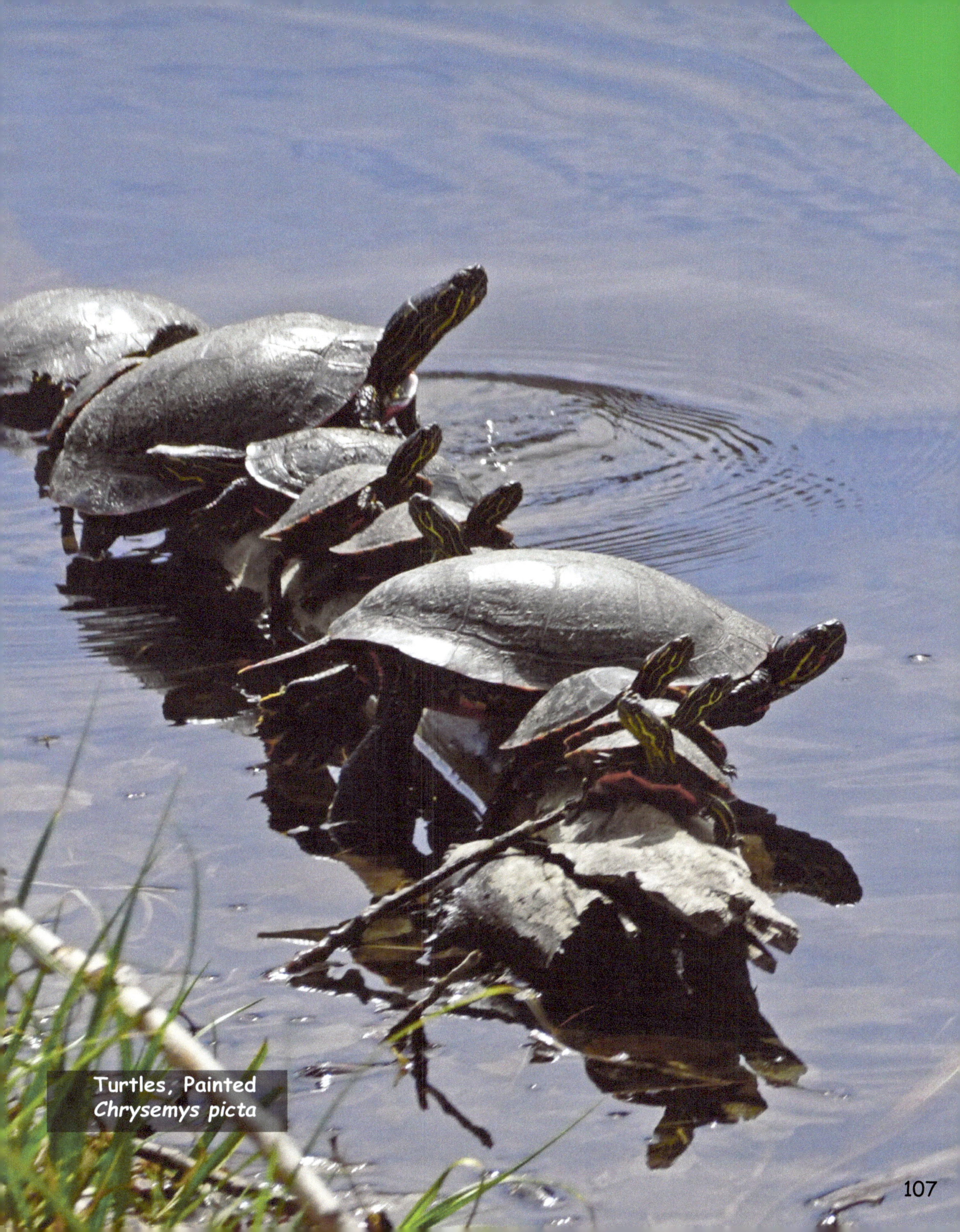

Turtles, Painted
Chrysemys picta

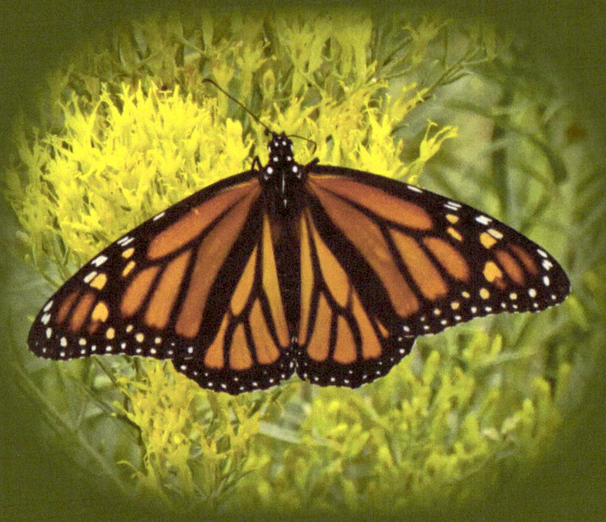

The **Monarch Butterfly** that we see in summer migrates to wintering sites in Mexico and California. The larvae feed on milkweed, making them distasteful to predators.

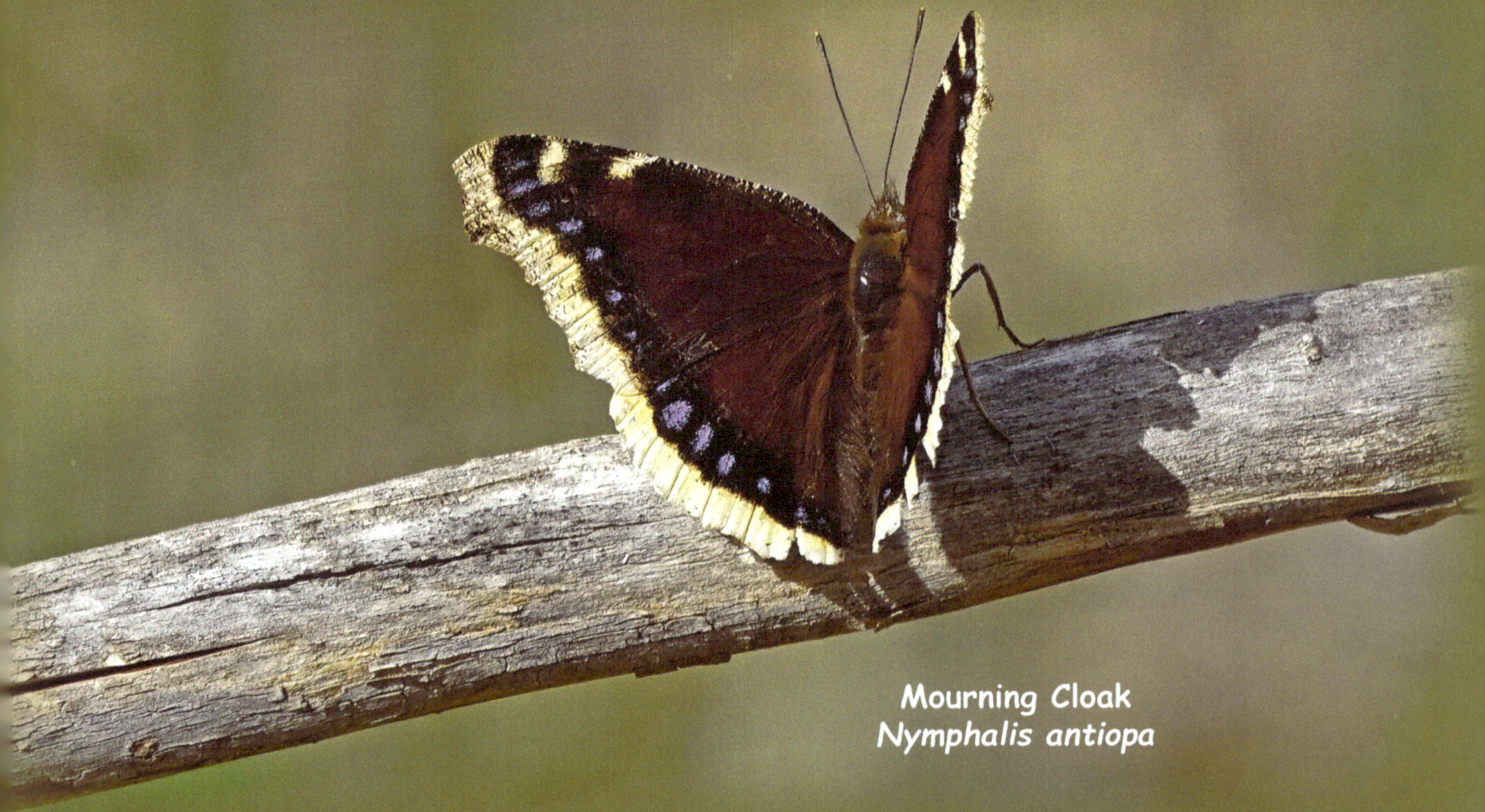

Mourning Cloak
Nymphalis antiopa

The **Mourning Cloak Butterfly**, unlike most butterflies, does not migrate to wintering sites but hibernates locally as an adult. They may be seen during mid-winter thaws or in early spring.

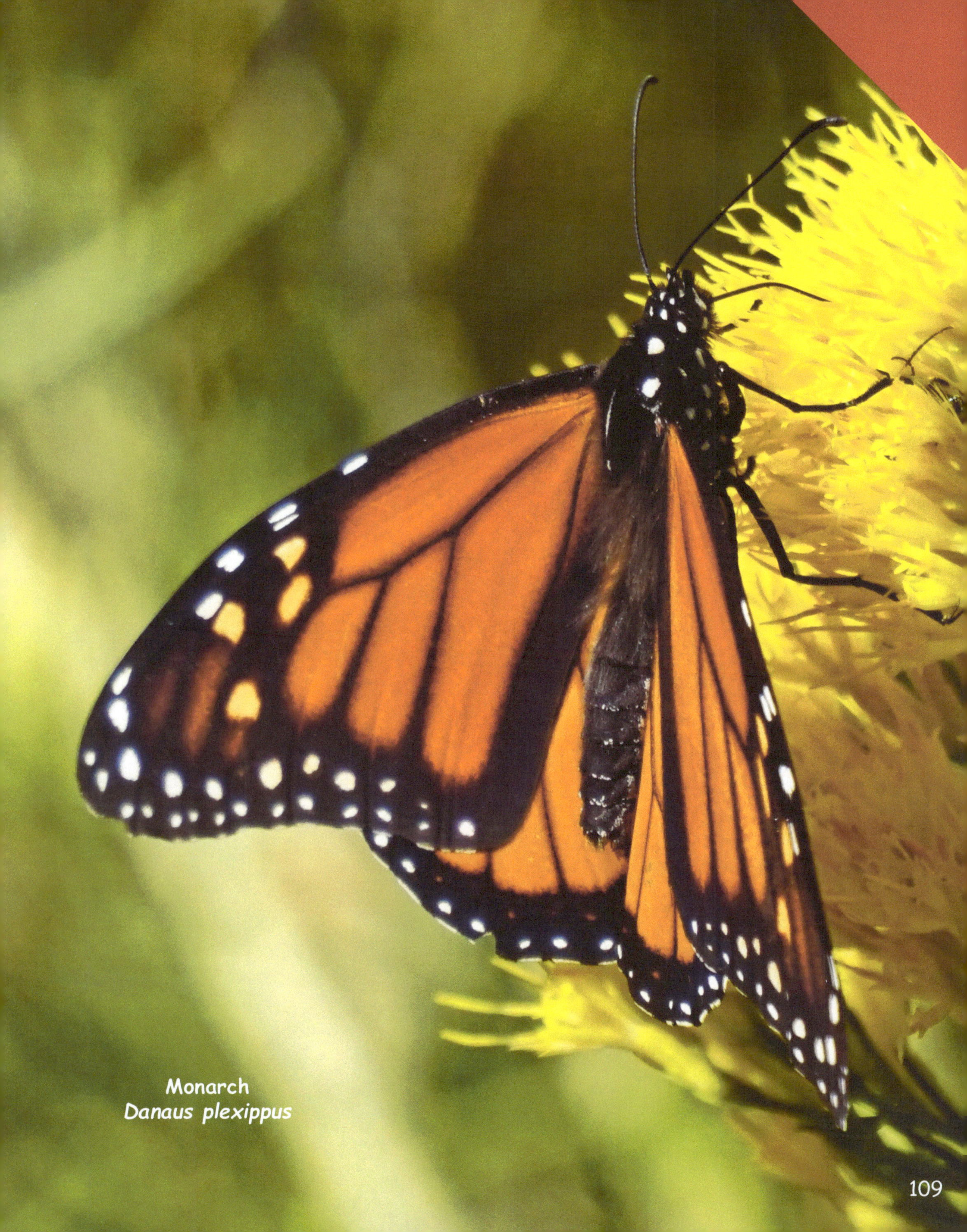

Monarch
Danaus plexippus

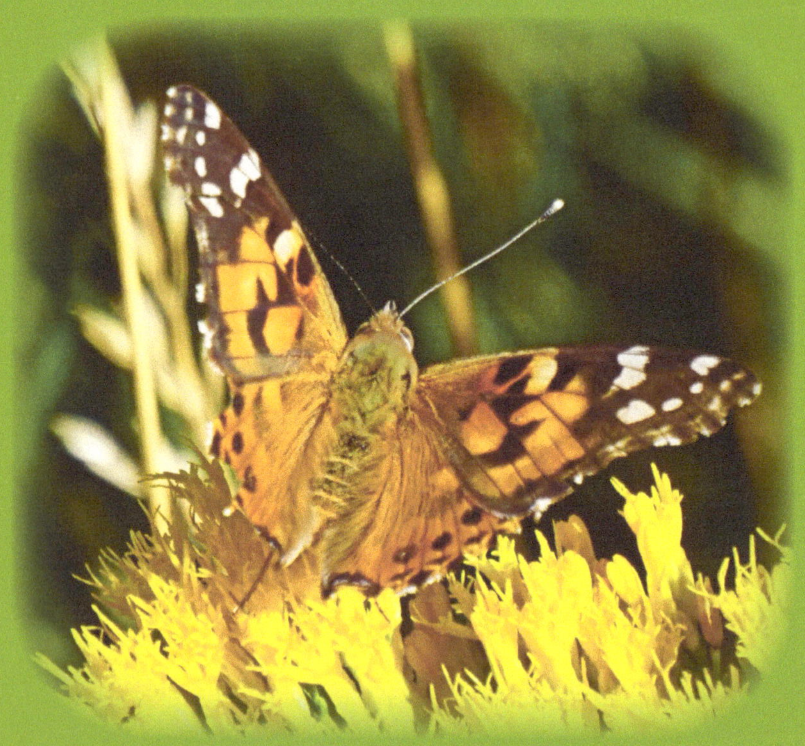

Painted Ladys are among the most widespread of all butterflies. They are found practically worldwide and are subject to mass "migration" with tens of thousands of individuals flying in one direction.

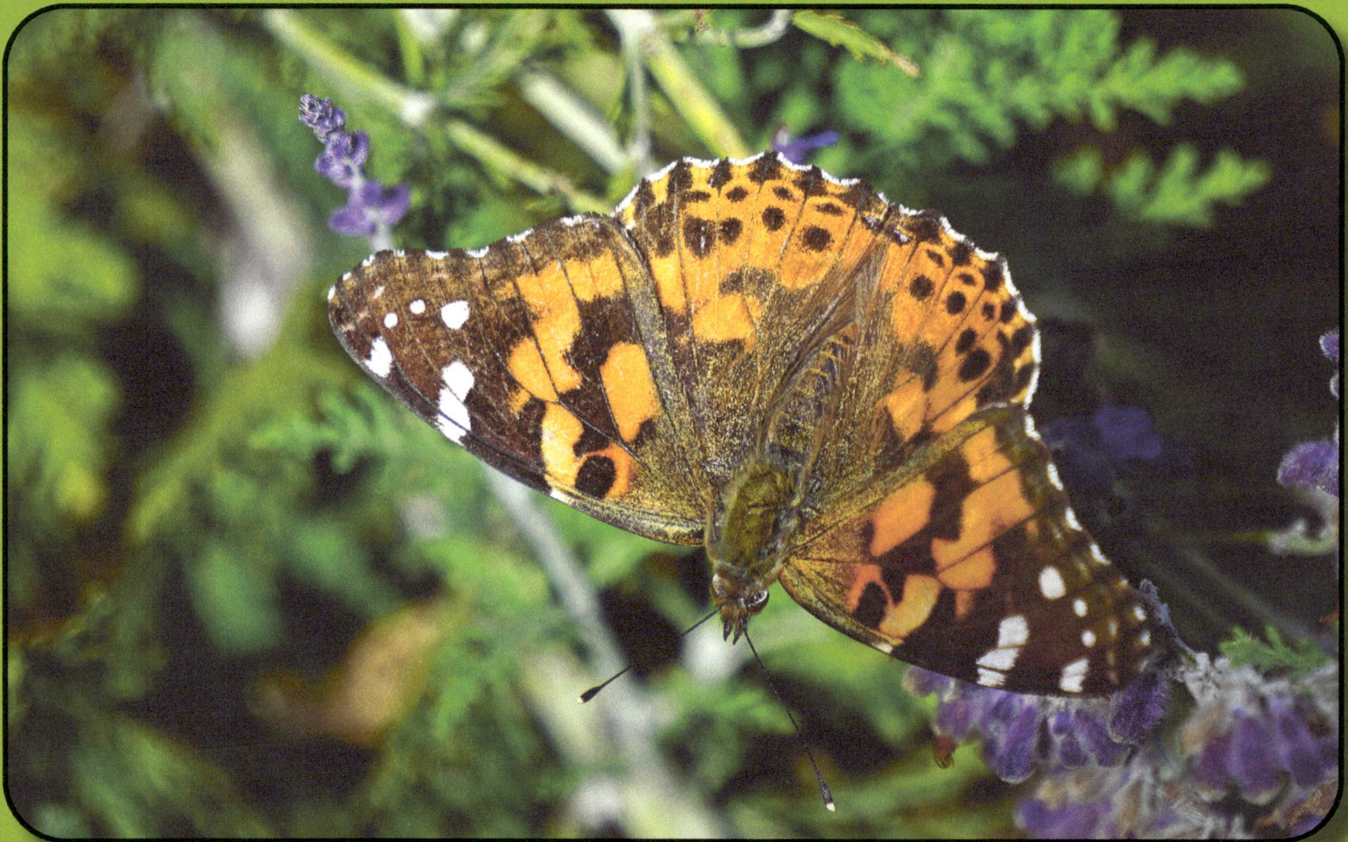

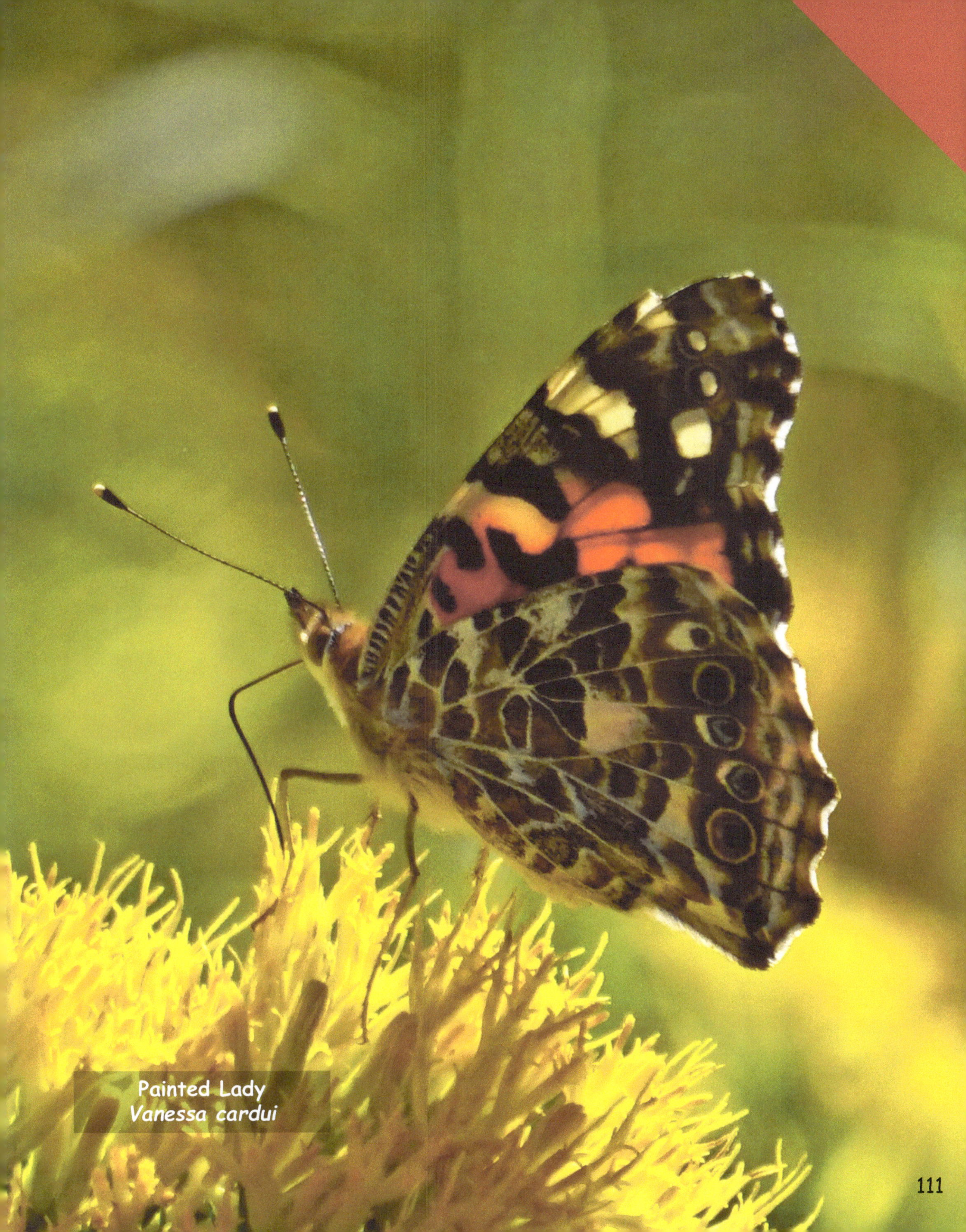

Painted Lady
Vanessa cardui

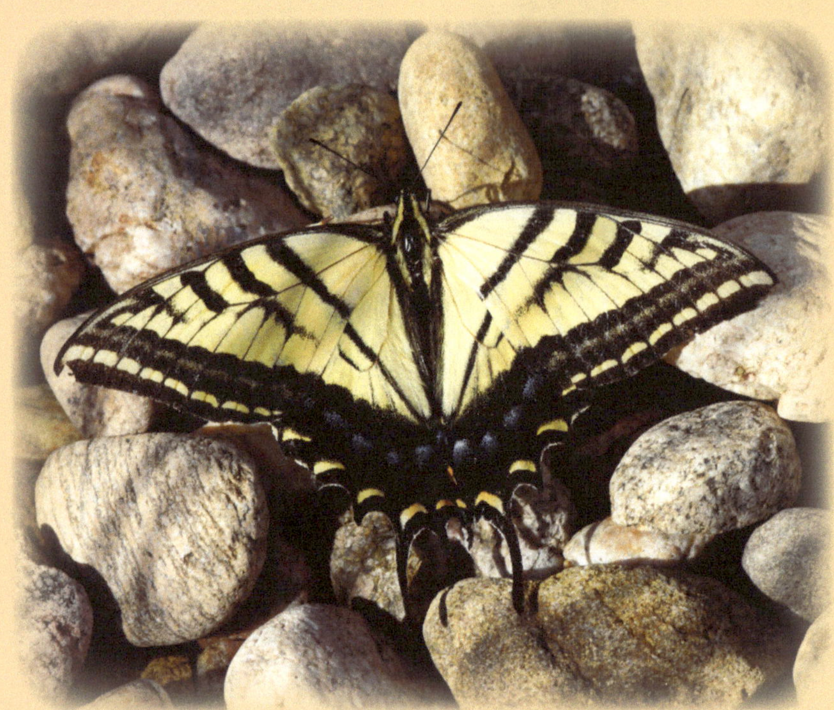

Eastern Tiger Swallowtails are common in our gardens and nearby open spaces in summer. The caterpillars feed on leaves of various trees, including Cottonwoods.

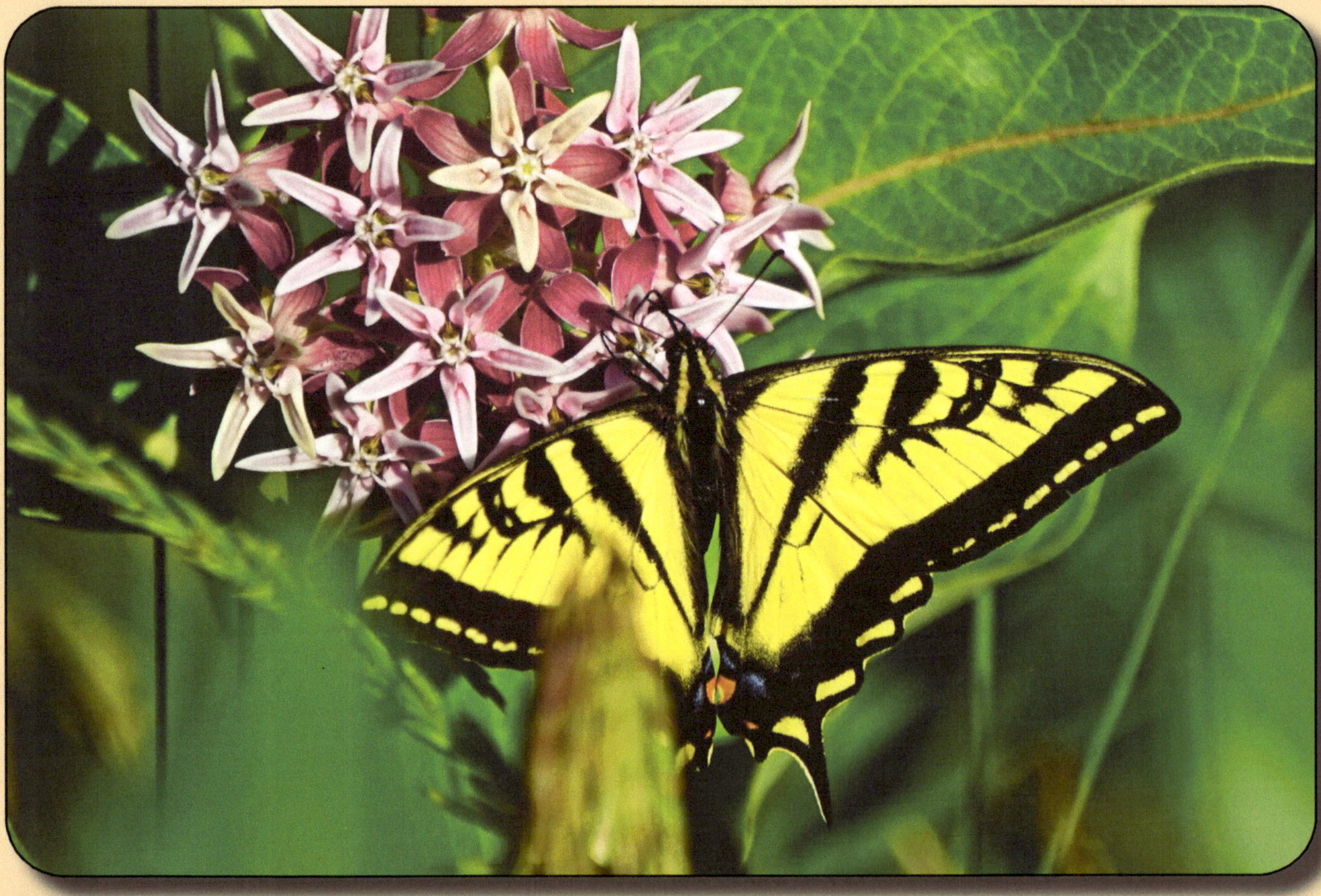

Eastern Tiger Swallowtail Butterfly feeding on Bitteroot flowers

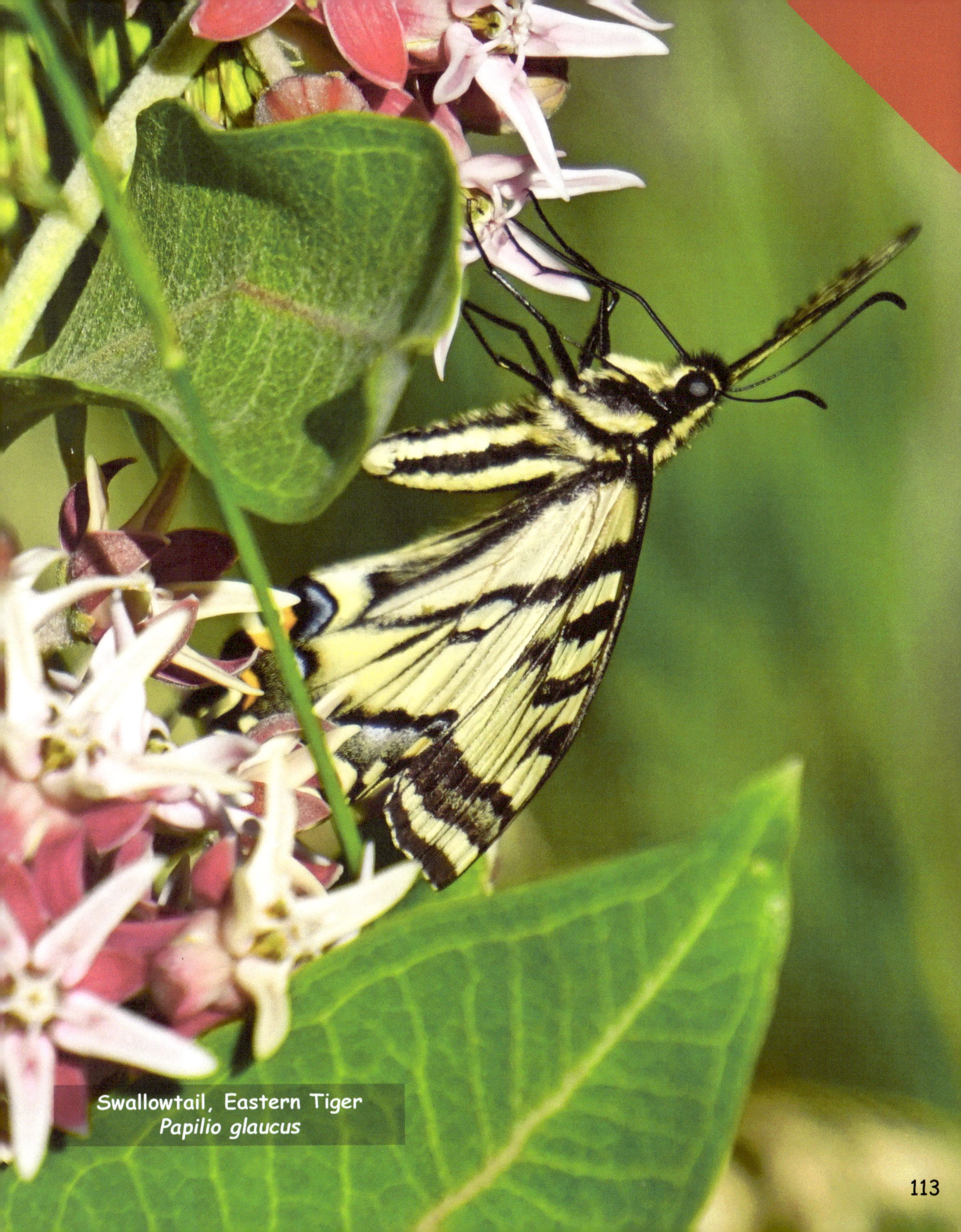

Swallowtail, Eastern Tiger
Papilio glaucus

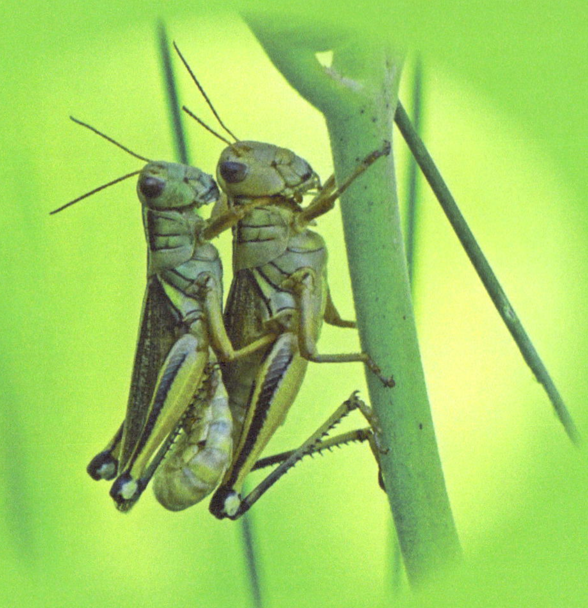

Two-striped Grasshoppers are widespread across the U.S. and are a nuisance for gardeners! They are found in thick low growth during summer and fall.

In favorable conditions, following good rains, they appear in dense numbers.

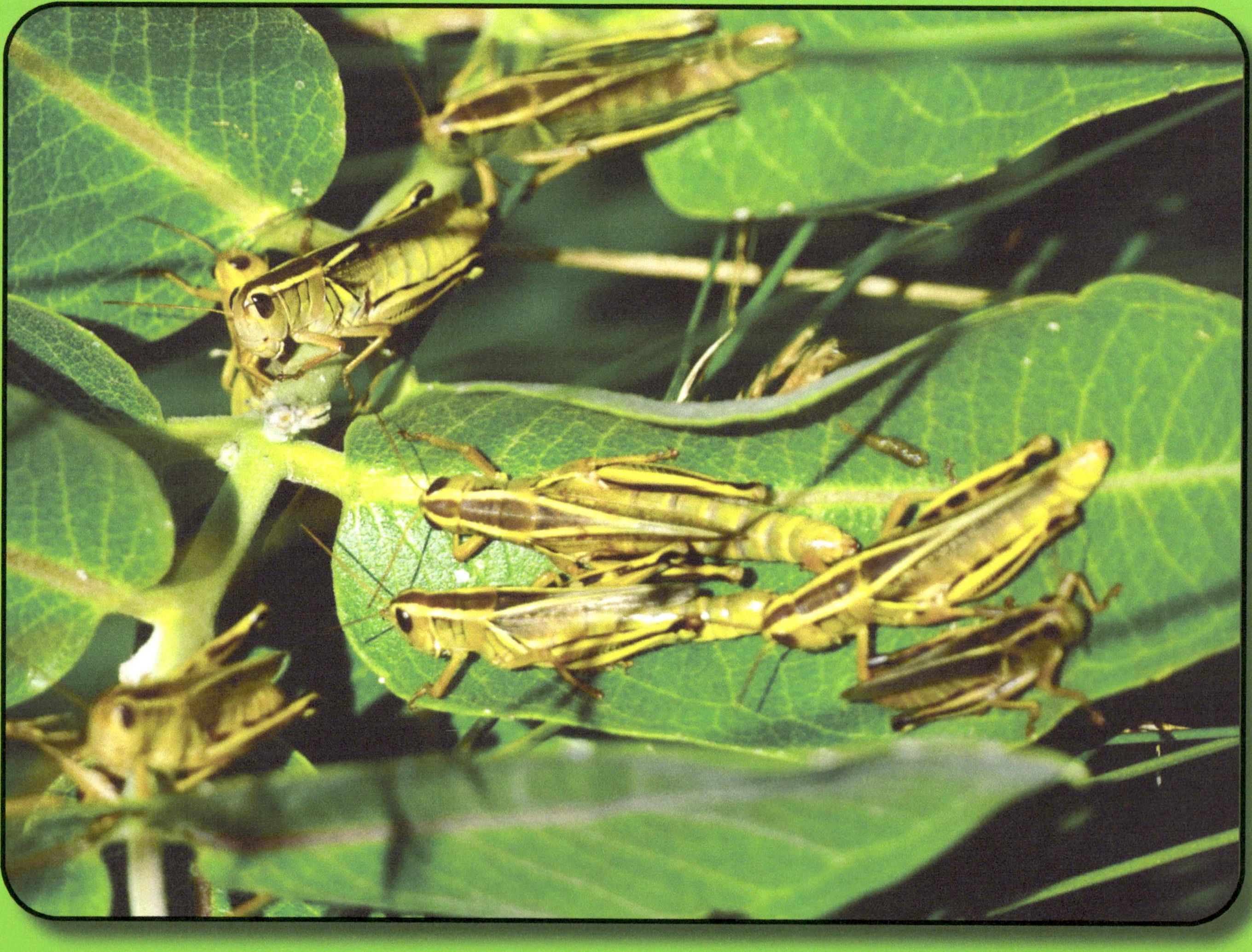

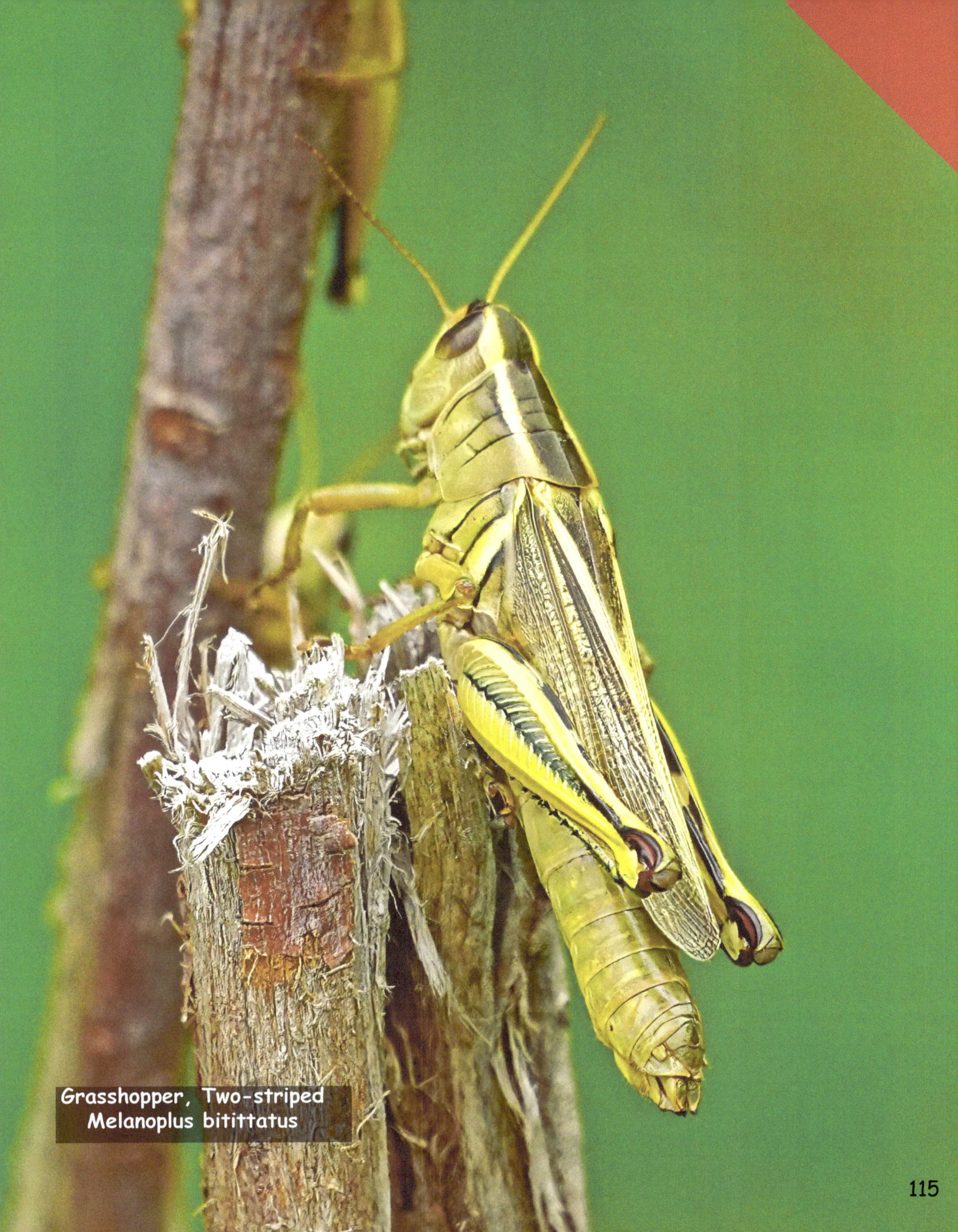

Grasshopper, Two-striped
Melanoplus bitittatus

The **Northern Leopard Frog** is the only amphibian in this book. They are *well-camouflaged* and abundant on the edges of ponds and streams. Breeding in the spring (March–June), up to 6,500 eggs are laid in water. Tadpoles complete development within the breeding pond.

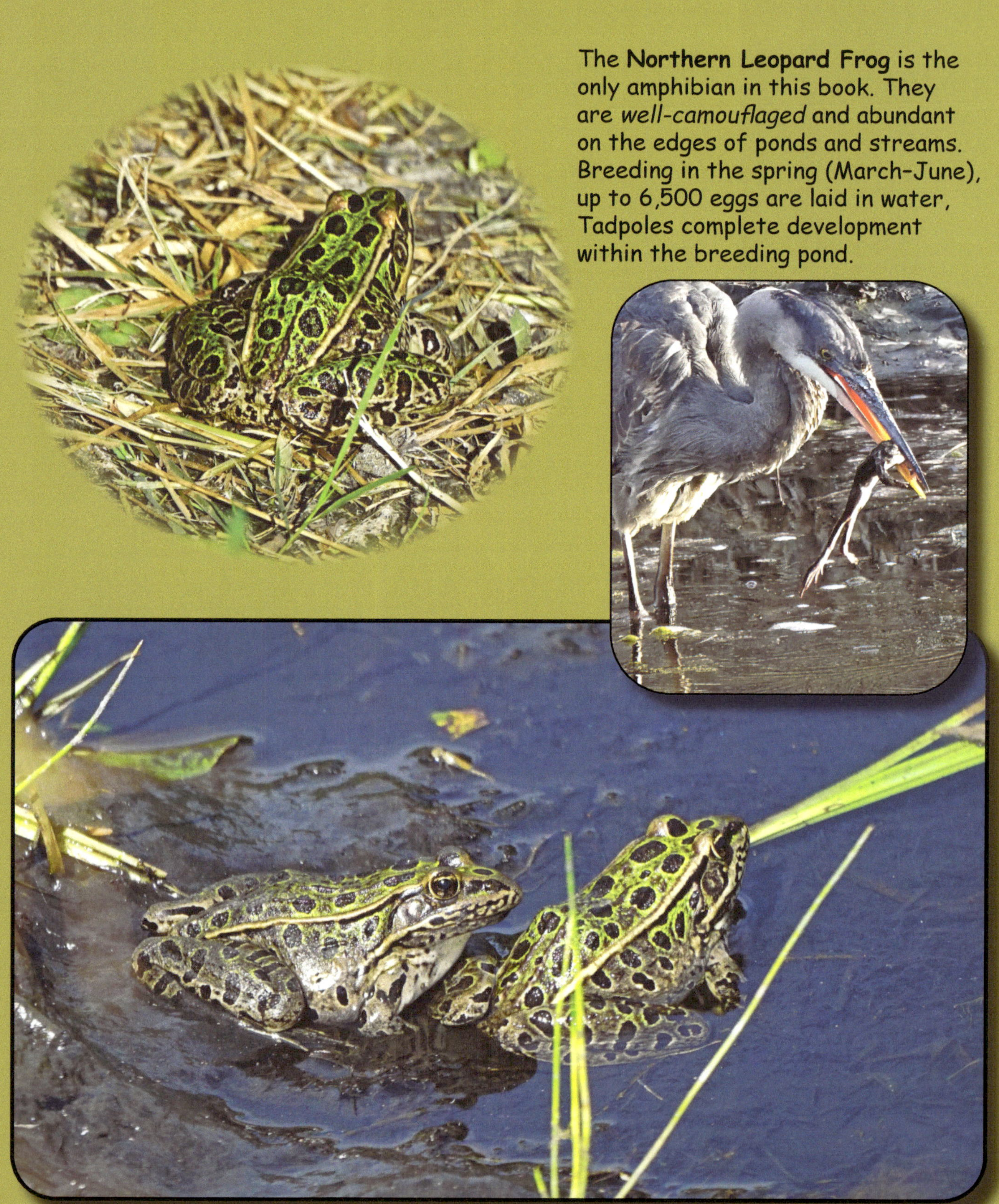

The distinctive markings of the Leopard Frog

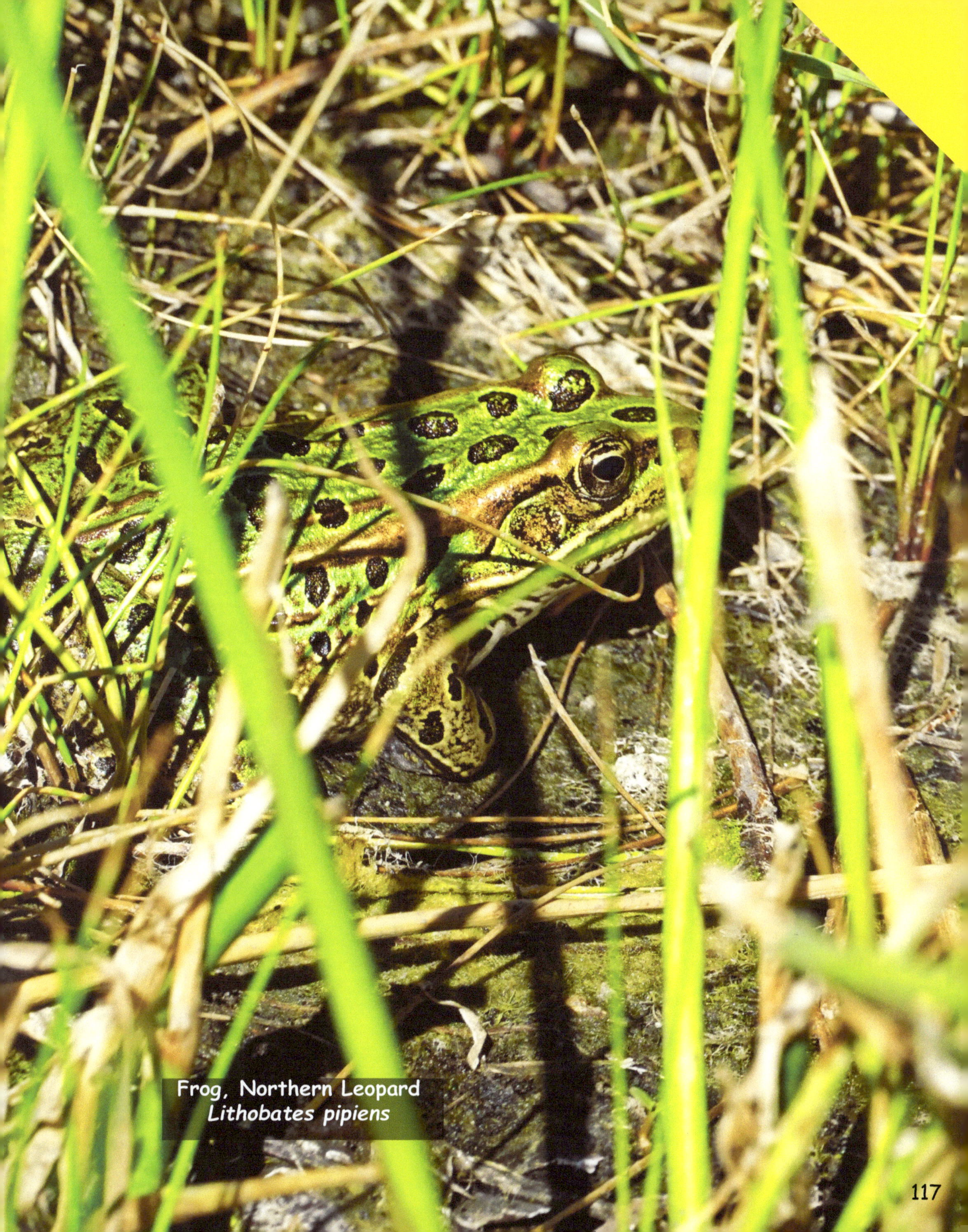

Frog, Northern Leopard
Lithobates pipiens

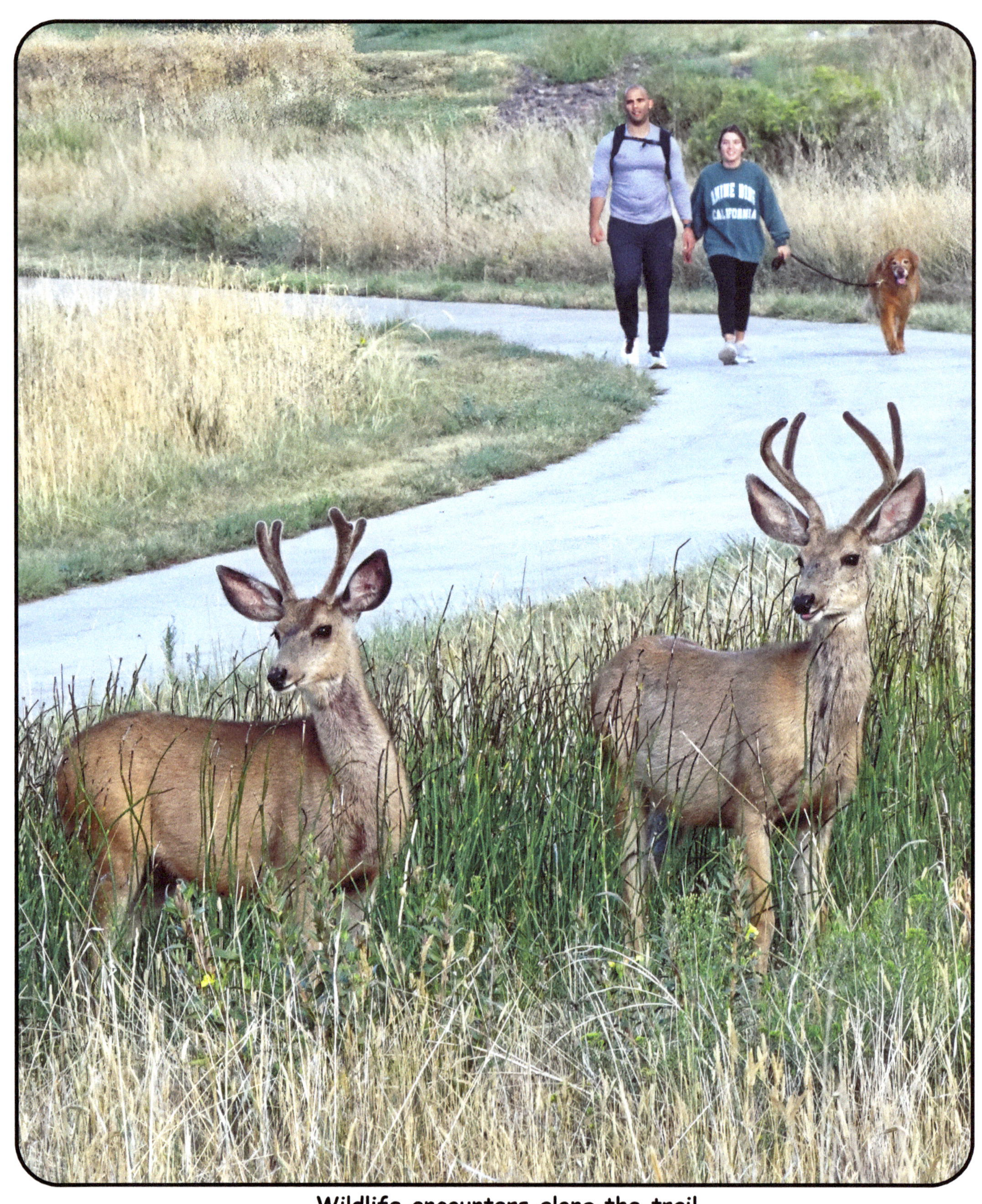

Wildlife encounters along the trail

Appendix

Harper Collins Complete North American Wildlife, A Photo Field Guide. First Edition
© 2003 by Gerard A. Bertrand, John A. Burton, and Paul Sterry.

Sibley Birds West, Field Guide to Birds of Western North America. Second Edition
© 2016 by David Allen Sibley

Kaufman Field Guide to Insects of North America
© 2007 by Hillstar Editions L.C.

National Geographic Pocket Guide to the Mammals of North America,
by Catherine Herbert Howell ©2016 National Geographic Society

https://parkerco.gov/

www.Wikipedia.org

Other Books by this author

Available from online bookstores:

Tallman Gulch Trail, A Collection of Nature Photographs.
© 2020 by Joe McDaniel
    ISBN 978-1-050647-51-4 Hardcover
    ISBN 978-1-950647-68-2 Softcover

Finding Wildlife In Colorado. Birds, Mammals & Reptiles.
© 2021 by Joe McDaniel
    ISBN 978-1-950647-77-4 Hardcover
    ISBN 978-1-950647-72-9 Softcover

Finding Wildlife On Safari, South Africa, Namibia, Botswana 2021
©2021 by Joe and Jan McDaniel
    ISBN 978-1-950647-94-1